"Whether you are a songwriter, producer, performer, or music enthu-siast, *21-Hit Wonder*, Sam Hollander's memoir and songwriting guide, is an essential read. His passion, perseverance, and love for all things music will motivate, educate, and entertain you. An exhilarat-ing lesson on why it's never an option to give up on following your dream and doing what you love!"

**—MATT PINFIELD (MTV VJ)**

met Sam Hollander when fate and/or a major airline employee s right next to one another on what is normally a terribly long -country flight. Sam started sharing his wildly entertaining story e off, and this may be the only time in my life in the air that I a journey took longer, so I could hear even more of Sam's still uch unfolding life story. Beyond all the obvious talent that has m such a wonderful and successful "21-Hit Wonder," Sam is a very witty, wonderfully revealing, and refreshingly honest r. And now with this book that you will devour and enjoy at you too can share an unforgettable and rollicking journey "

**WILD, CONTRIBUTING EDITOR, *ROLLING STONE***

## Praise for Sam Hollander and *21 Hit Won*

"Sam Hollander is a hitmaker extraordinaire, but you fin
also the king of cool when you work with him. Rock on
**—BILLY IDOL**

"Following Beckett's dictum, "Try again. Fail agai
Hollander's passionate pursuit through trial and erro
of the most renowned songwriters of today, will b
to any aspiring artist or music fan."
**—DAVID DUCHOVNY**

"Sam Hollander is the best prize a boy could
**—RINGO STARR**

"I met Sam in the back studio of my mar
2007. He was already deep in cooking
Goldilocks type of writer/producer—I
right. The right mix of dark humor, t
getting down to writing a big song.
grind" all the time in this business
the grind really is."
**—PETE WENT7**

"Sam is the 21-hit wonder—
comes out!! Bad mother****
**—BRAD JORDAN**

"This is a rags to *wish*
everything—he won't
managed to fail at fai
songwriters in the bu
which puts him in
writes about with
**—BOB GU**

# 21-Hit W🎵NDER

# 21-Hit WONDER

**Flopping My Way to the Top of the Charts**

## SAM HOLLANDER

Matt Holt Books
An Imprint of BenBella Books, Inc.
Dallas, TX

The events, locations, and conversations in this book, while true, are re-created from the author's memory. However, the essence of the story, and the feelings and emotions evoked, are intended to be accurate representations. In certain instances, names, persons, organizations, and places have been changed to protect an individual's privacy.

*21-Hit Wonder* copyright © 2022 by Rock Write Inc.

All rights reserved. No part of this book may be used or reproduced in any manner whatsoever without written permission of the publisher, except in the case of brief quotations embodied in critical articles or reviews.

Matt Holt is an imprint of BenBella Books, Inc.
10440 N. Central Expressway
Suite 800
Dallas, TX 75231
benbellabooks.com
Send feedback to feedback@benbellabooks.com

*BenBella* and *Matt Holt* are federally registered trademarks.

Printed in the United States of America
10 9 8 7 6 5 4 3 2 1

Library of Congress Control Number: 2022016503
ISBN 9781637741863 (hardcover)
ISBN 9781637741870 (electronic)

Editing by Katie Dickman
Copyediting by James Fraleigh
Proofreading by Sarah Vostok and Jenny Bridges
Text design and composition by Aaron Edmiston
Cover design by Brigid Pearson
Cover image © Shutterstock
Cover photography by Kamp Kennedy
Printed by Lake Book Manufacturing

Special discounts for bulk sales are available.
Please contact bulkorders@benbellabooks.com.

*Dear Casey,*

*I'd like to send this long-distance dedication to my dad. Pops, I don't know how strong the signal is up there, but if you're hearing this, keep your feet on the ground and keep reaching for the stars. This one's for you.*

*Signed,*
*Sam*

# Contents

# Contents

# Foreword

If you're ever lucky enough to spend a day writing with Sam Hollander there are certain things you can expect. First order of business—and the only thing he seems to care about working on—is lunch. He's pre-verbal until he's nailed down the what, when, and where of your culinary needs. He already knows what he wants. He'll expect a prompt decision. He's obsessed. It will be good and it will be healthy and it will be close by. Just don't expect anything sounding like social niceties until he's taken your order. There's a bit of "Aunt Martha" to Sam's style of caring for others that makes it hard not to love him.

The actual act of writing requires his collapsing into a position modeled after the early astronauts' launch recliners. Meeting at his current "feels right" retreat, the furnishings are usually early rehearsal hall, coffee tables that look toxic, great acoustics but a get-out-of-the-neighborhood-before-dark vibe. Sam's focus is quality and talent, not appearances. His wardrobe, and mine, would work on one of the Little Rascals. He covers fashion in an early chapter. It's hilarious. And true.

Any useable writing tools teeter on his lap and the best World War II decoder would probably have trouble deciphering his scratchings. He tends to mumble a bit, perhaps uncertain about sharing those early ideas. There's gold in those mumbles and the odds are high that there's something people will love listening to in those muddled notes. Sam's a remarkable songwriter. Billion-stream chart toppers usually indicate some impressive producing chops as well.

Avoiding struggle might be what Sam and I have most in common. We've been gifted with a steady stream of ideas, a kind of bubbling under rolling presence of "maybe-song." I endlessly hum. It's not pretty. Ask my wife.

Yes, it's a gift for sure, but sometimes exhausting. I suspect Sam's always writing. It makes using the word *work* to describe what we do a bit much. Yes, we put in the time, but there is a shared appreciation for the mystical slow drip or fire hose thought parade that we can't turn off and don't really want to.

Writing is easy. Most of the time. Starting to write requires adult behavior that we manage in spite of ourselves.

Note to self: You're writing about Sam .... Not you and Sam!

Ok, a recap. Do not expect all those face scrunching, forehead wrinkling, searching for the right word grimacing faces that actors playing songwriters make. Sam doesn't work like that. Sam writes songs like Freddie Couples plays golf. At a level that appears effortless. It's probably an illusion. Not the creative part. No, I get the feeling the real world keeps pulling on his pant leg. As the music he needs to make keeps nibbling at the hours, Sam has remained determined to make time for the family he adores and still meet the deadlines he's committed to!

It's the juggler that Sam has become that perhaps impresses me most. There's a level of "normalcy" that he manages amidst the insanity of major rock and roll success. And that's success at a level that most people only dream of. It's that 'Father Knows Best" devotion that makes me admire Sam, the man, as much as I marvel at his creativity. I love him and I like him. He's a great friend.

Muzoids love Sam. Want what he's got. I think it's his world class authenticity. He's eternally "one of the guys." A reluctant celebrity, Sam's real. And something about his friendship feels as good as the music he makes. "Feel" is everything when you wanna move bodies and open hearts. Sam does "Feel!" Get the feel right and you just might end up dropping a few billion-stream chart toppers too.

Sam's secret to writing massive hits remains Sam's secret. We really never talk about it. Or music really. What I can tell you is that there is joyful noise in his DNA—kindness in his actions, tenacity, respect, and originality in everything he does. Start turning pages and you'll see why heads turn when Sam walks in the room. And why the world smiles.

I can guarantee it'll be your pleasure!

Blessings and thanks,
Paul Williams

# Author! Author!

On May 27, 1977, the morning of his forty-third birthday, my father bounded down the stairs and proudly announced that he'd begun writing his first book. I was so happy for him. So in awe of him. I darted off to school and relayed this most exciting news to each and every classmate in grade two.

Today is January 1, 2022.

My pops never finished the book.

You see, just like Carl and Ellie's shattered journey in Pixar's animated *Up*, my dad's unfinished words died on his hard drive before he ever got to share them with the world. He lived such a fascinating life and, tragically, there's little record of it. And I guess that's what ultimately inspired the passages ahead—the fear that my own strange tale would inevitably end up lost on some faraway iCloud never to be passed down to my kid. So in tribute to my incredible old man, I decided to put my life on paper for posterity.

Now, there are several things you should know about me before we dig in. I've never sung anything on the radio except background vocals that are usually buried in the mix, so consider yourself blessed. I've never appeared in movies, though I was offered the nonspeaking role of "The DJ" in a Freddie Prinze Jr. flick that I immediately passed on when I learned "The DJ" had to spend two shitty weeks in a pit of extras with no special culinary options. I've had little TV exposure beyond an awkward talking-head soundbite on the lowest-rated episode of VH1's *Behind the Music,* plus a few holiday morning show performances where I bopped around with a keytar affixed to my chest with zero fucks left to give. I dress like a confused hybrid of '80s B-boy meets *The Odd Couple*'s Jack Klugman. My genetic features are large and my hairline is compromised. And as I have no crackerjack co-writer behind the curtain puppeteering my tale, you'll soon find that I'm a bit of a literary disaster as well.

All that being said, I do have one defined skill.

I can actually write a song.

If you're a popular music connoisseur, you've probably heard some form of my work in your everyday life. Maybe in your sweaty Zumba class? Possibly in some marginal movie or TV show that you streamed? Perhaps blaring in the background at some sporting event? Most definitely at your dentist's office!

Yes, somehow in this surprising run, I've created a bunch of tunes that have sneakily entered the wider consciousness. More interestingly, though, I've been blessed to collaborate with a stack of legends. Everyone from One Direction to Katy Perry; Carole King to Ringo Starr; Panic! at the Disco to Def Leppard. I know that sounds pretty slick, but trust me: it didn't begin that glamorous. In the front half of my career, I survived more calamitous flops, flats, and false starts than any living soul on record. Today, those creative scars have become my trophies. At this point, I've spent more than thirty years marathoning through the endless valleys and occasional peaks of musical miles, but in the end, I crossed that damn finish line. Once you've retraced my long strange journey, hopefully you'll be inspired to embark upon your own.

## CHAPTER 1

# Andy Warhol Was
# My Babysitter

I was born in Lindsay-era Manhattan. Family folklore has it
that upon receiving the first
smacks of life from the doctor, I
pissed all over my own face. This
set an ugly precedent. Shortly
after my arrival, my folks moved
my brother, Ben, and me out of
the savagely rotting Big Apple as
a means of protecting their flock.

Lil' me with transistor radio always on blast.

But after a few months at our new upstate New York accommodations, some junkie at the end of our dirt road threatened to kidnap my
four-year-old self.

My life was off to a rocky start.

We moved again and finally settled in Chappaqua, a sleepy Westchester County town that the stately Horace Greeley had put on the
map a century back. When we arrived it was a small, Clinton-less
suburban enclave with not much to show for it—well, except for a
local hospital that had birthed *The Love Boat*'s Captain Stubing.

Growing up in those lazy years, we lived the typical area code 914
existence, except we weren't typical. We were kinda like sideshow

freaks. Ben and I had different dads. He was the son of a blue blood who died when Ben was only one. His father's ancestry was some real *Mayflower* shit. He was even a direct descendant of John Adams. It was pretty wild. My parents were also some fascinating cats. They were quirky Ivy League academics who struggled to fit into the box of their surroundings. In his late teens, my pops went professional as a modern dancer with the famed José Limón troop, but after being forced into a premature retirement (having broken every toe on both feet), he resumed school, graduated from Yale's School of Architecture, and went to work first under Phillip Johnson and then later as a five-decade professor at Pratt Institute. Clearly the old man had a pretty heavy résumé. He was also a beautiful soul. Incredibly nurturing and ritualistically pragmatic. He'd get lost in his head for days on end, but was always the voice of reason when needed.

And Mom? Well, she sure as fuck wasn't your stereotypical '70s housewife. She didn't drive the carpool, she didn't have girlfriends, she hated Hallmark. She dug hard bop jazz and rebellion.

If Dad was my rock, Mom was my rock star.

A few years after graduating from Pembroke College at Brown University, Mom began her career as a small-time collector dealing nineteenth-century American furniture out of our house. She had a brilliant eye but, of equal importance, she was the most agile navigator. I loved the way she maneuvered through life. It was a literal master class. Within a matter of years, she had made a real name for herself in the antiques community by forming an interior-decorating partnership with a younger Manhattan collector named Jed Johnson. Their collaborations consumed her entire existence.

During that stretch, maternal instincts were few and far between; thus, I was the definitive Stouffer's Pizza latchkey kid. Since my brother had little interest in my shades of weird and my pops was always in Brooklyn teaching, I was frequently found wandering the neighborhood cul-de-sacs alone, talking to imaginary friends. I was so bored and lonely that, at the age of nine, I began volunteering for the Chappaqua Democratic Party, handing out leaflets at campaign rallies on the weekend. My parents weren't even registered voters. I aimed to perplex.

Now, around that stretch, Mom realized her lack of quality time with me could potentially be long-term damaging, so she concocted a Band-Aid of a parenting solution. She decided to let me tag along with her to NYC on the weekends as she scoured her go-to downtown antique shops. I think the fact that I was a generally polite and somewhat self-sufficient kid gave her the confidence to let me loiter in those work situations. Sure, it bored the hell out of me, but it was better than any of the alternatives. Unfortunately for my mom, though, this occurred right when I first got on hooked on music.

While most little kids of that era were initially seduced by the KISS Army, for me, at least, it was the Beatles and the Bee Gees that sucked me in, and soon I became singularly obsessed with building the illest of fourth-grade vinyl war chests. Packing tons of determination, I started hijacking those trips with my mom by pestering and pleading for East Village record shop detours until she finally acquiesced, which would inevitably narrow her (already slim) work window. This was obviously mad frustrating for her, so one morning she came up with a plan B. We jumped in the dirty Peugeot 504 (yes, my mom was a gearhead as well) and sped toward the city together, but when we exited FDR Drive at Seventy-Seventh Street, I started questioning the situation.

"Where we going?" I inquired.

She replied, "Babysitter."

I was livid. I could have stayed home with a damn babysitter. At least home would've guaranteed more of my beloved Stouffer's French Bread Pizza.

We pulled up to a townhouse on East Sixty-Sixth Street and knocked on the door. The babysitter slowly pulled it open.

Holy fuck.

It was Andy Warhol.

Yes, on that day, Andy Warhol was my babysitter.

You see, unbeknownst to my young, naive self, Jed Johnson was Andy's live-in boyfriend. As my mom and Jed began to ascend to the uppermost echelon of the international design world (clients included notables like Mick Jagger and Yves Saint-Laurent), it was now officially all hands on deck for my childcare. I guess Andy was a hand.

"Hi," I managed to utter.

I could barely speak. I knew he was uber-famous. I'd seen his photos in the newspapers and on TV. He was certainly the first celebrity I'd ever shaken hands with. Then Mom and Jed peaced out.

Now as you'd expect, Andy was super awkward in my presence. He guided me through his townhouse very slowly. I was definitely awestruck and hella nervous. When we finally reached the kitchen, Andy sat my ass down in front of a portable television and put on a Yankees game for me to vegetate with. I stared straight ahead at the TV, making sure I didn't exhibit my usual brand of social bumbling. He reclined in a chair on the other side of the room, alternately sorting mail or talking on the phone. Between us were two sweet housekeepers, Nena and Aurora, and two shorthaired dachshunds, Archie and Amos. Every hour or so, Andy walked over and made (very) small talk.

"Do you like Famous Amos cookies?" he asked.

Yes, sir.

Nena would proceed to mollify me with a cookie, the dogs would bark, and Andy would retreat back into his routine.

Now at this point, it's only right for me to mention that the previous week I had missed three days of school with a bad cold. I was still a total snotty mess. There was only one problem.

I had a strange aversion to tissues.

Looking back, it must've been my first streak of anarchy. I adamantly refused to use them. In fact, years later, in my early adult life, I randomly ran into a third-grade classmate, Anne Northwell, who instantly shouted, "Sam Hollander! Oh my God! I remember you . . . Booger Sam! You were the kid who always rubbed your nose boogies on your sleeve!" It was mortifying. She was right, though. In fourth grade, my sleeves were frequently coated in a greenish hue.

That day at Andy's, the slime began to flow sometime during hour two. In short time, my sleeve was a murky, Everglades-like swamp. I'd run out of sleeve space. I started panicking. Please stay lodged, boogies.

PLEASE STAY FUCKIN' LODGED!

Growing up is built on bad decisions, so I did the unthinkable. I began rubbing my green mini-rockets on the underside of Andy's majestic kitchen table. God, it was so wrong. But it was so essential. It was at least an hour of agony until the green stuff ceased. With my moist face now resting on the table in my even moister arms, Andy approached me one final time and asked me if I had any use for an autographed baseball. My eyes lit up like Luke Skywalker's lightsaber. This day was such an emotional joyride: fear, fun, everything in between. He casually handed me a ball signed by Thurman Munson—the captain of the Yankees. I could barely speak. I hyperactively thanked him while, luckily for Andy, avoiding all hand-to-hand contact with him. No boogers, no foul. It was my first taste of celebrity, and I loved all of the fixings.

The inner bliss of that day at the babysitter's lasted an entire week.

I floated through my Douglas Grafflin Elementary classes like a kite.

That is, until my dickhead brother and his friends decided to play Home Run Derby with my autographed ball and it landed somewhere deep in the pine trees behind our house.

I never saw the ball again.

Thurman Munson tragically died a few months later, and that old Rawlings probably would have paid a nice chunk of my kid's first semester of college tuition if it still existed, but, alas, such is life.

In 1980, Jed and Andy broke up, and my babysitter moved on. Seven years later, Andy passed away. Almost a decade after that, Jed tragically departed on TWA Flight 800 somewhere over Long Island. There is some light at the end of this dark bridge and tunnel, though.

Thanks to my mother (and the babysitter), I got an incredible head start in dealing with newspaper notables and glitterati. As I went off into the world and I was exposed to more famous folks, I was rarely, if ever, shook. Also, it's worth mentioning that although my

Andy Warhol and his dog Archie.

nose boogers are still alive and thriving, I've fully accepted the joys of Kleenex into my life.

RIP Booger Sam.

CHAPTER 2

# Kill Me in a Record Shop

y brain is incapable of turning off its songwriting mechanism.
I spend every moment soaking in this fascinating world and
then subsequently drowning my iPhone notes with indiscrim-
inate impressions of it. It's a total fixation. I think it all started the
night my mom and dad, usually on the reclusive end of the spectrum,
threw on their Saturday best and rallied down to NYC for a friend's
birthday party at late-era Studio 54. They usually ducked these soirées
the way I avoided all of my homework assignments. Nightlife and
socializing were never their thing. It didn't help that they had slightly
aged out of the 54 demographic. Factor in their general disdain for
anything designer drug or disco, and it was all a bad fit.

When they arrived that evening, they were introduced to a "super
cool" music-making fella. His name was Nile Rodgers. They instantly
recognized his handle from my jabbering. His Chic cuts were always
in rotation on my turntable. Since I spent endless hours reading the
credits on records like Scripture, I was well aware of the fact that
Nile had segued from artist to songwriter/producer for others (Diana
Ross, David Bowie, Madonna, and more), but I had no idea what a
writer/producer actually did.

Somehow, Nile was patient enough to chat with my parents for a
couple of hours without pause and they fell madly in love with him

Nile Rodgers.

that night. Who wouldn't? He's an incredibly charming guy. By evening's end, they could have written a lengthy account of his career exploits. The next morning, my parents recounted all the amazing play-by-play at breakfast before I dipped to school. I was completely freaking out. As they explained Nile's role in the recording process, the match was instantly lit. I realized songwriting and music production were more than a curiosity for me. They were meant to be my higher calling. The record was a movie, and I could be both the screenwriter and director. There was only one problem. I was just a dish of thirteen-year-old nothingness.

We'd moved again, to Bedford Hills, New York, a couple of years prior, and I still had zero bearings. I'd hop on the bus and attempt to connect with the neighborhood kids, but I always felt one step off kilter. Visually the prototypical Spock-eared dork, I was neither athletic enough to be special nor academically curious enough to run with the intellectuals. Basically, I was a rudderless floater. On most days, I rushed home from school and self-sequestered in my room and played with my crates of vinyl. The only thing I was interested in was my ever-expanding record collection. Well, and girls, but girls were way out of my (little) league.

Now, when you're dancing on the sidelines of cool, you search far and wide for your thing. My thing was endlessly scouring for 45s, 12-inch singles, and LPs. You'd have to kill me in a record shop before I exited without a purchase. My records were the only commodity that differentiated me from the rest of the kids and lifted me from the mire of my questionable social standing. Having a brother who was ahead of the curve was the game changer. In high school, Ben had little exposure to broader stuff, so he tended to default to

Molly Hatchet's "Flirtin' with Disaster" as the soundtrack of his first junked-up Z28. Then he went off to Boston University. When he rolled home on that first Thanksgiving break, his milk crates had magically transformed to all things new wave and no wave, 12-inches, and bootlegs. Suddenly, his tastes were impeccably cool. He introduced me to everything he knew. For years, my tiny record collection had been a part-time sanctuary. Soon, it was beginning to hook me like some *New Jack City* basshead.

On the days I wasn't digging in the proverbial crates, I'd take the bus to my neighbor George's house and melt into his couch for the next three hours studying each and every moment of MTV (Cable in my house? Never). After sprinting home and dashing through dinner, I'd settle into bed with the clock radio set to all the nighttime radio shows. WKTU. WAPP. WLIR. On the weekends, I'd wake up and immediately begin making lists of the songs and chart positions on Casey Kasem's *American Top 40* countdown.

I was on my way to becoming *the* music obsessive in my grade. My confidence grew, but as I roamed the halls, the name John McMahon was always looming. It seemed that he was truly the Grand Poobah of record collectors at Fox Lane Middle School. I had to meet this kid. From the moment we hung, we became instant buds. I had finally found a mentor and coconspirator for all things dripping in semi-geek. John had impeccable records and an actual working jukebox lined with stellar 45s. He also had a museum-worthy baseball card collection. He'd started this little hobby in fourth grade with the purchase of an elderly couple's complete set of 1939 Play Ball cards that he nabbed from an ad in our local pennysaver. That initial bounty was worth a ton. Remember, this was 1978, before *Antiques Roadshow* awoke everyone to the reality that there might just be cardboard gold buried in those old attic shoeboxes. By the time I finally entered the world of McMahon, he'd amassed a card and memorabilia collection worth over six figures. And he was twelve. He also had a VHS player. I had an RCA Videodisc Player. I was the only kid in the town with an RCA Videodisc Player. This wasn't VHS or Beta. This wasn't even a LaserDisc Player.

This was a fuckin' *RCA Videodisc Player.*

BONUS CUT

The RCA Videodisc Player was, hands down, the biggest piece-of-shit video playback machine ever to beset the home-video world. Of course, it was my anarchist (and selectively cheap) mother who refused to pony up for a VHS, even though my brother and I begged and pleaded. A natural-born contrarian, she always had to go against the grain. Right after her purchase, Ben and I raced to all the local video shops (which were soon collectively bludgeoned by Blockbuster) in search of Videodisc rentals. There were none. All we could muster up were five RCA Videodiscs available at a local liquidator: *Phantasm*, *The Blues Brothers*, *An American Werewolf in London*, *Midnight Express*, and *Emanuelle in Bangkok* (quite an eye opener). We watched each of them on loop until our eyeballs burned, but that was the least of our problems. You see, just like a cheap vinyl pressing, RCA Videodiscs would skip more and more after each viewing. Eventually, it was a stream of atrocious stutters. We had to junk each disc within months.

John's VHS, on the other hand, was sick. That shit was unflappable. One day after school, we were watching our absolute favorite film at the time, the Ramones vehicle *Rock 'n' Roll High School*, when he let me in on a secret. He and his father were about to set off to a White Plains parking lot for a very covert deal.

With Johnny Ramone.

Yes, the Ramones' guitarist had driven an hour upstate to deal '52 Bowman baseball cards with a twelve-year-old. You can't make this shit up. Suddenly, rock 'n' roll was even more real and seemingly obtainable. It was that Peter Pan awakening when you realize that adults can literally be just as ridiculous as yourself and exist in a beautiful, perma-kid purgatory forever.

Later that year, John and I finally made one trade between us. I parted ways with three mint-condition Mike Schmidt rookie cards in exchange for a stack of fifteen K-Tel compilation records. Though I knew I was dealing with a shark, I felt strangely compelled to do it.

Today those Mike Schmidt cards that I traded to John are worth about $800 apiece. The K-Tel records I received in return are worth a little less than five dollars for the entire batch. Five dollars! And you know what? I wouldn't change a single thing. That stack of wax compilations was my introduction to the seemingly illogical lumping of Nile Rodgers's disco, soft rock, Philly soul, novelty, hard rock, and glam all under one genre-less pop umbrella. And it's in that kind of grouping where I'd categorize the songs I write today. When I dig in to collaborate with an artist, my sole focus is on the tune at hand. Musical lanes and whatever production styles are in vogue at the time remain an afterthought. For me, at least, genres don't exist. As long as I'm connecting with the artist's point of view and crafting a tune that raises its hand, I get that very same twelve-year-old kid rush I did every time I unearthed a magical, elusive album in a record shop stack.

# CHAPTER 3

# Audio Concepts

As junior high wound down, there was only one ceremonial occasion left: the Fox Lane Middle School Shadowing Day. This would be my first musical step toward my future, and I had waited all friggin' year for it.

For Shadowing Day, we were required to list our top three dream vocations; then, if the fates allowed, we'd get to spend a day apprenticing the local professional of our dreams. If I remember correctly, most of the girls chose teachers or veterinarians. Most of the boys chose coaches or cops. Me? I chose "record producer." For my second and third choices, I chose "record producer." No plan B. I wanted to be Nile Rodgers. A week went by in a daze as I imagined myself mastering the craft in some recording studio that was wall-to-wall with Sunset Strip heavy metal groupies. I mean, it seemed plausible, right?

Finally, the day arrived.

We all squirmed at our desks as our teacher revealed the results. One by one, we were asked to walk up to the front of the class and receive our destination. When my name was called. I leaped out of my desk and hurried to my teacher's side.

"Okay, Sam Hollander—your turn."

*Fuck yeah*, I thought.

"So you asked to shadow . . . [extremely awkward pause] . . . a record producer?"

That's correct.

"Okay. Well, you are gonna be spending the day at [uncomfortable pause] . . . Audio Concepts!"

A couple of kids chuckled. One girl clapped politely.

"Audio Concepts?" I asked.

"Yup. You're obviously a music lover. Well, Audio Concepts did a bang-up job installing my husband's car stereo!"

Now, picture the biggest gut-wrenching loss in the history of the *Price Is Right* Showcase Showdown and multiply that shit times infinity. That's where I was. I guess in the musically ignorant mind of my eighth-grade teacher, record producing translated to car stereo installation. In all honesty, I don't remember walking back to my seat, because at that exact second my spirit was already murdered.

The following Monday, my pops dropped me off in the Audio Concepts parking lot. It was drizzling and brutally cold. I slumped my way into the store, where I was immediately shuttled into a rat trap of a side office. I sat there alone, melting under the fluorescent light for a solid hour as I eavesdropped on a couple of Skoal-tobacco-cheeked salesmen swapping tales of rude customers and "horny chicks." It felt like an eternity. I drifted in and out of consciousness.

Then my "mentor," Lance, entered the room. He was thirty-five and leathery with a Nicorette grin. "Follow me, kid," was the extent of his dialogue. As I quickly learned, Lance hated life but he sure loved the '80s metal band Krokus. He led me over to a dusty Cutlass Supreme in the parking lot and had me stand in complete silence by the passenger side as he began to dial in the stylish Pioneer KE-8300. Tiny drops of rain danced across my frozen Jewfro as Krokus's "Ready To Burn" blared in my ears. All I could do was daydream of a better place. A place with no rusty Phillips head screwdrivers. A place devoid of faceplates and Swiss heavy metal. Lance installed stereo after stereo that morning, never engaging me other than the occasional "Hand over the pliers, guy." After a few hours of torture courtesy of this tobacco-breathed clown, I feigned sickness and had my old man pick me up. When my pops arrived, I slumped into the car with tears welling up in my eyes. I could sense he empathized with my frustration. In that eight-minute ride up the hill toward home, I knew right there and then that I had no creative future in my town.

Four more years and I'd be history.

# CHAPTER 4

# The Bionic Homecoming

I met Huey Lewis at a Grammy party a couple of years back and I misted up. No lie. I'm sure he was a bit perplexed as my tears gathered, but to a Reagan-era youth who desperately attempted to find his cool, Huey was simply the smoothest dude in the galaxy.

Huey Lewis and my bawling self.

Growing up, I idolized all those early MTV gods. A few of them actually resided in my area code, which was mind-blowing for an aspiring music kid. At least half of Foreigner, a couple of Isley Brothers, Peter Frampton, Phil Ramone (Billy Joel's brilliant producer who I fanboyed) and John Waite of "Missing You" fame were all locals. I can still recall seeing John Waite loiter in front of his own albums at the record shop in the mall. I'm not sure if he was keeping a close track of his sales figures or if he was secretly hoping some rabid fans might start banshee screaming in his presence, but either way I felt like I belonged in his tribe. If I was ever gonna see my name in those same racks, though, I knew I had to put myself out there, so at the tail end of my junior year at Fox Lane High School, I summoned up the nerve to audition to be the singer in a rock band comprised of prodigious senior shredders. Though packing zero mic ability at the time, I actually made the cut through two rehearsals. Then they bounced me a week or so later. Probably a wise move on their end. Undeterred, I started my own group with my pals Dan Woods, who beautifully handled both bass and harmonies (and who we'll reconnect with later); Jason Young, who could, and still can, shred his face off; Neil Minsky, a brilliant punk rock kid who was also a bit of synth wiz; and Pete Kane, who'd just begun playing the drums, but held it down. Our ragtag outfit, The Psychoplathix, had one impromptu performance at some kid's party before we hastily decided we were ready for the mecca: the Battle of the Bands. My bandmates were up to this momentous challenge, but I totally sucked. My voice was pitchy and I yelled a lot. My stage presence was ultra wack. I was no Huey Lewis. We finished in a soul-crushing seventh place out of eight groups. Immediately after, we packed it in.

**BONUS CUT**

> The eighth-place finishers were a super tight, stoner rock outfit led by my future pals and musical cohorts Don Lunetta and Tyler Roe, who were rightfully disqualified for sneakin' in a thirty-year-old ringer on rhythm guitar. If those greedy jerks had just played by the damn rules, they would've leapfrogged us by at least six spots.

Now with no other band options and in desperate need of some sort of peer validation, I gave football a toss. My brother had been a pigskin star, so I figured it had to be in the genetic code. Man, my calculations were off. The coach was a guy named Big Ed, who seemed to get endless pleasure mocking me in front of the entire squad. This fella was just awful. He actually had the gall to tell a few of my football star pals to steer socially clear of me as I was simply a dirtbag who'd inevitably amount to zero. Ouch! Though I really worked my ass off to improve at the sport, it didn't help my cause that I struggled to buy into his witless rah rah bullshit. At the end of the day, as a semi-athletic insurgent, on-the-field greatness was my only potential positive outcome. Alas, greatness, or good-ness for that matter, never materialized as I was routinely benched and clowned by Big Ed until my spirit finally rotted away and I tossed in the towel.

The Fox Lane halls were lined with golden retrievers and chocolate Labs.

The chosen ones.

The desirables.

Sadly, I was never the first pick in any litter; academically, musically, athletically, even with girls, shit was always an uphill grind. So, at that fragile age, the stacking of all of my collective non-achievements really began to demoralize. I started skipping out of school and sneaking home early for two-hour depression naps on the daily. My folks didn't know how to deal with me. In an exasperated fit, they summoned the help of their friend Rashid Silvera in the hopes that he could be the Tripper to my Rudy in *Meatballs*.

Rashid Silvera? He was the most fascinating of fellas. First and foremost, he was a much-beloved teacher down county at Scarsdale High School, where he was known to be a life-altering motivator (picture Robin Williams in *Dead Poets Society*). Randomly enough, at the same time he was also a groundbreaking male model. His mug graced the covers of *GQ* and *Essence*. He was charming and super smooth. He dated both civilians and celebrities, all ridiculously hot.

One night during that depressing stretch, in an attempt to boost my plummeting morale, Rashid phoned the house and asked me if I wanted to join him to watch the heralded Fox Lane versus Scarsdale homecoming football game festivities the following afternoon.

"No thank you, sir," I replied.

Then he dangled the carrot:

"Oh, that's too bad. It'd be you, me, and Lindsay Wagner."

My jaw hit the floor.

Lindsay Wagner?

*The Bionic Fuckin' Woman?!*

She was huge. I mean, she had already graced multiple *People* magazine covers and starred in more TV movies than humanly

The Bionic Woman.

possible! Just a few summers earlier, I had slurped from a Lindsay Wagner thermos at the town day camp. Now I had the opportunity to meet her?

I took a deep breath. "Sure." Translation: "Hell yeah!"

I woke up mad jittery the next morning and raced down the Saw Mill River Parkway toward Rashid's White Plains home, my goosebumps pumping as Huey Lewis's "If This Is It" blared on the radio. I pulled into Rashid's driveway and holy shit, there she was in all of her gorgeous glory! My nerves were completely on fire. I managed to mumble a pathetic "Hi." Then we all crammed into Rashid's Honda and set off on the twelve-minute trek over to the high school. My mind was plotting like crazy. The moment we stepped out of the car, Rashid was immediately mauled by a report-card-questioning student.

"You guys go ahead," he said. "I'll meet up with you in a second."

Lindsay and me.

Alone at last.

The game was already a few minutes underway, but somehow my unearned swagger began to awaken. Slowly, we glided toward the field, chitchatting like old chums. Then, on some slick shit, I steered us on a roundabout path that ended with a deliberate strut behind the Fox Lane team bench and directly in front of the bleachers filled with my classmates. We slid by in cinematic slow motion. I made sure to continue jabbering away, so they'd all just assume we were besties. I was successfully pulling a *Can't Buy Me Love* Ronald Miller and scamming myself up the pecking order with every step. Honestly, it was my finest work to date.

When we finally set up a picnic on the adjacent hill, the packed stands began turning away from the field and fixing their gaze on us. A couple of girls ran over and begged for an intro. Some idiot even not-so-casually whispered in my ear that he used to jerk off to her poster. I felt like I was on top of the damn world, but I hadn't even hit the apex. My dopey ex-coach finally averted his eyes away from the field and glanced in my direction. His puzzled and pummeled reaction is still frozen in my brain. I gave him a Huey Lewis–worthy wink, and continued gabbing away with Lindsay Wagner. Farewell, Big Ed. Thanks for the kerosene. This was one of the first moments when I realized the power of celebrity transcended all. I was hooked then and there. I wanted to play in THAT game.

## CHAPTER 5

# The College Drop-In

Sometime during those last dog days of high school, my buddy Jill Cohen forged the following note for me: "To whom it may concern: Please excuse Sam Hollander from gym today. He's fighting a nasty cold. Thank you. Judith Hollander." Quite simple and direct.

Those words freed me to race straight down to the city to catch Daryl Hall, music attorney Allan Grubman, and then–Hall & Oates manager Tommy Mottola keynote a panel at the New York Public Library about breaking into the music business. By the time I finally exited my seat, I'd learned more in those two hours than the entire previous year or so in classrooms.

Because of that early (and gratis) intro to the business, I've never once taken a penny to speak at high schools and universities. I figure if those distinguished cats could find the time to inform without lining their pockets, I should always do the same. Funnily enough, I still proudly stow that now slightly illegible and frayed get-out-of-jail note in my wallet as a reminder of all the sacrifices, dreams, and schemes it took to break down barriers. I can only hope my kid chases whatever passion she has with the same intensity. If she skips school a couple of times to color outside the lines, she won't have to forge an excuse; I'll write the damn note for her.

Now, many music folks I've met through the years had horrific high school experiences. That just wasn't the case for me. Truth be told, I really dug my hometown and my group of high school friends, but eventually claustrophobia started to grab hold of my throat, and I needed to seek more musical stimuli. I began spending all of my free time on the Metro-North lines rushing to the city to catch any possible concert. I saw everyone from REM, the Smiths (who broke my heart when they blew that night), and Echo & the Bunnymen to Run-DMC, Doug E. Fresh, and UTFO. Some days, I'd just roll down to the Village and loiter around Tower Records and The Wiz just to hear all the eclectic records booming out of the Jeeps on lower Broadway. The electricity was wild. It was obviously bound to be my home.

So, as high school wound down, I pleaded with my folks to let me apply for my first record label internship in the city. I'm sure they thought I had a next-to-nothing shot, but I cold-called every record company number I could find in my stack of 12-inch records anyway. Most of these were indie dance and hip-hop outfits. Then, after a week or so of leaving long, awkward messages, I finally got a call back. This deep-ass voice on the other end seemed a bit mystified as to why I was inquiring about a gig. He grilled me about my intentions until he realized my kid heart was in the right place.

A couple of Mondays later, I took the after-school train to 125th Street in Harlem and walked some dark, circuitous path to get to the DNA Records office located at the corner of 141st and Malcolm X Boulevard. This was when Public Enemy and Boogie Down Productions ruled the streets. Consciousness was everywhere. So was crack. Probably not the best time for wide-eyed Westchester kids traversing the mean streets and alleys near the Rucker. I didn't sweat it. I wouldn't let anything stop me from getting in the game. But when I arrived at DNA, it wasn't exactly what I had envisioned. No gold records. No leather couches. No elaborate phone setup or cigar-chomping mogul. Just a cramped apartment cluttered floor to ceiling with 12-inch singles.

After a quick introduction, one of the employees set me up at a dusty-ass card table, where I began the arduous task of assembling cardboard shipping boxes and stuffing them with vinyl to ship to radio stations. It redefined mundane. I found myself watching the second hand on the clock limp along, just as I had during the previous fifteen years of schooling. It took only a couple of days for me to realize that this factorylike vinyl packing gig would be my glass ceiling at DNA. None of the older cats working there acknowledged my existence. I didn't want to overstay my welcome, so after a brief run on 141st, I bounced.

As I careened toward high school graduation, I was buried in the bottom third of my class. My SAT score was anemic, so my folks signed me up for the Kaplan Test Prep course. Somehow, when I took the SAT a second time, I did significantly worse. How that was even possible?! Undeterred, I delusionally applied to a dozen colleges. And that spring, I got ten rejections back—one thin-ass envelope after another. NYU was an absolute crusher: I was waitlisted, but they never called. My only acceptances were from Temple University in Philadelphia and the University of the Pacific in Stockton, California.

What?

You've never heard of the UOP?

**BONUS CUT**

> Famous UOP alumni include jazz pianist Dave Brubeck, *Psycho*'s Janet Leigh, and Bridget from that creepy Playboy Mansion series *The Girls Next Door.*

Now, you might wonder how I discovered this lesser known West Coast shipping port school. It certainly wasn't from the academic wisdom of my befuddled but kind guidance counselor, Mr. Krupberg, who strongly recommended the local community college for me (while simultaneously hitting me up to DJ his daughter's bat mitzvah for a discounted fee). No, I actually discovered this higher-learning hub in the back of a worn-out college guide at the town library that I frantically scoured for any possible college with a music production major. At that time, there were only a few options, the bulk of which were way out of reach of both my talent level and GPA. If I truly wanted to learn how to mastermind records, the University of the Pacific was probably my only option, so I sequestered myself in front of our Apple II computer for a week spitting out the most passionate application ever to UOP. I pitched my wares as an "aspiring" song-writer/producer. I mean, I had journals of song lyrics. I could DJ a little. Music was my singular obsession; I just needed to connect the dots. Basically, I begged.

It worked.

After four years of disgraceful underachieving, the acceptance letter I received from the University of the Pacific was the most inspiring moment of my young life. It came from the dean of the Music Production school. It read something like this:

> *Dear Sam,*
>
> *It is my pleasure to offer you admission to the incoming Class of 1992 at the University of the Pacific. This opportunity to join one of the most outstanding music production programs in the country comes in recognition of your immense musical gifts. From your essay submission, it is quite obvious that you are so uniquely talented. Not just a brilliant artist, but a musical prodigy who will be a breath of fresh air . . .*

It floored me. I couldn't believe this man saw all of this potential in my essay alone. Shit, no educator in my *high school* had ever identified any real promise in me whatsoever, except my senior year philosophy teacher, who once walked me down the hall and said the

Go Tigers!

following simple words that cut me to the core: "I don't think you get it yet, but Sam, you're much brighter and significantly more interesting than you think."

Thank you, Dr. Berman. At the time, I needed to hear that more than you could ever understand.

Still, I couldn't choose between my two college options. I mean, Temple had just been in basketball's Elite Eight. That was pretty sick. And America's favorite dad at the time wore the school's sweatshirt on

*The Cosby Show* every few episodes. He sure seemed like a swell ambassador for the university. Thankfully his sweatshirt privileges have since been revoked. I was vacillating. I spun the proverbial Bartles & Jaymes wine cooler bottle and chose the west side sight unseen on the weather upgrade alone. Since I was the first of the old gang to ship off to college (a good three weeks before any of my classmates), I threw the most epic of early August going-away ragers. A couple of hundred loaded revelers celebrated my departure. My hands finally made contact with a very long-sought-after set of boobies. It was the best farewell ever.

My parents dropped me off at JFK Airport early the following morning. Why they weren't actually accompanying me on this crazy cross-country move was a bit of an unspoken weirdness, but our relationship was somewhat fraught at that time due to my years of underachieving, so I chose my battles wisely. We awkwardly hugged goodbye as I set off for my Pan Am multi-connection flight. First stop? Detroit Rock City. The plane landed briefly in Motown as four or five slightly disheveled stragglers hopped aboard. A pink-mohawked chick slid into the one empty seat next to me. Inclement weather kept us grounded for another hour. We began to chat. Her name was Kelly. Guess where she was headed.

The University of the Pacific!

Craziness, right? Even nuttier, she pulled out her admission letter, and it was a carbon copy of mine. All that personal shit about my being a musical prodigy? It seemed we'd both been rooked.

Four hours later, we landed in San Francisco for our second connection. After another brutal layover, we disembarked at Stockton Metropolitan Airport completely shredded. As we walked toward the terminal, we exchanged a half-hearted *Breakfast Club* high five: "Go us!"

---

The airport was desolate.

Where were the smiling California sunbaked faces that blanketed the school's catalog? Where were the palm trees? Where was any actual living human?

We anxiously made our way over to the pay phone to call the school for a little assistance. No one answered. In a panic, we decided to split a taxi to the campus. After a forty-minute wait, a driver from the local fleet arrived. He seemed a few years older than us but, man, he looked worse for the wear. We kicked it with him the entire ride, and guess what? It turned out he had graduated from the very same music production program two years earlier! Then he couldn't find a job. Struggling to pay the bills in a city in fiscal ruins, our cabbie had been forced to start hacking while concurrently developing a nasty crack habit. He was three months sober and mildly optimistic.

"Um, it's a cool program, I guess. I don't know, man. The town is pretty messed up. Did you get into any other schools?"

Silence.

We pulled up to the university's main entrance, paid our cab driver $25, and wished him well with his sobriety.

"Every day's a rehab rainbow," he replied as he sped off.

We were now both completely tweaked out ourselves. Then, it got worse. The main campus entrance was a solid half-mile away from our respective dormitories. Again, with no helpers in sight. And it was jet black outside. That's when we began the joyless task of pushing our respective duffel bags across the campus—one yard at a time. We'd each sweatily push our first duffel bag a few feet. Then stop. Walk back and kick our second to the same spot. This took a solid hour. No lie. We must've passed two hundred students and faculty. They all ignored us. I couldn't recall feeling more broken. I parted ways with Kelly at my dorm. It was the most emo goodbye ever.

When I finally crawled through the entrance of my room, I threw both of my duffel bags down on the floor, but I felt restlessly trapped and rushed back outside to get some air. I started getting a *this was an awful fuckin' idea* feeling in my gut. I walked the campus for an hour, surveying the scene and becoming more depressed with every step. I just wasn't emotionally ready for this kind of a transition. I desperately tried to calm myself down, but my fight-or-flight reflex was screaming, "RUN!" I knew I had to get out of Stockton, or the movie would end real badly.

I called my parents, bawling my eyes out. They hung up on me. I called five more times. I begged and pleaded on the answering machine. I promised I'd enroll in a community college back home (Mr. Krupberg had apparently been on some Miss Cleo psychic shit). I vowed an honest-to-goodness academic awakening. After a stern, lengthy lecture from both of them, they bought me a one-way ticket out.

The following morning, I lay in the grass alongside the Stockton Airport runway and stared at the sky, Canal Street–knockoff Ray-Ban shades blanketing my eyes, pondering my questionable future. I still remember that moment of revelation vividly: I had spent eighteen years dicking around. I really had to get my shit together.

When I landed, my folks refused to acknowledge my presence. We rode in complete silence back to the house. I was now also the official laughingstock of my town. Since I'd set off for California early, the rest of my classmates hadn't even begun packing for their freshman exodus. Therefore, ladies and gentlemen, I was technically my grade's first dropout! That was quite a dubious distinction. It was a gruesome weekend.

The following Monday, over the most uncomfortable of breakfasts ever, my beyond-disappointed parents finally let me out of the timeout corner and broke some beautiful news. Since they knew I was still operating at the maturity level of a ten-year-old at that point, they'd been so convinced that my stunted self would hightail it out of Stockton in a flash that they had actually mailed in my signed Temple enrollment offer with a deposit a few weeks prior as a fail-safe. They knew I wouldn't be able to survive the West. It felt like *Trading Places*'s Randolph and Mortimer Duke had made a $1 bet on my futility. I began jumping up and down and bear-hugged them.

Now, Temple was a substantial upgrade for my fragile psyche. Just being in the orbit of the Philly Sound was inspiring. From Gamble and Huff and Hall & Oates to Schoolly D, the Hooters, and the Fresh

DO YOU HAVE WHAT IT TAKES?

IF YOU RAP, MIX, OR SING; DO YOU WANT A CHANCE AT SUCCESS?

Send A Well-Made 2 Song Demo-Tape To:

STP Productions
Peabody Hall - Rm. 114
2029 N. BROAD ST.
PHILLY, PA 19122

(include name, age, and a picture)

The world's saddest ad.

Prince, the city was dripping with music greatness, and I nerded out on that kinda thing. Week one, feeling mad inspired, I strolled over to Kinko's and printed up three hundred (mortifying) flyers that read, "Do you have what it takes? Send A Well-Made 2 Song Demo-Tape to STP Productions." STP was short for "Sam the Producer."

Yes, "Sam the Producer."

I walked around the Center Street area for five hours, taping these things to telephone poles. I had, and still have, no idea what service I would've been able to offer anyone who inquired, but blessedly for all, I didn't receive even one response. To quote the late D. Boon of the Minutemen: "I must look like a dork."

Temple was also a huge transition from home. The campus was surrounded by sketchy blocks on both sides. The dorms were real grimy. The rooms resembled horizontal telephone booths—possibly 150 square feet of space. There were also very few music options in the curriculum. I settled on the Radio-Television-Film major, but that felt like a general waste of time for what I was chasing. Needless to say, I knew I had to move on from Temple pretty quickly as well.

About two weeks into the semester, I made a weekend break back home and unearthed my NYU waitlist letter. It was signed by someone named Maryann Collins in admissions.

Thus began my courtship of Maryann Collins.

I persistently pounded Maryann's extension. Every Tuesday morning at ten. For some reason, she always made the mistake of answering. We became fast friends—or, to be more precise—she couldn't hide. I was always on the other end, spouting all my woeful tales, from the sweet architecture student down the hall who got jumped on the corner of Broad Street and limped back with a completely rearranged face, to my sweet, gentle giant of a roommate's dead cheesesteak wrappers, which left a nightly smell of carcass wafting around our Playmobil-sized room. I pled my musical dreams. My fears of failure. My general loneliness. I spewed anything I was feeling at any given moment. I just couldn't shut up. It was a therapy of sorts. In time, I began to get the sense that she found these weekly updates mildly amusing. Occasionally she'd pull in her coworkers, who I'd hear giggling on the other end on speakerphone. Then one day, she finally laid down the gauntlet:

"Okay, if you get a 3.2 this semester, you're in."

I hung up and screamed louder than a piercing lawn mower! I knew I had aced freshman lit. I had slayed a twentieth-century history class. Completely cruised through some sociology thing. That left only one essay. An intro to film history, a class I actually appreciated, but struggled in mightily. There was no way I was gonna slay that dragon. I sat there furiously scheming a way out. Then the way out magically appeared within minutes! A kid from down the hall looking for some cash to cop an ounce of weed offered to sell me his film history essay from two years ago. I gave him $40, retyped his A-graded offering, and man, I was ear-to-ear grinning. I could see myself sipping coffee on MacDougal Street with my NYU Washington Square roomies within a matter of weeks. The dragon had been slayed.

But the following morning, I got the worst call of my young grifter life. The professor dialed my dorm room extension and demanded to see me in his office at 1 PM. When I arrived, a kid named Alvin, who I vaguely recognized from the dorm's cafeteria, was sitting in the hall waiting as well. It appeared our douche of a dormmate had decided that one ounce of smoke wasn't enough, so he pawned both Alvin and myself the same damn essay. We were totally screwed, but somehow in that moment of duress a spin was birthed in my terrified mind. I locked eyes with the kid and whispered, "Let me talk."

Within three minutes, we were summoned inside. This was a life-defining moment. The professor cut right to the chase.

"Gentlemen, you both did quite well on your essays. Too well, actually. Your papers are 100 percent identical. I'd love an explanation if you have one."

Deep pause.

Then I let loose.

"I'm so sorry for the confusion, sir. Of course, our papers are identical. We collaborated. We thought that was acceptable for the assignment. We had no idea that wasn't cool." (Now, in all fairness, we had been allowed to partner up with a classmate for one exercise earlier in the semester.)

Alvin nervously nodded, but he sold it convincingly enough.

"I mean, we'd have to be absolute idiots to hand in the same paper when we're best friends!"

Then Alvin and I shot each other perfectly unscripted knowing glances, like Eddie Murphy and Dan Aykroyd at the end of *Trading Places*, that said, "It's true, we really are the closest of homies!" My heart was pumping like German techno. The professor remained mum.

Finally, after about twenty seconds of treacherous silence, he replied, "Okay. That makes more sense. These misunderstandings do happen every semester with freshmen. You both did such a solid job, though. I can't give you a perfect grade, but you'll do just fine. Oh, and guys, in the future, no collaborating unless I specifically give those instructions. If we have this talk again, you're done!"

We both thanked him profusely and stepped away from that office. I winked at Alvin and just kept on walking. I had a 3.3. Within a week, it was "Philadelphia Freedom."

## CHAPTER 6

# Only in New York, Kids, Only in New York

I was so ripe and ready to bite the shit out of the Apple as I hauled my now thrice-moved college duffel bags into the Tenth and Broadway NYU dorm. That first night in the city, I linked up with my old hometown pal Jaik Miller, who I'd met a year or so earlier when I caught him busking curbside in front of the Mount Kisco Ben & Jerry's. Though he was goofy-looking like me, he was surrounded by a mini-mob of cute, riveted girls as he blew through an incredible set of Cat Stevens covers. Man, I was jealous. In that thirstiest of moments, I knew this kid would play a huge role in my life. We both crashed Manhattan during that same January and ran around catching every concert in town together. I felt like we were two wacky cops in a buddy movie trolling the clubs night after night.

Jaik was such a unique and brilliant talent. He'd been writing original songs since middle school! During the last few years at Fox Lane, I'd begun messing with songwriting in a primitive form myself—mainly filling journals with bad teenage stanzas that read somewhere between Run-DMC and suspect Beat poetry. Those pages became the one safe place where I could emotionally spew, but I never really knew what to do with them. Jaik inspired me to believe I could take it all a step further.

When you take that first scary leap into songwriting, and spouting lyrics in particular, you'll undoubtedly find inspiration everywhere you look. Shitty relationships, hatred of your parents, Peter Pan syndrome—all that primal angsty shit. At some point, though, you will exhaust that initial internal mess of options, so to combat the inevitable creative K-hole that follows, I highly recommend a lengthy '80s-high-school movie binge (even '90s TV like *My So-Called Life* or *Dawson's Creek* should suffice). For all of you hipper-than-thous, you can fast the fuck forward, but John Hughes, Cameron Crowe, Amy Heckerling, Savage Steve Holland, et cetera inspired a heavy portion of my first dives into song. Though the bulk of those films recycled the same clichés—the cooler kid falling for the out-of-the-mix weirdo, the glow-up of the nerd who's magically transformed by a haircut and/or contact lenses, and the unholy pressure of the prom date pick—the all-encompassing themes of unrequited teen love and the general feeling of knowing you belonged someplace better, but never knowing where the fuck that was, were such relatable topics to me that they always fueled pen to paper when I needed the creative boost.

As the semester kicked in, my academic pursuits were on life support. I tried to absorb the required reading for the NYU music business and technology major, like M. William Krasilovsky and Sidney Shemel's *This Business of Music: Definitive Guide to the Music Industry* and Don Passman's *All You Need to Know About the Music Business*, but every time I cracked open one of those industry bibles, my ADHD would engulf me. The only course read that really blew my skull was Fredric Dannen's *Hit Men: Power Brokers and Fast Money Inside the Music Business*. The book was an inflammatory deep dive into the industry and all of its ruthless vendettas, insatiable greed, and nasty ambition. It was so dark and riveting. It was like a blueprint of all of the awfulness that would ensue if I ever actually permeated the game. I devoured it three times cover to cover.

Feeling the need to master the business outside of the classroom, I began to forsake social stuff and spent the bulk of my dorm room hours typing letters to any production company, recording studio, or label I could find in search of another internship. For a few weeks there were zero responses, but then I finally caught a break. A tiny indie called Big Beat Records decided to give me a shot. Big Beat was a small downtown NYC house music label started by a recent Brown University alum named Craig Kallman. The label first made some noise with "The Party" by Kraze, which sold 250,000 units worldwide. Soon after, Kallman signed Tara Kemp, who had a big radio tune. In time, Big Beat would be acquired by Atlantic Records; now, a hundred years down the road, Kallman is currently the chairman of Atlantic Records.

My stint at Big Beat lasted a full semester. My role there was similar to the Harlem gig at DNA, but Craig was actually receptive to my jabberings and gave me the leeway to learn the entry-level inner workings of the machine. I was one of two interns. The other was a kid named Adrian Bartos, who, under the moniker Stretch Armstrong, would go on to become one of the most influential DJs in hip-hop history. He was clearly way cooler than myself.

As I loitered around the Big Beat offices, I spent hours on end pondering my own creative path in this industry. In all my plans and schemes for reaching songwriting and production mastery, I'd never even calculated any real route to a career. I knew I definitely didn't have the makeup of a "label guy." I was too much of a shit stirrer to thrive in that machine. Then it finally walloped me one afternoon as I sat in the empty Big Beat hallway purging overrun trash cans and rodents: What if I followed the lead of Def Jam creator Rick Rubin and began writing and producing some hybrid of rap myself? On paper, it felt like a tremendous stretch, but I wondered, if I blended hip-hop with alt-rock and pop, maybe that could be my entry point into the club. For the three previous years, I'd kept a copy of the Rick Rubin *Village Voice* cover story profile, "He's the King of Rap, There Is None Higher, CBS Execs All Call Him

Sire" in my backpack, tailing me everywhere I went. Now it was all starting to make sense. As a senior at NYU, Rick birthed the home of T La Rock, LL Cool J, and the Beastie Boys in his dorm room. He released records that completely transformed the genre. We were both suburban kids with wicked diverse musical knowledge, so why couldn't I follow suit? Sure, I knew these thoughts were a stretch at best, because there were obviously a few gigantic potholes in my résumé that I needed to fill:

1. I didn't have any demonstrable writing or production proficiencies.
2. I had about three chords at my disposal, with zero theory to back them up.
3. I had no industry connections.
4. I was just kinda wack in general.

My pals and eventual collaborators, Arrested Development, titled their Grammy-winning debut *3 Years, 5 Months and 2 Days in the Life Of*, a reference to the amount of time between the band's conception and its first record deal. It actually took me three years and a few months myself to enter the stage. It certainly wasn't for lack of trying.

It all began the day I bought A Tribe Called Quest's *People's Instinctive Travels and the Paths of Rhythm*. I spun the record over and over for hours on end. Q-Tip's wordplay. Tip and Ali's beats. That shit was incredible. Tip was exactly my age and was already creating skull-melting boho soundscapes—the sophistication was so humbling on a myriad of levels. I questioned if I could ever concoct anything so fresh, but I sure as hell wanted to take a stab at it.

I placed a classified ad looking for cheap recording time and I got a response from a session drummer/programmer named Jim Mussen who had built a living room studio on West 111th Street. I booked my first session that very same day. When I arrived uptown, it was pretty obvious to Jim from the jump that I knew nothing, so he patiently guided me through some basic recording fundamentals. I brought a couple of records along to loop up. The first was the *Fat*

*Albert* theme; I wanted to jack the "Na na na, gonna have a good time" part. The second was the isolated recorder in the intro of Bob James's "Angela's Theme." Jim showed me how to "sample" fragments from these records in his Akai S900 sampler and then build the rest of a track around it. Once the bed of music was tight, I would write placeholder rhymes and hooks over it.

It was the craziest rush of my life. I began crafting cuts up there day and night at $15 an hour for studio time. Sometimes, the wonderful Jim let me hang around for free. It was all a bargain. It became the only thing in life that I cared about. I started skipping classes at NYU and hopping the uptown train with a knapsack of records on my shoulder. I made daily trips to off-the-grid vinyl liquidators around the city in search of fifty-cent cutout gems.

I just needed an MC.

I put feelers out all over the city, but I couldn't find a single interested rapper. I begged my boy MC Profit, the one truly gifted MC in my hometown, to give it a go. He spit one verse and ghosted. I never saw him again. Then a friend introduced me to a middle school teacher from New Haven who had ridiculous bars and charm. After we spent a magical day in the lab, he told me that he'd be down to keep going—if I wrote him a check for $5K! My bank account had a solid $120 in it at the time. That sure as fuck wasn't gonna happen, so on that most desperate of whims, I started laying down my own verses. Instantly, I felt unleashed. I literally spewed out my demons and issues for hours on end. You see, at the core, most writers feel like we're on the outside looking in. We use words and melodies to stitch up all of our broken inner mechanisms. From the first poems I ever wrote, the pen and notebook became my primary form of catharsis. Obviously, I didn't aspire to be an MC, or whatever the fuck I was doing, as I knew I lacked both the verbal believability and a marketable tone.

**BONUS CUT**

When I blessed the mic, I sounded like Nicolas Cage .

But as I began to tie-dye all of my influences, I started to see a MSNBC Steve Kornacki–worthy path form: In my warped psyche, I began to believe my pop-rap-alt-rock amalgamation might just be my winning ticket for writing recognition in a rapidly diversifying industry.

To help fund my "artist" efforts, I took a job "bouncing" at the famous downtown club the Bottom Line. During the club's first fifteen years, a slew of highly notables graced its stage, from Eric Clapton, Neil Young, and The Boss to Miles Davis, the Police, and Prince. When I arrived, however, the spot's luster had all but faded. It was now primarily just a hub for folk artists and '70s mainstays. My gig primarily involved the delicate art of gently coaxing drunken ex- and still-hanging-on-for-dear-life hippies, most of whom were my folks' age, to dial it the fuck down when they danced on tables or did rails of blow on the bathroom sink. This was not a particularly taxing gig, but the pay was shit: $35 a night plus occasional tips, free cheeseburgers, and risky fries from the kitchen. I should've called the Better Business Bureau, but instead I sucked it up for the sake of my burgeoning art. In the end, it was an excellent introduction to the Village, and I genuinely loved it.

Around this time, I made a new friend named Kennedy, a kid from Massachusetts who was stoking the same delusional microphone fire as me. Yes, Kennedy was also a rap dabbler. He was hoping it would be an entryway to his true passion: music video directing. He lived in a mammoth industrial loft on Twenty-Third and Seventh the size of a gymnasium. He shared it with four friends and a plumber named Joe who'd shown up one day for a quick shower installation and never left. Well, that's not exactly true. Eventually he did leave. Disappeared, actually, with Kennedy's checkbook in his back pocket. Years later, we learned he'd looted some other checkbooks as well, but from far scarier folks. He was eventually found swimming with the Hudson River fishes. No lie. To quote Cindy Adams, the era's preeminent gossip columnist, "Only in New York, kids, only in New York."

It was the wildest scene at Kennedy's, though. He threw rent parties every month and a fascinating cast of downtown freaks would partake. I loved every second of it. Since we both had fairly enormous aspirations, we began to collaborate on tunes, and Kennedy would pimp them all over town. Unlike myself at the time, Kennedy was uniquely magnetic. I knew it was only a matter of time before he got a nibble. It took less than two months. He hooked up his first record label meeting with an older fella named Hal who ran a small uptown reggae label. Though on a musical tip it seemed a strange fit, Hal bought Kennedy's phone pitch and agreed to meet with him. Since I produced Kennedy's track in question, he let me tag along.

That Friday morning, I rushed up to the label's Midtown office for the meeting and sat nervously on the reception area's pleather couch. It was my first real taste of grown-up shit. I melted in the fluorescent hell. I began to sweat profusely.

Where was Kennedy? WTF?!

Then the receptionist called my name and walked me through a grim hallway until we reached a midsized, nondescript office. Hal was sitting behind a narrow desk. He was fifty-plus, midsized, and nondescript as well.

"Have a seat," he said.

I did. And that's when the eerie silence kicked in. The room went completely still.

Then Hal slowly lowered his head toward the table.

He laid his head in his hands and began to groan repeatedly.

Loud moans.

This was a first for me. Even if I'd read *All You Need to Know About the Music Business* cover to cover, I'm not sure it would've addressed how to proceed when you're in your first-ever record label meeting and the executive sitting across from you seems to be in midst of some dark, catastrophic shit. I knew I should've just rolled with the weirdness and remained on mute, but I couldn't leave it at that. I was so amped up that I clumsily attempted to break the hush.

"So, umm, how's your week been?"

The words landed like a lost meteorite. It was probably another thirty seconds of awkward agony (with a few last sighs interspersed) before Hal mumbled that soul-shattering response that still rings in my brain today.

"How's my week been? Really? Um, how'd your week be if your wife was dying of cancer?"

Yup.

Dying of cancer.

Stephen King couldn't have scripted anything more perversely awful. I stammered something along the lines of, "Oh wow, I'm so sorry, sir," but there was no turning back. Between his gritted teeth, he mumbled, "Oh sure, I BET you are."

My heart was darting in a full-on fit of terror. I honestly thought this dude might just hop over the desk and try to choke me out. I knew I had to break the fuck out of Hal's mental hospice pronto, so I slowly lifted my sorry limbs from my chair and excused myself to the restroom. I grabbed the key for show, but I sailed straight past the bathroom door, ran to the elevator, and anxiously pounded the down button. After a damn eternity, the doors shot open and I jumped in, desperately praying they would glue shut. Blessedly, they did.

Forty seconds later, I landed on the curb . . . where the tardy Kennedy was cheerily sitting on a fire hydrant, removing his roller-blades for the meeting. I couldn't even speak. I just glared at him and exclaimed, "It's over, man. Go home!" Kennedy attempted to calm me down, but I proceeded to speed-walk south at a Flo-Jo pace. I couldn't stop. It took me only ten blocks or so to realize I'd completely jacked Hal's bathroom key. There would be no returning it. I kept that key in a sock drawer full of musical scars for years to come. From that day forward, it became obvious to me that the music business was gonna be chock-full of bizarre interactions that would test my psyche on the daily, so I had to master resilience.

CHAPTER 7

# The Boy Who Cried Turtle

Growing up, I was way into the electro-funk band The System (David Frank and Mic Murphy), so as I desperately searched for labels to heave my musical wares, I found their production company's info, jotted it down, and mailed them my first demo. It was worth a shot, right? The group was red-hot, coming off a monster self-produced hit called "Don't Disturb This Groove." At that point, my demo tape was four tunes bathing in a blend of pop culture and nostalgia. Admittedly, this was not five-mic material from *The Source*, but at least I had my own (somewhat weird) thing.

> **BONUS CUT**
>
> From the moment I began writing and did my first real deep dive into wordplay, I knew it was crucial for me to come from a super-detailed, gripping place to be competitive. Since my vocal abilities and flow were hella suspect, I had to spout the most unique verbal imagery if I wanted to rise from the literal bottom. I wrote about shitty red-sauce restaurants, lonely diners, Chevy IROCs, and dreary high school landscapes. Suburban malaise. I knew my words and concepts had to be a cut above to disguise my other shortcomings.

Then one day, it actually happened.

I got a message on my dormitory answering machine from The System's sweet studio manager, Todd. It seemed the duo had invited me over for a sit-down. I was literally shaking as I rewound the message over and over. Their studio was located in the famed 1650 Broadway building at Fifty-First and Broadway, usually referred to as the Brill Building. The actual Brill Building was located around the corner; that spot was the hub of the Tin Pan Alley greats, as well as Leiber & Stoller and Pomus & Shuman, but 1650 was where Carole & Gerry and Barry & Cynthia shaped the pop landscape.

I took that first nervous step through The System's office doorway, and it was obvious there was an undeniably fresh energy to the place. Electro-Funk music pumping. Lots of action. I was shepherded into the group's A room studio and I almost died. I'd never been in a real studio before. The flashing lights dancing across the SSL board. It looked like a 747 cockpit.

David and Mic were seated on the studio couch. Only a year and a half earlier, I'd danced to "Don't Disturb This Groove" at my prom. Now I was in their place of business. They both greeted me warmly and gushed about my lyrical creativity. I was flabbergasted. After much back-and-forth babble, they offered me a production deal on the spot. A production deal meant:

1. I'd receive no advance whatsoever.
2. The guys would retain my recording rights for the next fourteen years or so in return for a retail record royalty of only 3 to 5 percent.
3. I'd give them 50 percent of my merchandising income.
4. I'd have to hand over the administrative control of my music publishing and 50 percent of my publishing income to their company, which at the time wasn't a full-service music publisher (a music publisher is responsible for exploiting a songwriter or composer's music through both the license of songs and collection of royalties).

Sounds shady, right? Honestly, it wasn't! For an unknown like myself, in the '80s and '90s, these types of production deals were the industry standard. In return for my musical soul, The System guys were contractually obligated to shop my music to record labels and find me opportunities. Through the hookup of an NYU dorm-mate, I found a lawyer and signed the paper within a week.

**BONUS CUT**

Note to young aspiring creatives: ALWAYS hire an entertainment lawyer. Having zero industry blueprint at nineteen, I haphazardly settled on a discount personal injury lawyer to handle this first deal for me. He was a nice gentleman with next to no knowledge of the industry. He would have been infinitely more helpful if I'd been hit by a fuckin' bus. The music business has its own twisted legalese. You have to find someone who speaks it.

Okay, so it was now December '89, and I was only a few months into The System deal when they presented me with the proverbial pot of gold. Under the moniker Orchestra on the Half-Shell, David and his composer friend John Du Prez had created "Turtle Rhapsody," the end-title song for what would be the first Teenage Mutant Ninja Turtles movie, and they needed a sixteen-bar rap on it. They gave me a weekend to write it. Cowabunga! The Ninja Turtles were already a cultural phenomenon, so I sensed this film was gonna be huge. I spent hours pounding liters of Coca-Cola, polishing my words to perfection.

I arrived early the following Monday morning and sat in the lobby, silently freaking out. When David rolled through, I hopped off the couch and freestyled my lyrics for him like one of these determined kids who bumrush Kanye in parking lots while TMZ films. He seemed to love it. He sent me directly into the booth. I'd never actually been in a real vocal setup. The closest I'd come to that sanctified fortress was Jimmy Mussen's bathroom on 111th Street, where I was once forced to lay down a verse due to his living room being overrun with dirty laundry.

As the playback kicked in, I was literally shaking.

At first, I struggled to ride the beat correctly. Then I began to lay back in the pocket. After about twenty takes, I finally started to nail the flow. I couldn't believe how meticulous David was. He wouldn't let me stop. When we finally wrapped, David generously let me hang around to watch as they comped my verse and then brought in DJ MoJoe from the Palladium nightclub to chop up my vocal using razor blades on the 2-inch tape. He achieved this by manipulating the tape area corresponding to the beginning of my voice and swaying it back and forth over the playback head. When MoJoe found the money spot, he marked the edit point with a white pencil and sliced the tape with a razor blade. That portion of the tape was then slowly fed through MoJoe's fingers to the position of a previously marked edit spot. One more cut, and the two pieces were fused together with some magical editing tape. Sounds complicated, but it was fascinating. Suddenly my vocals stuttered like Max Headroom or the Nu Shooz "I Can't Wait" jam.

I left that afternoon on top of the world. The film was set for worldwide release just three months later, so I headed home for the holidays and blustered about my accomplishment. At that point, I was so desperate for any positive acknowledgment in life, I just couldn't keep my mouth shut. When everyone asked me how my second year of college was going, I verbally spasmed, "Honestly, I'm only focused on my music right now. Did I tell you I'm gonna be on the *Teenage Mutant Ninja Turtles* soundtrack?!" It really was a nice flex.

In early January, I returned to NYC riding the high, and everything was majestic. I strutted through a bitterly cold uptown to the studio every day, just so I could count the *Teenage Mutant Ninja Turtles* movie-poster snipes that hung along the endless construction sites and on billboards dotting the skyline. Up at 1650, David and Mic gave me the coat closet in the back as a space to create. This was not the SSL room. It smelled like a moist slew of $2 bodega umbrellas, but I was super jazzed to devise in my own spot. For the next two months, I wrote day and night, but something was definitely amiss. David and Mic barely communicated with each other. Or me. They seemed like they were always in a rush to get out of there. I couldn't quite read the energy, but it was off. I didn't care. I was already trying to wrangle red carpet tickets to the Ninja Turtles premiere.

I was buried in the closet attempting to finish a demo during the second week of March, about five days before the release of the movie and soundtrack, when, on a bathroom break, I noticed a shiny, unopened cassette sitting on the receptionist's desk.

The official *Teenage Mutant Ninja Turtles* soundtrack on SBK Records. I started bouncing up and down. I had to do it. I slid the plastic wrap off and yanked out the booklet. I scrolled straight to the credits. And there it was—the last song on the soundtrack.

Orchestra on the Half Shell's "Turtle Rhapsody," written by John Du Prez and David Frank.

Hmm?

I grabbed the cassette and ran it back to the closet. I jammed it in a boom box and swiftly fast-forwarded to my moment in the sun. The song began. Long intro. My heart was racing. My verse in 3, 2, 1 . . .

Nothing.

It was just an instrumental section with a few random dialogue samples from the movie scratched in on top. What the actual fuck? Was this a mastering error? Had someone mistakenly muted my brilliance, or had my words died on some gruesome Hollywood cutting-room floor? It had to have been a mistake. As I was now completely losing my shit, I barged into the SSL room. David was deep in focus laying down some synth part.

"Um, David," I anxiously interrupted.

"Hey, Sam. I'm kinda busy here. What's up?"

I reached into my sweatshirt and pulled out the cassette. "My Turtle verse? It's not on here. Did I get cut?"

He paused and started rubbing his temples. "Oh my God! I'm so sorry. I can't believe I forgot to tell you. They decided that your rap didn't really work. We've had so much crazy stuff going on up here. I totally spaced."

I began to hyperventilate. I was a steaming pile of sadness, yet I sensed David wasn't bullshitting me about any of it. Unbeknownst to myself at the time, he and Mic were in the midst of a musical divorce and, under that tension, the slashing of my verse was probably just another lost (minor) detail in days of duress, but man, it just gutted me to the core.

The film was obviously gigantic.

The soundtrack exploded as well.

And guess who wasn't part of any of it.

The boy who cried turtle.

You see, many of my childhood friends bought tickets to the movie as a show of support, but soon discovered I was a two-bit liar when the credits rolled. My name was mud. It took years (and a bunch of hits) for anyone back home to ever believe any of my music tales again.

That day I left the studio wrecked, as I knew that my relationship with The System was pretty much doomed as well. Sure, I was crushed about the tune, but I sensed that as their partnership was beginning to buckle, I would be the first to get lost in the shuffle. I didn't want to be an afterthought, so on the "Free Britney" tip, I cold-called a young music attorney that a girlfriend had randomly met at a party and begged him to get me out of the production deal. After a few weeks of legalese, David and Mic were super generous

**BONUS CUT**

Fast-forward to 2008 and a phone call from my Yoda, Jonathan "JD" Daniel of Crush Management, who will enter the picture in a bit. JD told me that his act Gym Class Heroes had been offered the end title for *TMNT*, the long-awaited sequel to *Teenage Mutant Ninja Turtles*, and asked me if I wanted to create it with them. I leaped at the opportunity. We threw down "Welcome to Shellshock" over a long weekend. For the band, it was probably just another easy grab, but for me, this was closure on a whole 'nutha level. This time, the tune made both the film and soundtrack. You see, everything comes full circle in this brutal game if you can just keep your pulse beating long enough.

and let me skate. They could have been real dickish about it, but they handled the situation with total class.

Shortly thereafter, David packed up his belongings, moved to Malibu, and eventually wrote the gigantic Christina Aguilera–launching "Genie in a Bottle," among other big hits. He's still a super sweet guy. I owe him a ton. And Mic has made tons of business and real estate moves and can still sing his face off. He's also a superb soul. If you're not familiar with The System's discography, definitely go on a deep dig. They were so ahead of the curve. I owe them eternally for giving me a shot.

All right, so my glorious mic debut had been hacked and I was back to square one. Through trial and much error, though, I began to hear an even more defined musical bed in my head—crazier samples mixed with live instrumentation and my vocal stylings on top. I furiously filled notebooks with lyric scribbles on my brother's fire escape, which loomed over Eighth Avenue. Ben and his wife, Julie, were incredibly supportive, letting me post up in that spot for hours on end. Sure, I was a bit of a stoney, social recluse at the time, but it was during those lonely, introspective days that I really began to believe I'd finally found my voice. Now I just needed a tight unit of musician compadres to help me bring this vision to life.

Don Lunetta was my first choice. He'd previously been the bassist in Jaik Miller's band, Out of Context, but after grindin' together for a couple of years, Jaik had decided to scrap the project and go in a darker, heavier direction. Don was now living with his folks, figuring out his next move. I begged and pleaded for him to join me. With no other options in the nonexistent hometown scene, he caved. He turned out to be a great accomplice, blessed with a solid foundation of snark that nicely balanced my ping-ponging neuroses. We shared a four-hundred-square-foot studio apartment on West Seventy-Second Street. For privacy, we stacked my floor-to-ceiling vinyl collection as a makeshift wall. We spent the days locked in the lab together and created a full-on sonic cacophony in the studio. Adding everything from distorted bass to chopped-up Moog bits to sampled '60s bubblegum pop, it wasn't the most joyful of noises, but it was definitely unique.

**BONUS CUT**

When you begin creating your first song demos, remember that minimalism is an essential discipline. Personally, I've never been able to master it. The process of developing a project with Don was a precursor to so many of my future writing and production fails. It was the start of my overproducing. I could never step away from a song without drowning it with clutter. Learn from my errors. Keep shit sparse and focused.

After much working and reworking, Don and I finally wrapped our first acceptable demo together. We just needed a proper handle. First I toyed around with "Mayday Malone," a nod to the *Cheers* bartender, but everyone I ran it by was underwhelmed. Then I went with the short lived "Sam Ace," which I nabbed from the '80s indie classic *Hollywood Shuffle*.

**BONUS CUT**

*Hollywood Shuffle* was a film about the racial stereotypes that Black actors face—thus I'm sure it was a bit of a head-scratcher when I gawkily introduced myself to the film's star, Robert Townsend, at a club one night and told him I wanted to use his character's name for my Caucasian rap experiment. I can still recall his muted expression. Those were indeed wobbly days.

Finally, I settled on the name Sam-N-The Swing as a subtle nod to the '60s Tex-Mex garage kings, Sam the Sham & The Pharaohs. It didn't blow me away, but at least it was passable. What now? We had zero road maps. We did, however, live above a newsstand, so I spent hours on end reading *Billboard* magazine cover to cover, taking copious notes in a little diary. I stalked every executive's photo like that Fatal Attraction bunny butcher Glenn Close. I memorized both names and faces. I knew it was time to get off my ass and start hustlin' on our behalf, so I packed up a knapsack and set sail for the Black Rock Building on Fifty-Second Street and Sixth Avenue. Black Rock housed both CBS and Epic Records, as well as a bunch of powerful subsidiaries. Two blocks away, Warner Brothers, Atlantic, Elektra, and Atco stood, equally behemoth. I set up shop outside these record labels' revolving doors once a week between 5 and 7 PM. I'd like to think my facial recognition from those *Billboard* shots was that little bit of extra due diligence that separated me from the other demo hawkers. I stalked. Then I struck. I approached each A&R executive slowly and respectfully attempted a dialogue.

"Excuse me, are you [insert name here]? Hi, my name is Sam from Sam-N-The Swing. I'm a big fan of the [insert name here] record you A&R'd. Is there any way I could give you my demo?"

Then when the day was done, my good pal Tyler Roe would pretend to be my manager and leave follow-up messages with these folks on my behalf. In the end, everyone was very gracious and took a tape, but responses were few and far between.

**BONUS CUT**

A&R is short for "Artists and Repertoire." A&R is the record label department that's responsible for discovering talent to sign to recording contracts. Once the artist is signed, the A&R gig transmutes into finding a delicate balance between the talent's artistic goals and delivering a marketable record for the label. These are the proverbial gatekeepers. On any given day, A&R are a songwriter's savior or kiss of death.

Undeterred, I continued to network at clubs and gigs. I hounded every single contact I made over those first three years in the city. Lawyers, managers, publicists, low-level A&R. Everybody knew somebody. As the rejections mounted, I did receive a tiny publishing deal offer from a German indie. Unfortunately, it involved moving to Deutschland. Though I debated it for a minute, out of ancestral respect, that sure as fuck wasn't gonna happen. Nächste!

Then Buddah Records got ahold of our tape.

Buddah was launched in 1967 by Kama Sutra Records's head, Art Kass, who'd soured with the distribution deal he had at MGM Records. He partnered with his original Kama Sutra cronies Artie Ripp, Hy Mizrahi, Phil Steinberg, and Sonny Franzese. Then the label hired Neil Bogart (the legendary soon-to-be founder of Casablanca Records and the most exciting character in the aforementioned Hit Men) as head of operations. Buddah had been one of the coolest pop shops of the early '70s. They were the masters of bubblegum pop. From the Ohio Express to the 1910 Fruitgum Company, it was pure pep 24/7.

That was then.

By 1991, Buddah had lay dormant for years. All the other partners were gone. It was just Art in a somewhat empty, dust-bunny-lined office, guarding the remains of his astonishing catalog. But I didn't care. I was just thrilled that he was interested. I walked through the door, and Art offered up the warmest of greetings. After a brief office tour where he unearthed some amazing artifacts of his glory days (Lovin' Spoonful and Bobby Bloom gold records!), we got down to brass tacks.

"Sam. I'll be honest with you. When I heard your music, I got so excited. You're a real throwback. But modern at the same time!"

I could barely contain my enthusiasm. My pulse raced like a last-lap Seattle Slew! Was Art actually about to offer me a recording contract?

"Honestly, I really want to sign you."

!!!!!!!!

"But I've gotta be honest with you: I'm not so sure I'll be able to make it happen."

Tire screech.

My face froze.

Art continued, "You see, last week, I saw these two Brooklyn kids in a Spike Lee–directed Levi's commercial. They were speaking in a backwards language. That's the only way they communicate. Turns out they rap as well. This backwards thing feels real 'next' to me. I just reached out to them about a potential deal. If they sign, unfortunately I'll have to pass on your band."

My life was suddenly devolving into a David Cronenberg movie right in front of my eyes. I attempted to sit silently and process Art's words, but I couldn't let it go.

"Okay. So let me see if I got this right . . . You're saying these two guys rap in reverse?"

"Correct."

"Can I hear it?"

And then Art played me their demo. He wasn't lying. It was three minutes and forty-seven seconds of backward rapping. It was quite possibly the oddest shit I'd ever heard. It was the musical equivalent of Reverend Jim from *Taxi* snorting Latka's cocaine cookies. I squirmed in my seat watching this sweet, enthusiastic fella nod his head to the verses. The second the track faded, I politely thanked Art for his time. This pairing was obviously not meant to happen. He was very kind though. We both agreed that we'd touch base soon. We never spoke again.

As I slunk back to the avenue, I made a pledge to my sanity. There could be no more backward bullshit for Sam-N-The Swing. It was straight on or bust.

**BONUS CUT**

> Sadly, we were stuck in reverse. A friend slipped the red-hot producer Eddie F (Heavy D, Mary J. Blige) our demo, and I was invited to his crib for a sit-down. I drove across the Tappan Zee Bridge that day with an unbridled joy that I can't express. I pulled up to his split-level ranch, and some minion greeted me and told me to wait in his kitchen. I sat by myself in that kitchen for three fuckin' hours. I'm not kidding. Though I could hear his voice talking upstairs, Eddie F never came downstairs to meet me. It was a pretty harsh afternoon. Finally, with zero self-esteem left, I dejectedly crawled back home.

One night shortly thereafter, I braved the worst Chelsea rainstorm on record to dash to the post office and cold-mail our demo to Ultrax, a division of SBK Records (uh-oh, Ninja Turtles flashback). All you sloths out there, keep this in mind: In those dark prehistoric days, there was no internet! You couldn't just touch a button and shoot your demo link to a master email list of industry contacts. If you wanted to get noticed, you braved the slick pavement to the post office, even when the Doppler forecasted buckets of rain on your tortured dome. I had already been doused on so many occasions that I was completely numb to it, but this one time, it seemed the damn raindrops magically transformed into a rainbow.

Yes, within a week or so of receiving our cassette, Ultrax's head of A&R, a lovely gentleman named JW Sewell, reached out and offered to fly me down to their corporate offices in Plano, Texas. Crazily enough, they seemed interested in signing our little group on the strength of the demo alone.

There was only one problem.

It was finals week at NYU, and I was already hanging on for academic life.

I crashed the office of Cindy Reese, an absolutely stunning former touring background vocalist who'd shifted into academia and was now running the music program. From the day I had arrived at the university, it was quite obvious that Cindy didn't back me. Could you blame her? At that point, I was just a moderate talent with Ferris Bueller–like delusional fearlessness. I'd drop by Cindy's office, plop down across from her, and commence tossing my under-thought and overreaching musical schemes, hoping for some sort of validation or insight. She'd just sit there in a half-listen with a look of horror tattooed on her raised eyebrows. She seemed to find some sadistic joy in lobbing brief, negative responses in every one of our exchanges. It was never a warm hang.

On the afternoon of the Ultrax call, I begged Cindy to let me postpone a final so I could seize my big break and hop a plane for the Lone Star State. Yet again, she refused to look me in the eye or even comment after this most passionate of pitches. It was obvious she didn't believe a single word spraying out of my mouth. She reeked of integrity. At twenty, I hated integrity. I was so frustrated that I stormed out of her office, shitcanned my finals, and took the trip to Plano, anyway.

**BONUS CUT**

> Ultrax had been launched by Dallas nightclub owner Tommy Quon as a local indie label, but after discovering the chart-topping Vanilla Ice (the same Vanilla Ice whose "Ninja Rap" had been the first single from the aforementioned, PTSD-inducing *Teenage Mutant Ninja Turtles* soundtrack—if you can't beat 'em, join 'em, right?), the label was flush with newly minted cash; thus, they rolled out the reddest of carpets upon my arrival.

I spent three days running around the Dallas region with these sweet cats. It couldn't have been more enticing. From boating on an endless lake to enjoying a ridiculous BBQ under the stars, it was my first honest-to-goodness courtship. The possibilities seemed endless with this crew. I was particularly inspired by the mammoth storage vault in the office, which housed every possible Vanilla Ice merch item ever concocted: pencils, lunch boxes, action figures, and tooth-brushes. If I'd dug deeper into the glory hole, I'm sure there would've been a line of "Ice Ice Baby" vibrators looming around. It was all a brilliant slice of American cheese and I had zero fear of the Velveeta.

On my last night hanging with the Ultrax gang, they invited me to a record release shindig for their newest signing, the Mac Band. Now, the Mac Band wasn't new. They'd been kicking around the Dallas area for years, having already cut two full-lengths for MCA. I believe they were older than their new jack swing contemporaries by a solid decade or so. To the music nerd in me, their signing felt like a reach, but that's who Tommy and JW were. A pair of sweet, local loyalists who cultivated a roster full of Dallas-area music-biz castoffs seemingly out of friendship more than any potential fiscal victory. It was a bit of a cautionary tale, however, because inevitably none of these other acts blew up.

Many years down the road, after a stretch of success, the NFL invited me to speak to a bunch of music-industry-curious players about songwriting. Oh, the irony, Big Ed. As I stepped up to the makeshift podium, I passionately pounded the following message: "When scouting for talent, do your best to avoid signing family, neighbors, friends, or friends' extended cousins. It's impossible to gauge their true abilities with any real context. Ninety-nine times out of a hundred, it'll be a tremendous waste of time." In my experience, at least, star searching and nepotism have usually made for the ugliest of bedfellows.

The Mac Band were the real deal, though, and seemed like genuinely solid guys. I sure was having a swell time at their party. Then Tommy Quon grabbed a microphone and, after a gushing introduction, had the soundman kill the lights and turn on a gigantic TV monitor as he debuted the quartet's new music video. The song was cool, I knew that much, but the video itself was fairly generic. I began to turn away from the monitor when my inner *Saved by the Bell*'s Mr. Belding whispered, "Hey, hey, hey. What is going on here?" Something strange had most definitely caught my eye. The scantily clad babe in the negligee looked eerily familiar. She was writhing around with the lead singer while teasing a pearl necklace with her lips. I whispered in one of the Mac's ears, "Who's that model? I swear I know her."

He replied with words that I still cherish to this day:

"Some girl named Cindy from New York. I think she's actually a professor or something."

Yes, it was Cindy Reese.

I'm not kidding.

The following Monday, I knocked on her office door with a shit-eating grin that I can only describe as *Three's Company*'s Mr. Roper–ish.

"Hey, Cindy!"

I had her in the crosshairs, and I was gonna enjoy every wicked second of this shit.

"Yup," she responded without looking up.

"So I just got back from meeting that record label in Dallas!"

Cindy replied with a terse "Cool," giving me zilch—as usual.

This was truly a momentous moment in my human development.

"Man, it was so wild. They offered me an album deal on the spot! My lawyer's negotiating it this week!"

"Oh, nice."

Still no eye contact.

"I even got to go to my first video release party! It was for these guys, um, wait, what was their name . . . Umm."

3, 2, 1.

"THE MAC BAND?!"

Then the air completely vanished in the room.

Cindy slowly pulled her frames away from her pupils and blasted a lethal glance at my smirky-ass self.

"So let me make this very clear. What I do in my personal time has nothing to do with my work here, and it's none of your damn business. You understand?"

Oh, I understood all right. Though I was painfully aware that I might also have to spend my life working side gigs to keep the music alive, I no longer trusted the outcomes of academia.

I dropped out of NYU a week later.

Surprisingly enough, I've always been tremendously conflicted about my decision to ditch college. At the time of my bailing, I was such an ambitious pinball that I couldn't possibly fathom stagnating in a dorm for four years when I could be chasing dreams on the street. It probably took me twenty-something years till it finally dawned on me that missing out on those pivotal semesters of socialization ended up precluding me from becoming a fully formed human. I'd like to think Cindy's tough love was just a somewhat well-intentioned attempt to shove me toward maturity. The irony is, a lifetime later, though I am making progress, I'm still attempting to de-stunt myself.

## CHAPTER 8

# Select Ebola

Within days of returning to the city, my lawyer began the record deal negotiations with Ultrax, but then a sexier dark horse entered the race and shook the whole thing up. A publicist friend slid my demo cassette over to Select Records, a rap division of Atlantic Records. The label's head of A&R, Greg Riles, flipped out on the demo and hit me up in a flurry of excitement. At the time, Select was red hot. From Kid 'n Play, who were full-blown movie stars as well, to Chubb Rock and UTFO. Rap masters!

We set up a showcase for the following Thursday, November 7, 1991, at 6 PM. Myself, Don, our new drummer, Jason Linn, and a sweet singer from New Rochelle, Nicole Alifante, who hit the hooks, practiced 24/7. We were finally a biscuit away from glory and we weren't gonna blow it. We walked into the rehearsal space at 5:30 PM. We set up our gear, then loitered in the lobby, nervously watching the small color TV as we waited for the label folk. At 5:56, the suits sauntered through the door. We all exchanged somewhat awkward pleasantries. Then, suddenly the lobby TV interrupted:

"Breaking news: NBA superstar Magic Johnson is about to give a live press conference."

Thirty seconds later, Magic told the world he had HIV.

We all stared, silent and stunned. It was that old, ominous feeling again. In the '80s, my folks lost the bulk of their friends to this dreaded disease. This is no exaggeration. They had such a tiny social circle and it was completely decimated. Magic's announcement was an instant flashback to those not-so-distant ghastly days. Unfortunately, the second the press conference wrapped, we were forced to shift gears into showtime. Somehow we had to casually move past this bombshell and summon every bit of our smiley-faced, goofball energy. It was a next-to-impossible undertaking. We went balls to the wall, but it was obvious that our heads were elsewhere, mine primarily pondering all the safe-sex choices I'd ever failed to make. What an emotional shitshow. The faces on the Select execs remained expressionless. I was getting used to numb reactions whenever I rocked the mic, so honestly, it didn't faze me, but God, we were a hot mess that day. When we wrapped our final song, I was sure it would be yet another pass, but the label's president, Fred Munao, slowly made his way over to me, smiling, and said, "I know that wasn't easy, Sam, but I loved the passion. I'd like to sign you guys if you're interested?"

I kept it together and replied, "Absolutely, sir."

We all shook hands, and they bounced.

I stepped away from Don and Jason, walked to the bathroom, and started crying. Bawling, actually. It was such a grueling afternoon. The next day, I mustered up the courage to call JW and Tommy at Ultrax and had a heart to heart with them. They were such lovely humans, and their intentions were so pure. It was somewhat gut-wrenching, but we both promised to remain in contact.

**BONUS CUT**

One of the keys to survival in this job is having the guts to initiate a tough conversation. In a business of passive aggressive bullshit, be the one who comes correct.

After a seamless negotiation, I signed my very first actual record deal with Select. When it came time to physically record an album, the process itself was basically a more expensive, juiced-up version of the demo process. We moved on from Jimmy Mussen's bare-bones $15-an-hour living room setup straight to the swanky Platinum Island studio on lower Broadway, where the label shelled out $600 a day (100 percent recoupable, obviously). We recorded for four straight months. Looking back on it, I still don't understand how a musically naive, manager-less twenty-one-year-old was handed a six-figure budget to oversee, but man, it made for a solid on-the-job tutorial as I learned how to properly conduct myself and run the room in a real studio environment.

Select Records signing photo. Back row: Scott Francis, Harry Getzov, Greg Riles (RIP), Stan White, Wyatt Cheek. Front row: Don Lunetta, Fred Muneo, giddy me.

Once our basic tracks were laid down, we moved locations again to mix the record at the original Chung King House of Metal. A few years earlier, the Beastie Boys and Run-DMC had put this revered, shabby Chinatown spot on the map. In a budget-saving maneuver, I booked us on overnight sessions, while the daytime rooms were brimming with the Golden Era hip-hop gods like LL Cool J, Leaders of the New School, Brand Nubian, etc. Sadly, we rarely got the chance to fraternize with them.

**BONUS CUT**

Overnights were fuckin' bizarre.

1. On many occasions, I had hallucinatory visions swarm me right around 5 AM or so, and I'd start to see rats scurrying everywhere I looked.
2. I was guzzling 32-ounce Cokes all night just to stay engaged—thus I gained the proverbial freshman fifteen during the process.
3. I did cop weed from the Beastie Boys's legendary photographer, Ricky Powell. That was some real downtown NYC badge-of-honor shit.

4. Our engineer took a different tack: he snorted heroin every hour on the hour. Notwithstanding this, somehow his mixes seemed to dramatically improve the harder he rode that horse. I still refer to those nights as the Belmont Stakes.

5. Most of the rap cats kept communication real brief with us, but Leaders of the New School were pretty sweet fellas. They were always down to kick it and we peeped each other's tracks. Boy, those hangs were some sadistic shit, though. By that point, I'd awkwardly altered my vocal performances in an attempt to emulate the infinitely more badass Ice Cube. Since no soul in the entire fuckin' universe was checking on my now puzzling, thugged-out Nicolas Cage microphone style, it was yet another in a series of dubious calls. You can't imagine how brutal it was listening back to my pedestrian mic deftness through the blaring speakers while these significantly more gifted kids attempted to maintain a straight face. Charlie and Dinco were beasts lyrically, and Busta Rhymes was a burgeoning superstar. It was like a bantamweight sparring with a trio of Mike Tysons. Thankfully, one night, Busta was so zooted that after two verses of my strained, marginally competent flow, he jumped up and screamed, "Man, that shit is so dope!" Secretly, I knew he was probably deep in some twisted phantasmagoria pondering the secret code that lies buried inside a Lucky Charms cereal box. Still, I enthusiastically took any nibble of acceptance I could get.

After we completed the mixing and mastering of the record, it was supposed to be shipped to stores immediately, but we ended up spending an entire frustrating year in limbo. There were just too many larger acts on the roster, so we were forced to wait our turn. It totally sucked. Finally, after twelve agonizing months, we got our big official release date. It was a sprint to the finish, so one afternoon, I popped by the Select offices to sit with my rad new pal, Gail Ghezzi, in the art department to check out the mockups she'd made for our album cover. Suddenly, I heard a loud voice from down the hall.

"Yo, dude. You are funny, man!"

I looked up. It was Play from Kid 'n Play fame. He was pointing at me and laughing. The rest of the office all surrounded him like the conquering House Party hero he was.

"Me?" I inquired.

"Yeah, you, dude. You are funny!"

That was an odd comment.

I was confused.

Play started strutting toward me.

It began to feel like the fight scene in Three O'Clock High as the whole staff followed him down the hall toward my direction.

What had I done to agitate this fella? Was I really that wack?

Play was now three feet away from me, looking me straight in the eye.

The tension peaked.

Then suddenly, at a decibel-shattering level, Play screamed, "HEY JERKY!"

What the fuck was happening here?!

Gail whispered in my ear, "Oh my God. They didn't tell you? We just signed two guys from Queens. They're called the Jerky Boys. They make prank phone calls. He thinks you're a Jerky."

"A Jerky?!"

Then the label's in-house counsel, Harry Getzov (real name), spoke up and further clarified the misunderstanding. Everyone laughed hysterically.

Me?

Not so much.

From the get-go, I had been the lowest priority at the label, and now it appeared I had been leapfrogged again by a couple of prank phone-calling dudes who The Howard Stern Show had blown up. I didn't have any Howard Stern in my corner. I didn't even have Joe Franklin (give yourself a well-deserved pat on the back if you understand that reference). I had to convert some believers in the building ASAP.

Since the rest of the roster were primarily MCs who performed live with only DJ accompaniment, I thought we could generate some label heat by performing our record with a tight eight-piece band. At least it would be a spectacle. Alas, Select had no budget for that Full Monty of a setup. We were only allotted dollars for a percussionist. A percussionist! That was like an eighth of a Monty or some shit. We also received zero budget for rehearsals. Thankfully, Jason Linn's saint of a dad owned a button factory in Long Island City, so he let us use the space to practice after office hours on the roof. Okay—keep in mind this was pre-gentrified early-'90s LIC. As we blasted our noise from the three-story roof, we were the official soundtrack of the local junkies, pimps, and crack-smoking prostitutes. God, the horrors we saw. The littered Trojan wrappers, pipes, and needles.

We put the word out for a percussionist everywhere. About six guys showed up to audition on the roof. They all underwhelmed. I stumbled home in despair when the phone rang. It was my new friend Doug DeAngelis, a super-gifted young programmer/engineer who had also gotten his start under the tutelage of Mic Murphy and David Frank. He was certainly the most connected of my peers at that point. Doug alerted me to the fact that his Berklee School of Music suite-mate, percussionist Dave "Duke Mushroom" Schommer, was moving to NYC from Detroit. I met Duke the next day.

Duke Mushroom—what a fuckin' hurricane!

He was a few years older than me with a shaved head, long beard, and a slew of swagger. He strolled in with large congas and set them on fire. He was a walking metronome. He truly could do it all. Any instrument. And he sang beautifully. Suddenly, our strange little "alternative" unit was up and running.

**BONUS CUT**

You see, "alternative" was always my safety word for Sam-N-The Swing. Anytime anyone even insinuated that I was jacking rap, I'd make it clear we were an alt band to avoid any hip-hop confusion. "Alternative" basically said, "Bitch, don't you dare label my quirky art." To a major extent, it was true. This was not hip-hop music. Sadly, it was a bit too weird for pop. I really didn't know what it was. I just hoped that I'd find an audience of eccentric kids who'd appreciate it. I did reference the Minutemen, Joe Jackson, and *Blazing Saddles*. Someone had to dig my strange creativity . . .

Someone did.

Her name was Michelle Mills from somewhere in West Virginia. She sent me the one and only fan letter to ever arrive at the label's office. God bless her misguided soul, wherever she is now.

The truth is, we really did try to make a go of it live, but our first booking was a bit of a head scratcher. Somehow we got asked to play at the Universal One-Stop urban music convention in Cherry Hill, New Jersey. This convention was a chance for younger artists to get exposed to the owners of mom-and-pop retail outlets. I didn't understand how this specific convention would help our cause genre-wise, but with only a week left before our record was hitting the streets, any promotion was fair game!

The day got off to a dazzling start. We were shuttled across the bridge to the Garden State in the back of a dirty-ass cargo van. And they say this biz is all airbuses and limos. After a ninety-minute trip filled with classic soul sing-alongs, we arrived at a hip-hop record store in Philadelphia for an autograph signing. Not only was this place completely devoid of signature seekers, the store managers and cash register kids hid from us as well. It was a grim look. Then our jaunt continued to the convention center, where we were escorted into a giant ballroom and seated uncomfortably at card tables with posters and 12-inch flats of our album cover serving as a backdrop. Our job was just to sign autographs for the attendees. Sounds glorious, right? After a ten-minute setup period, the doors opened. I had my Sharpie in firing position. Can you imagine being one of those company folks attending this south Jersey convention and being pressed by the higher-ups to ask for token autographs from some wack new artist you couldn't give two shits about? You'd probably get plastered first. Well, one by one, adult beverages in hand, the attendees trickled into the room at a snail's pace. We were among forty or so other up-and-comers scattered around the floor praying for a taste of adulation, and almost immediately, a cruel pattern began to take shape. All of the birds began to flock to the next booth over. I couldn't make out who was posted up in it. I was too embarrassed to ask. Whoever this fella was, he had the whole room standing in line waiting to meet him. Our line? Nonexistent. Guys would approach our table, smile at me, and then do a subtle cha-cha slide over to Nerissa, our significantly hotter label-mate, who was signing a few feet away. Girls? They completely avoided us. It seemed we had musical cooties.

As my embarrassment ebbed, enough was enough. I stood up and marched over to my competitor's overflowing booth. There had to be seventy-five people waiting patiently to meet this mulleted man. His name?

Kid Rock.

I recognized his face immediately. Two years earlier, I'd watched him open a show at NYU in a pair of red, white, and blue Speedos, where he debuted his laughable first single, an ode to oral sex, "Yo-Da-Lin in the Valley." He was immediately booed offstage and pelted with loose change (New York does not play). Now he was back for round two on some new indie label as the mullet-y, trailer park–skateboarding MC. I turned away and laughed.

> **BONUS CUT**
>
> It was just six years later, while sitting in my apartment eating bonbons of jealousy, that I watched this now-superstar headline and completely slay Dick Clark's New Year's Rockin' Eve.

I digress.

After an hour of these humiliations of the autograph variety, it was showtime. We were slotted to perform fifth in the lineup. The waiting went on for a couple of hours. The first three acts were R&B vocal groups. Honestly, they were all kinda whatever. I began to feel that we might actually survive the gig. Then the as-yet unknown Fat Joe performed, and the room went wild. The hardcore Joe would be a tough act to follow with our candy-ass shit, but as we were setting up our gear onstage, I came up with a kooky eleventh-hour idea. Toward the end of our set, when we played our single, the Chicago-sampling "Sweet Four U" (as I type this, the Prince fail of a title makes me nauseous), I'd toss our cassettes into the crowd to stir the Universal One-Stop troops. We had a punk sensibility (barely). Let's give them a taste of our utter disregard for corporate shilling. Well, that's how I rationalized it.

The set started with a resounding thud.

The less-than-amused crowd seemed to be debuting the McKayla Maroney meme a solid two years before the gymnast's actual earth birth. We did slog on, though. Between songs you could've heard a pin drop. Finally, it was "Sweet Four U" time. I led with some half-hearted introduction: "Thank you, Universal One-Stop family and all of you record shop people! You guys fuckin' rock!"

Crickets.

Then suddenly, as I wrapped up my underappreciated banter, the side doors swung open. All heads swiftly shifted toward a quadriplegic gentleman being wheeled in our direction. While Don and Duke launched into our single, my eyes stayed completely fixed on the wheelchair and I blundered my cue. Don and Duke were less fazed. They just jumped up and down and pounded away. Finally, I snapped out of it, regained my chi, and began thriving off their collective energy. Alas, so much misplaced heart.

The cassette singles?!

Shit, I had totally spaced them!

I kept rapping as I shuffled side stage, grabbed the box, and subtly placed it in front of me in one seamless motion. And so it began. I started whipping the cassettes into the crowd with sniper-like precision. Rapid-fire hurls like Buddy the Elf snowball-tossing in Central Park. Faster and faster. People politely caught them—or at least made a valiant effort to. My adrenaline was next level.

Finally, I was down to the last damn cassette. I obviously wasn't content with my previous flings, so my fingers let this one fly behind my back with a little extra vigor. Unfortunately, the tape slid off my fingers and veered right—wide right. I can still see it sailing away in slow motion. Holy Scott Norwood! Every last mouth in the room gaped as the cassette single sped directly toward the man in the wheelchair's poor innocent head. I remember his eyes vividly.

The horror.

The fear.

Nooooo . . .

The cassette just missed scalping this poor man's dome by a solid sixteenth of an inch at best. Completely grazed him. I locked eyes with the fella and all I saw was distress. His scowling aide immediately smacked the door open and wheeled him out for safety.

The gentleman in the wheelchair?

Teddy Pendergrass.

**BONUS CUT**

Teddy, originally the lead singer of the Philly R&B kings, Harold Melvin and The Bluenotes, went on to become one of the most renowned solo vocalists of the '70s and '80s, until he was tragically paralyzed as a result of a horrific car crash. By this point, his public appearances were few and far between. That's why the entire room was gawking in his direction.

There would be no polite applause. I mean, I'd almost decapitated a Philly king. Folks began booing. I saw a couple of inebriated dudes pick up a pair of water glasses and debate tossing them in our direction. We wisely pulled the plug right then and there. As we exited the stage, our label deftly avoided us. We didn't have musical cooties. We were Select Ebola. We hightailed it to the back of the lonely cargo van and waited in shame. For over an hour, actually. Eventually our mortified label crew hopped aboard, drunk enough to mercifully pay us no mind.

The ride home was just the worst. I think everyone involved had reached the glum realization that our group wasn't gonna connect. There would be no more soul sing-alongs. As the sun set behind us, we pulled into the George Washington Bridge tollbooth just as the KISS FM DJ introduced Teddy Pendergrass's soul hit, "The Whole Town's Laughing at Me."

A week or so later, our album limped out into the universe. Well, I wouldn't really say our album was released so much as it just sort of escaped. Within days, I stumbled on a stack of our CDs at St. Mark's Sounds in the East Village in the discounted 88-cent sale bin. It was like finding a razor blade in a candy apple. This happened to occur while I was on a much-anticipated date with a girl I'd crushed on since high school. We both awkwardly chuckled about it. It was a terrible look.

**BONUS CUT**

Fear not, you can still find copies of the consigned-to-oblivion Sam-N-The Swing cassette languishing in the depths of eBay. Surprisingly, the reserve price is typically around $25. How 'bout them apples? Also, contrary to what you might surmise, I wasn't the only Jewish hip-hop experimenter chasing the Beastie Boys' Amazing Technicolor Dreamcoat in the city at the time. My friends Ali Dee and Jessie "James" Itzler both got deals that same year and dropped records in a similar vein. In the end, though, none of us ever really moved the pop-rap needle, I guess it all worked out okay. Today, Ali is one of the top writers of television and film tunes in the game, and Jessie and his wife, Sara Blakely, are billionaire entrepreneurs who just happen to own the Atlanta Hawks. There's your Hebraic mic drop.

## CHAPTER 9

# 10 Things I Hate About Time Warner

I hate Time Warner. They're a dream-crushing conglomerate. First and foremost, I blame them for the worst merger in the history of the music business, which left a good bunch of my industry friends jobless, but on a more personal tip, I still hold them indirectly accountable for so many of the creative obstacles I faced at the time.

In the mid-'90s, as my record deal ultimately capsized (yes, Select Records was a Time Warner subsidiary), I fought like hell to stay afloat in the industry. I immediately formed and fronted a new, organic alt-hip-hop outfit called Midnight Jones, but it was fairly obvious after a few months of shows that we weren't destined to connect. Then, after a cross-country road trip with Don Lunetta and Tony Arkin (son of Alan Arkin, also a fantastic actor), we formed a slightly avant-garde spoken word project called Phat Mack Kerouwack. The tracks we birthed were actually quite interesting, but we received zero label interest and packed it in, but that's when Doug DeAngelis reentered the picture. As I mentioned earlier, Doug was already a first-rate engineer and programmer who'd done a little work on my disastrous debut. We decided to try writing together one day on a lark, but I came down with vertigo mid-session. I spent the next forty-eight hours in bed, spinning into the apocalypse. It was probably an indicator that our partnership could spin out as well, but I never read omens correctly at that age.

When I returned to Doug's to attempt collaborating again a few days later, the song we wrote was pretty tight. It was kinda acid-jazzish since we both loved Jamiroquai, Brand New Heavies, and the like. I started to get a little geeked about the prospects of us as a jazzy songwriting and production duo. We recruited a dope vocalist we knew named Wanda Felicia, and together the three of us created a really vibey EP. Soon, an indie acid-jazz label called Smash Records gave us a small deal. Score! Then seemingly overnight, their phones were disconnected and we never heard from them again. Though slightly unnerved by this, Doug and I kept collaborating like crazy. He handled the programming and engineering, while I focused on our creative direction. In the process, we became really close pals. Together we hustled all of our combined contacts, which resulted in us getting hired to hit a few indie label remixes. The first remix we did was for some British trip-hop band on TVT Records. We spent two days on it and walked away with $6K. It was a cakewalk.

Our second remix gig was for Chris Connelly, an industrial rock guy who was signed to Wax Trax! Records, the home of all things dark and twisted. Chris had done time in the Revolting Cocks, as well as Ministry. Enter the silky-smooth acid-jazz newbies! In most remix situations, the remixer is sent the song's acapella stem, as well as the rest of the individual recorded tracks, and let loose creatively in his or her own space. That was not gonna be allowed on this one. If we wanted the gig, we were told that the remix could only be done at the label's studio in Chicago. It seemed like a strange ask, but within a day or so, we were TWA bound. We couldn't believe we were actually getting paid and nabbing a twenty-four-hour trip to a stellar city.

We landed in Chicago at 5 PM and excitedly rushed to the studio. It was one of the sickest recording spots I'd stepped in to date. This was the big time.

But instantly, shit got weird.

When the artist and his hangers-on arrived at the studio a few hours later, they appeared to have done a ton of smack, crack, and/

or euphoria (the mythic Beverly Hills 90210 drug that psycho Emily Valentine spiked Brandon Walsh's drink with) and proceeded to fall asleep across the mammoth, extremely fragile $100,000 SSL console in a preemptive strike to kill our rocket of a remix before launch. I guess they were so appalled with the idea of two no-name musical cheeseballs taking a stab at reimagining their angsty brilliance that they did their junkie equivalent of a peaceful sit-in. We negotiated back and forth with these guys for hours, until at 2 AM or so, we were finally allowed to start our mix. Needless to say, it was a bad trip.

**BONUS CUT**

The late, great music publisher Chuck Kaye once told me a Tahitian tale about his time trolling the island with Marlon Brando. Supposedly Marlon had invested in a gigantic hotel resort; later, he was approached by locals in a dive bar and alerted to the fact that the hotel was being built on sacred ground. Marlon Brando woke up the next day and joined these guys on the picket line. Yes, he picketed his own hotel! I've never been able to verify the story, but if I could go back in time, maybe I would've have protested us too?

When we returned to New York, as Eurodance was now becoming the new thing, we waved goodbye to Acid Jazz and wrote a Hi-NRG tune called "Step Up To The Line" with a singer named Kimberly Blake. We had such a swell time with Kimberly, who was truly the coolest, that we decided to form our own new group together called Mighty Reel. My role in Mighty Reel was to rap with a slight German accent. The thirst was real. Kimberly's friend Joe Riccitelli (eventual president of RCA) randomly pitched "Step Up To The Line" to the music supervisor for the Whoopi Goldberg movie *Eddie*, and it actually made the cut! If you happen to catch the film at 3 AM in a fit of Netflix insomnia, you can hear it muddle in the background for a couple of seconds while fiesty Coach Whoopi berates one of the Knicks. Since the song also landed on the soundtrack, alongside the likes of Jodeci, Coolio, and Dru Hill, Joe Riccitelli—who was, and is, a total sweetheart—got us all invites to the *Eddie* soundtrack release party. Man, we were so pumped. A real soundtrack release party! That night at the celeb-filled, jam-packed soiree, however, the club's douche of a DJ decided to blast every single jam on the soundtrack except ours. I'm serious, every last one. Each time it got to our tune in the sequencing, he'd just abruptly skip over it. Was my Düsseldorf flow really that wack? After two hours of this bullshit indignity, we sheepishly called it a night, and soon after, Mighty Reel called it a day as well.

As these things go, *Eddie* also turned out to be the point of no return for me and Doug DeAngelis. One morning, he summoned me to a diner on Twenty-Third Street, where, over a pair of stale blueberry muffins, he musically dumped my ass. He said I wasn't carrying my weight in the studio, I was immature, occasionally toxic (well, in all fairness, at the time that was probably true), and he questioned my musical abilities altogether. That was the dagger. I had never had anyone disintegrate me like that. Honestly, it broke my fuckin' heart. When I exited the diner and stepped outside toward Seventh Avenue, I had the first of a thousand existential panic attacks in my adult life. For one moment, I actually missed vertigo: it would've been immeasurably more pleasant. In the months that followed the demise of our short-lived partnership, I wished him some form of musical dismemberment, but then one day it finally hit me: Doug was completely correct. Both my talents and emotional growth were in no way where they needed to be if I wanted to make something of myself. I was impulsively ricochetting through my early twenties with piles of ambition but only a lump of ability. In my collaborations with Doug, I'd been primarily relying on his chops out of fear of being exposed as a musical lightweight. His years of theory had been carrying us. His charm as well. I resolved then and there that I would never be carried again. To be taken seriously in this business, I had to both master the craft and become a better, infinitely more evolved human, and I didn't care how long it took.

That was the first watershed moment of my career.

I worked at it day and night. I began to hang around friends' sessions and pick up tricks. Sure, I was an untrained musician, but

I began to realize there might actually be a built-in benefit to this reality. Since technically suspect musicians like myself were pretty much devoid of theory, all rules got tossed out the window, which aligned with my mutineer spirit. I just had to create my own lane. I wrote lyric after inspired lyric and messed with beat making too. I spent hours a day on an E-mu SP-1200 sampler that only allotted a less-than-whopping 2.5 seconds per sound. As the machine's sample time was ridiculously limited, it forced me to create musical beds that were quite often just a two-chord loop of whatever dusty old record I decided to chop up. That provided a concise challenge. To craft an entire topline over two chords max, it really forced me to expand my melodies to keep (potential) listeners engaged. It immediately elevated my craft. Aspiring writers, I highly recommend you take a few stabs at creating your own tune with these limitations.

During this musical moment of salvation, the bulk of my free time was spent soaking up biographies of my songwriter and producer idols. At night, I'd grab Tyler Roe and we'd sneak into each and every industry showcase in town, hoping to make some connects or meet like-minded creatives. As I got more comfortable in my own skin, I started making some new incredible friendships. I also speed-dialed every single human I'd ever previously met in this less-than-forgiving business, searching for any dollop of opportunity. That first crucial crumb came from JW Sewell, formerly of Ultrax, who was now running Intersound, a small label in Alpharetta, Georgia. He had begun dabbling in a new musical genre: Booty bass.

Booty bass was a strictly Southern phenomenon. An offshoot of the late '80s Miami bass craze, those mostly faceless records were a wonderful exercise in restraint. Just 808 drums and some vocal sample chops. That's it—this was a case study in sparse. JW was pressing and releasing a couple of booty bass long-plays per month. "Bass Headz," "Bootleg Booty," and "Booty Mix" were a few of his releases in this speaker-tweakin' genre. Each record was more successful than the last.

I hopped a plane to Atlanta, where JW kindly put me up for a weekend, and I desperately pleaded my case. Truthfully, I knew nothing about this shit, but by the time I angled JW, I was a well-studied booty expert, dropping knowledge of the boom like an AP science teacher. Eventually I wore him down. He agreed to give me one record—with a $10,000 budget! All anyone really needs in this business is two or three people who believe in you, and you have the infrastructure to make moves. Early on, JW was one of those people. Man, I owe that swell fella for it. I took the $10,000 and bought a bunch of new equipment. I pounded the record out over an eight-day, Diet Dr Pepper–fueled, booty bliss bender. I titled the resulting album *Bass Crimes*. It was complete and utter garbage, but it sold a few copies, and suddenly JW opened up the coffers.

**BONUS CUT**

Fun fact: Around that same time, the Beastie Boys' magazine *Grand Royal* published a fascinating feature on my old pal Kennedy, who had retired the microphone himself and was now in the midst of a epic run directing some of the booty era's iconic music videos. It was titled "The Hitchcock of Hoochie." If you can unearth it, it's some Pulitzer-worthy stuff. Crazily enough, one of his booty clips featured a Gary Coleman (*Diff'rent Strokes*) cameo. Knowing that on the trivia tip I could freely recite quotes from the former child star's long-forgotten TV flick, *The Kid from Left Field*, Kennedy actually let me loiter around that shoot, and toward the end of the day, I got to kick it with Gary for ten challenging minutes during a break. It was an extremely uncomfortable hang. He didn't seem like a particularly chipper fella. I felt like a dick for bumrushing him.

So with JW's wallet wedged slightly open, I phoned Duke Mushroom up and gave him the hard sell. I told him there was a ton of potential work at Intersound Records. It wouldn't be the sexiest of gigs, but the quick cash would free us to keep scheming up greater projects. I thought the Teddy Pendergrass debacle might've put a barbecue fork in my credibility with him, but blessedly he hopped in a cab with his sampler and Juno-60 synth.

The Pop Rox duo was born.

Yes, over an inspiring lunch that day, we created an official partnership. Duke was totally cool with letting my creative vision guide our thing. His musical chops were so nimble and well versed that we paired perfectly. I think we both completely believed we could be the next Chapman and Chinn, the next Kasenetz-Katz SuperCircus—shit, the next David Frank and Mic Murphy. We began banging out more booty tracks. Then trip-hop tracks. And drum and bass tracks. Basically, anything JW asked for, we delivered. One of the records we cooked up, "I Am The Freshmaka," actually caught a little buzz in L.A., and *LA Times Magazine*'s Jill Barrett booked me to model in a fashion spread. Sure, they spray-painted my first bald spot jet black and I was styled up like some weird-ass blend of *Zoolander* meets *Thriller*, but I did own it.

> **BONUS CUT**
>
> I sat beside Meatloaf in the hair and makeup trailer. If I remember correctly, he was a grunter.

It was around that time that I began two other relationships that entirely revamped my life. After a year and a half of relentless courtship, I finally landed a date with a girl named Jen Abu, who I'd met one night while gyrating around the Village. From that very first hang, I knew Jen would be my BFF and, in time, significantly better half. I wasn't the least bit deterred by the fact that she found me somewhat repulsive. Sure, neither my failed white-rap career nor booty-record pedigree were much of an aphrodisiac, but I held my damn ground like a wad of gum on a shoe sole. There's always been a tenacity to my terrible. Jen was razor-sharp, levelheaded, and super beautiful, but most importantly, she was willing to go on a date with me to see the casts of *Real World* and *Road Rules* speak at the Beacon Theatre. That was some ride-or-die shit.

BONUS CUT

We were only backstage at the Beacon for thirty seconds or so when a ballistic Puck from *Real World: San Francisco* randomly ran up to me and tossed a busted acoustic guitar at my chest, screaming, "Hey you! Hold this fuckin' thing for me NOW!" In an instant, I understood why this dick was evicted from the SF house.

That same month, I met a young manager named Bret Disend. We were both loafing outside Brownies, the East Village rock pit, when we were introduced by a mutual friend. Bret had recently moved to the Financial District from Boston to set up a music management shop. He was a brilliant balance of tactical and sympathetic, and he swiftly became a loyal friend in a business of slick. He asked me what Pop Rox's goals were, and, with zero hesitation, I told him that I wanted to cast a stable of acts who would sing my and Duke's songs. After much time assessing the game, I'd arrived at the conclusion that this was gonna be the only possible entry point for me and Duke as aspiring scribes. Bret loved the idea and said he'd shop and manage each act. That was 1998 or so.

BONUS CUT

Somehow, he remained my manager for another twenty-two years. That was a pretty impressive run. I'm not an easy one.

Since neither myself, Duke, or Bret, for that matter, had a direct pipeline to any blue-chip talents, we absorbed Billy Beane's *Moneyball* philosophy. We weren't necessarily looking for home run sluggers. We just needed kids who could get on base.

Our first Pop Rox act was a seventeen-year-old single mom from the Bronx named Sabrina Nieves. She was a dancer on *Club MTV* and she was ridiculously attractive and sweet. Though she wasn't really that interested in chasing a singing career, she gave us a shot.

I rechristened her Sabrina Sang (an ode to that '70s one-hit wonder, Bee Gees protégé Samantha Sang), and through Kennedy's connect we were able to land her both an audition and a subsequent record deal with Tommy Boy Records. It was a whirlwind. Duke and I received a check for $100,000 to commence recording! A week or two later, our ragtag production company moved out of my studio apartment, and we leased an office on 20 West Twentieth Street.

Ahhh . . . 20 West Twentieth Street. What a marvelous hot mess of a building. It harbored a gun range in the basement and a strip club on the ground floor. The rest of the space was a hodgepodge of industries. Our walls backed into a children's modeling agency. There were more than a few evenings when I rode a jam-packed elevator with sweaty strippers and ten-year-old models, their stage moms aghast, all spiraling toward the lobby in the most uncomfortable of silences.

On the Saturday when we first moved into the building, I made a terrible judgment call. For a little extra creative inspiration, I ingested a couple of pot brownies in the morning and then set off to the Janovic Paint shop to pick up two fresh containers of Martha Stewart white. When I entered the building, a rush of lap dancers excitedly exited the elevator, and one bumped into me full force. In that flurry, I began to juggle the gallons awkwardly, and they fell hard from my hands, banging onto the lobby floor and sounding like gun blasts from the basement. Somehow, the velocity of impact blew one of the gallon lids wide open. The paint flew everywhere, spraying the strippers like a Mafia-movie Uzi. Everyone began to scream and holler. I'm serious. As the chaos ensued, I panicked and sprinted ten flights up the stairwell and dashed through the doors of our new studio, breathlessly laughing while covered in paint. I hid behind the couch as my heart raced a mile a minute. Duke was mortified. I was sure I was Attica bound. After sobering up for a couple of hours, I returned to the scene of the crime, and thankfully all paint remnants had been magically scraped away by a (better) Samaritan. That episode set an ugly Pop Rox precedent.

Sabrina's record set an ugly Pop Rox precedent as well. It got shelved.

We put so much work into this electro-leaning debut, delivered the finished album, and then . . . crickets. Whenever we'd inquire about a release date, our A&R at Tommy Boy (a division of Time Warner) would go cemetery silent, so in fits of desperation, we'd record a few new songs and deliver them in a whipped-up frenzy. Zero response. After a year of this forth with no back, Tommy Boy mercifully placed one of the tunes on their lucrative Jock Jams compilations. That record sold a few million copies, so we received our first platinum plaque.

For Jock Jams.

Yes, Jock Jams.

**BONUS CUT**

Obviously, I purchased a second Jock Jams plaque for my mom.

She proudly displayed it above the dog bowls.

Sabrina was the best. We absolutely adored her, but Tommy Boy cut the cord and set her free. We tried shopping her (now label-less) album elsewhere, but we couldn't find any takers, so Sabrina wisely moved on and joined a reboot of the '80s freestyle group the Cover Girls.

Before long, Duke stumbled upon our next muse. Her name was Tarsha Vega. I believe she worked in the CBS Television accounting department. From the moment Duke brought her by the studio, I knew we had something. She was quite striking, but mad guarded, which gave her a sexy, aloof vibe that captivated everyone she met. Most importantly, Tarsha also had complete and utter faith in us. That was huge. She hadn't really entertained the notion of rapping, so she let me play the role of Cyrano with zero pushback. I began crafting verses for her day and night, trying to concoct a lyrical uniqueness. Tarsha became the natural extension of my own failed rap career. (I secretly loved the idea that my character morphed from an average-looking suburban Jew to an uptown Puerto Rican bombshell.)

And the industry bought it.

My incredible lawyer, Lisa Socransky (twenty-four years and running now!), sent our Tarsha demo over to Joe Fleischer at *Hits!* magazine, and he featured it in his "Wheels and Deals" column. Within a week or so, we had six legitimate record-deal offers. We ended up closing the Tarsha record deal with Bob Jamieson, then chairman of RCA Records, and set off on the record. And the best part? We seemed to bamboozle the entire business into believing that Tarsha was the lyricist. A publisher even gave her $150,000 for 1 percent of the album's publishing. One percent! We were so maniacal about making sure this record reeked of "artistry" that we slid Tarsha that sliver of pub so her name would appear with us in the credits.

**BONUS CUT**

Alas, that believability took a huge early hit when a member of Tarsha's management team interrupted our first RCA full-label digital marketing meeting by loudly exclaiming, "I would prefer if we refrain from talking about the World Wide Web. I actually invented the internet, and I'm in the process of suing to get my patent straightened out." No, he was not joking. Now, I'm not referring to that cat in particular (who I actually kinda liked), but I would say 95 percent of all managers are terrible. Think about it: Anyone can wake up and claim "manager" status. There's no bar of entry for the job. Most people blame labels for a record's failure, but in my experience, a meddling manager (or "fanager," who believes their client can do no wrong) usually plays a huge role in a flop.

Thankfully, we survived that potentially litigious afternoon, and almost immediately after, we landed the white whale. A music supervisor sent our Tarsha songs to Sandra Bullock, who, upon one listen, supposedly lost her mind and requested our single "Be Ya Self" as the end title song for her upcoming comedy, *Miss Congeniality* (distributed by Time Warner). Excitement in the RCA building built.

Everyone was over the moon about this project. Months of strategy ensued. Then one morning, Bret and I got summoned up to the Nipper offices. We sat down in the slight office of Jimmy Maloney, the marketing director in charge of our project. Jimmy was so giddy, he looked like he could burst.

"What's going on?" Bret inquired.

"I have amazing news! We passed on *Miss Congeniality* last night," Jimmy replied.

Huh?

"Yup. You're not gonna believe it! 'Be Ya Self' is going to be the end-title for *Rocky & Bullwinkle*. Starring . . . Are you ready? . . . Robert De Niro and *Seinfeld*'s Jason Alexander! The movie is gonna pay for a $350,000 live-action music video. It's gonna feature an animated dancing Bullwinkle. Tarsha's gonna dance with Bullwinkle!"

Bret and I glared at each other in horror. We loved De Niro. We loved Costanza. But this was fuckin' Rocky and Bullwinkle! We begged and pleaded our case to no avail. The die was already cast. A month later, we dashed up to the label to screen the final cut of the $350,000 music video. When we arrived, Jimmy looked extremely distressed. He pushed play and swiftly exited the room. For the next three minutes, we viewed what might've been the wackest music video of the year 2000. The clip featured a break-dancing Hasid. As I began to hyperventilate, Bret looked at me and in his usual monotone snark whispered, "Dancing Hasid. Dude, this shit is deceased."

It was.

Though the video did make the film's credit roll, Tarsha was dropped soon after and her debut never saw the light of day.

The movie was nominated for a Razzie Award, so at least we had that.

Within a year or so, Jimmy exited the music business and took a job at *TV Guide*.

BONUS CUT

One night, Bret, Jen, Duke, and myself were eating at Nobu in Tribeca when we were overwhelmed by a loud, drunken table right next to us. It was Sandra Bullock and the entire cast of *Miss Congeniality* enjoying a celebratory wrap dinner! Crazy, right? We spent the entire evening ogling them in a sake-fueled stupor. When a slightly inebriated Sandra Bullock slid by us on the way to the restroom, we had to take a stab at closure. Duke and I jumped up and clumsily introduced ourselves as the folks who wrote "Be Ya Self." She looked at us with puppy-dog eyes and said, "Aw, whatever happened to that song? We loved it so much! We were so bummed when you guys pulled it from the film." Then she moved on.

Feelin' kinda humbled and in need of some quick pocket dollars, Duke and I accepted a seemingly innocuous cash gig. Duke's neighbor was directing a Time Warner cable commercial, and he hired us to create the music. We were offered a couple of thousand dollars apiece. It was bullshit pay, but as we both needed the dough infusion, we dug in and hit it furiously. The end result was some cable-friendly brilliance. Unfortunately, we weren't getting paid enough to afford a legal fee, so we signed the one-sheet deal memo sans representation and moved on.

When we delivered it, Time Warner flipped. I mean, they really loved it. They ran it for the next four years. 24/7. But guess who didn't make one additional penny. Yes, we'd completely signed away our rights on the song as a "work for hire," including our writer's royalties.

That meant zero dollars, ever!

If we'd only maintained a smidgen of writing or publishing royalties on the tune, we would've walked away with years of rent. Instead, we got nothing but constant reminders of our foolishness. This ate at us every day. We couldn't avoid it. At home. The gym. Everywhere. The tune was ubiquitous. One night in the early millennium, Jen and I fell behind on our bills, and Time Warner promptly cut off our cable. Hello, irony! I called the support line frantically. The line rang busy for thirty minutes. I sat on hold. The hold music? You guessed it. Our little Time Warner jingle had reared its hurtful little head again on loop. As I sat there sadistically listening to our sad little tune over and over, I had to take a deep breath and reassure myself that it wouldn't stay this shade of bleak forever.

## CHAPTER 10

# Celluloid Zero

There's an episode of *Seinfeld* that shows Cosmo Kramer racing down Seventh Avenue in the back of a taxicab as a loop of exterior B-roll footage of early-'90s downtown NYC floats by in the distance. Suddenly, the frame freezes on the exterior canopy from Michael's Muffins. Be still, my insatiable heart. Michael's Muffins was located on Nineteenth Street and Seventh Avenue and had the greatest homemade pastries I ever tasted. I lived at that counter for two years, adding pound after precious pound. I just googled it, and there seems to be only one mention of its existence on the entire interweb. It's like that magical spot has vanished from time and space. Whenever I stumble upon that clip, I get homesick for a long-forgotten city. At this point, I barely recognize the place.

As I came of musical age in Manhattan, it was this crazy, blank page of opportunity, both professionally and socially. I began to meet so many like-minded downtown freaks with similar pursuits. I owe a major part of this to Duke Mushroom. Having grown up in the Chicago suburb of Evanston, he'd graduated high school with a Hollywood-chasing cast of friends: John Cusack, Jeremy Piven, and a bunch of others that all ended up succeeding in film and TV. I was so jealous of their collective. Thankfully, through Duke's endorsement, I was initiated into the big-screen gang, even though I myself was only a celluloid zero.

At the time, John Cusack was on top of the world. Between *Say Anything* and *The Grifters*, he was something of an icon. He moved to the city to film Woody Allen's *Bullets over Broadway* and threw some much-needed cash Duke's way to be his PA for the shoot. For some inexplicable reason, Johnny took an interest in me immediately and began letting me tag along everywhere in the kid brother role. It was a tremendous initiation into celebrity and the warped headspace of fame. We ran wild. Bars. Restaurants. Illegal gambling parlors. Sporting events. One curious trip after another. That was life with Cusack (and Piven, for that matter). How about drinks with Matt Damon, Ben Affleck, and a super-chatty Lars Ulrich immediately after *Good Will Hunting* hit the zeitgeist? Or hanging at some mid-'90s MTV Awards after-party with Billy Corgan, Marilyn Manson, and Courtney Love? Cusack even joined us for Thanksgiving at Grandma Hilda's apartment. That evening ended with me, Johnny, Piven, and Uma Thurman all dancing on the steps of the Metropolitan Museum of Art in the pouring rain. It was definitely some dreamlike, cinematic shit, but yet another in a series of "one of these folks doesn't belong here" snapshots that defined my younger life. I'd run home from these hangs in a euphoric state that was immediately followed by hours of uncomfortable stirring. I felt very unfulfilled in the entourage. I knew I desperately needed to make a name for myself.

On the night Evander Holyfield fought Ray Mercer for the world heavyweight championship, I met Johnny over at Mickey Mantle's restaurant on Fifty-Seventh to soak in the festivities, where we were joined by a crew that included the lovely Liam Neeson, Natasha Richardson, and Dan Marino. When the Holyfield fight wrapped, Johnny suggested that three of us—me, Johnny, and his aspiring Hollywood screenwriter pal whose name sadly escapes me—roll over to Scores, the notorious

NYC late night with John Cusack, Uma Thurman, and Don Lunetta.

strip club tucked a dozen blocks away. We hopped into his town car and within minutes, saddled up to the famed jiggle joint. It was apparent immediately that the doorman was a big *Better Off Dead* fan. He shuttled us off to a private banquette with a perfect semicircular view of the room. I sat down and posted up in the middle of the booth with Johnny and the screenwriter on my left and right, respectively. Suddenly the floodgates opened: a dozen revved-up dancers standing a solid twenty feet away, all whispering and pointing in our direction. As they began to saunter toward us with the slowest, most cinematic of steps, I began to think of my friends back home. There was no way they'd ever believe that a goofball like myself could ever high dive into such a spectacular sea of silicone. Nah, they wouldn't believe a word of it. Johnny sat there slightly expressionless, just as cool as a cucumber. The screenwriter had a shit-eating grin. I was completely mesmerized by the moment. But then something weird happened.

The strippers parted down the middle like Moses and the Red Sea.

Six swept to the left.

Six swept to the right.

Johnny was swarmed.

The screenwriter was swarmed.

Me?

Nada.

This was quite possibly the most humiliating moment of my adult life: the girls all desperately jockeying for the attention of my infinitely more desirable cohorts. I was left blowing in the wind. I began to wig out. I had to be the only living boy in New York who couldn't attract a lap dance with dollars in hand. I stood up and pretended to walk to the bathroom, but then I made a clean break for the door. As I rushed toward the exit, I was stopped by a slightly sympathetic cocktail waitress who attempted to engage me conversationally out of pity. She gave me a knowing hug. Then, with zero pride left, I ghosted. As I'm sure you can surmise, in the months and years to come, Johnny stopped inviting me anywhere. I was no longer in the nook. My weak stripper game was obviously a deal breaker. I've never once set foot in a gentleman's club since.

Looking back on it now, we really had a great crew of showbiz-bound underdogs building in the Village back in the Pop Rox days. Morgan Spurlock and Mick Reed were posted up in an office on Little West Twelfth Street. I had the best time running around with those fools. Morgan had a relentless motor. Since I had similar, non-stop creative machinations, I dug him from the jump. He always had pitches, pilots, plots, and schemes. We had great hangs discussing all of it. Mick Reed lived on a houseboat on the West Side. One night he invited eight or so of us out onto the slip to meet his new girlfriend under the beautiful city sunset. When we arrived at the pier, there were paparazzi waiting. I was befuddled. I figured the shutterbugs must've missed the memo because they were definitely trailing a bunch of nobodies. And then it all made sense. There she was. Mick's new girlfriend . . .

Monica Lewinsky.

This was right at the absolute height of the Clinton scandal. I still can't recall being more disturbingly starstruck. We hopped on board, and she strode over and stuck out her hand in the friendliest manner.

"Hi, I'm Monica!"

Yes. Yes, you are.

I had this perverse feeling that we'd all end up like Natalie Wood, capsized into the Hudson by a vindictive Secret Service, but thankfully we survived the night. For whatever it's worth, she was very sweet.

Duke had another friend that I really dug, J.J. Abrams. When he first showed up on the scene, J.J. had already written a screenplay, *Regarding Henry*, which easily made him one of our more successful pals. We used to sit around the basement of Duke and Tyler's East Village apartment riffing on music and film for hours on end. When he sold his first television show, *Felicity*, we all linked up at the Odeon restaurant in Tribeca to celebrate. When the show made it to air, he invited us out to hang around the set and take it all in. Jen and I spent hours sitting in his director chair, watching take after take unfold in front of us. He even shouted out me and Duke on the show by naming the record label that offered Amy Jo Johnson's character a demo deal "Pop Rox." He really was the kindest guy in the world. Now, of course, he's J.J. F'N ABRAMS—the heir to all things Spielberg. I haven't seen him in a good decade or so, but I will tell you this: He was wonderfully supportive back in those early, scrappy NYC days. Honestly, all of these guys were. I'm still so grateful to each and every one of them for exposing me to bigger ideas and greater possibilities.

## CHAPTER 11

# Sesame Street on Acid

**W**hile Duke and I continued the uphill song climb, we began clocking some side-hustle dollars remixing tunes for Def Jam Records working in tandem with our pal Matt Stein. I know that sounds like an incredible opportunity, but it wasn't as exciting as you'd think. These were low-budget techno remixes (as the electronica genre was having its first—brief—moment in the US), so the only folks who got to hear the fruits of our hard labor tended to be glow stick–waving rave kids stumbling on ecstasy. We didn't care. We were just hoping the gig would continue for a minute, as it did kick to the rent, but then Eminem loudly proclaimed that "Nobody listens to techno!" and soon it was RIP techno and our brief Def Jam remix run.

As I look back on that batch of track flips, my favorite was unquestionably our rework of DMX's "Party Up (Up in Here)." I have to say, it was pretty solid! I was kinda hoping we'd get to connect with DMX in person when it dropped, but alas, it wasn't meant to happen. That being said however, I do have a brief DMX tale.

DMX moved to my hometown of Mount Kisco, New York, sometime around the late '90s. As I alluded to earlier, it's always been a pretty sleepy suburban spot. Thus it was kind of a big deal that he decided to post up there. Whenever I visited my folks, I'd roll by his golden-gated house on the stalker tip and marvel at his front yard full of hoopties on blocks, but I never actually caught sight of him. Then one particularly mellow afternoon, I tagged along with my mom while she went dish shopping at the Dansk store downtown. As Danish dinnerware wasn't really my thing, I trod around the shop in my usual BlackBerry-engrossed stupor. Suddenly, I heard the loudest booming sound I'd ever heard. Literally ear splitting. It was like a vicious mob of 808s. I sprinted outside to peep the source of the noise, and my jaw fell to the sidewalk as an Impala convertible came hopping down the empty-ass street in my direction. Now when I say "empty," I mean tumbleweeds. No other living soul was around to witness this visual. As the Impala eased closer, I realized that it was jam-packed with a crew of little kids—and DMX was driving!

But it gets better.

They were all screaming along to a DMX record.

DMX included!

He winked at me as he cruised by. The five or six tiny dudes waved and yelled as well. This shit was seriously like *Sesame Street* on acid. Then he hit the switches and the car bounced off into forever. I'd always been a fan, but now I was entirely all in.

## CHAPTER 12

# The Slot Machine

So you want to have your first minor international dance hit? Just follow these simple steps that worked for me!

1. Make sure the phone has stopped ringing altogether. It'll help if the studio rent is due and you have zero dollars coming in.

2. As eviction looms, you should recklessly ignore your pressing fiscal concerns to enjoy another day of nothingness.

3. Hey, why not get blitzed and sift through your dusty crates of records? You might just stumble upon an ill little funk snippet.

4. What if you chop and screw that joint up on your sampler and then proceed to dance your face off to this greasy loop you made?

5. When your musical coconspirator enters the room, maybe he'll be so inspired by your bouncy brilliance that he'll turn on his '65 Gibson Falcon tube amp, mic up the Fender Rhodes, and begin jamming chords over it.

6. Wait, this is beginning to sound real fresh! You guys have clearly created twenty seconds of throwback funk-disco brilliance. What do you do with it?

7. Maybe you should make it the background music behind your studio answering machine's outgoing message. Even if

no one calls besides your exasperated manager and angry landlord at this point, at least they'll both give you props for the nastiness you've concocted.

8. That being said, you never know, though. You might just get a message from your long-lost hipster indie rock pal who's been slugging away in bands for years with little to show for it.

9. Big news! Turns out your indie rock pal has reinvented himself as a DJ.

10. DJ loves the outgoing background tune on the machine. He inquires about it.

11. "It's just us fuckin' around, man," you reply.

12. DJ respectfully asks for the Pro Tools files of this jam. He wants to mess with the stems.

13. You happily hand them over.

14. Over the next few weeks, DJ puts a four-on-the-floor kick drum behind it.

15. Boom. Boom. Boom. Boom.

16. Then he adds a couple of layers of synths.

17. Jeez, it sounds way nastier. Is that even possible?!

18. DJ shops your newly completed four-minute answering-loop track to record labels.

19. An indie label pays $2,000 for it.

20. Well alrighty then!

21. The label folds.

22. Shit.

23. DJ buys the master back from the indie label's carcass for $2,000 out of his own wallet. That's a bold commitment. Somehow, you wisely avoid digging in your own pockets.

24. In a last-ditch effort, DJ sends the track directly to a contact at the BBC.

25. Crazily enough, the BBC playlists it on Radio 1!

26. Since the song is now devoid of a record label, a fierce bidding war ensues.

27. You own a third of the master. For once, you've done this correctly.

28. Guess what? It's actually a hit.
29. You get your first sizable royalty check.
30. The rent is finally paid.
31. Your answering machine promptly breaks.

## CHAPTER 13

# I Write the Songs that Make the Whole World Sleep

I was nearing the age of thirty and was already a grizzled veteran of the washout. Completely calloused, actually. All of my life ups seemed to be immediately followed by tremendous downs in a Bob Fosse–choreographed sequence. One bright spot, however, was that every false start had resulted in the opportunity to clock a bit of time with the real record-biz kings. The titans of the industry—Jimmy Iovine, Seymour Stein, Donnie Ienner, Chris Blackwell—bona fide kings. At various points, each of these industry icons courted, and then usually shelved or passed on, one Pop Rox act or another, but I did get to spend a few hours of priceless time in their orbit that provided me with some tidbits of career-altering insight.

The one elusive meeting, however, was with Clive Davis.

For the unaware, Clive Davis completely shaped the modern music industry as president of CBS's Records Division and as founder and president of both Arista and J Records. From Carlos Santana and the Grateful Dead to Whitney Houston and Aretha Franklin, Clive was widely considered the most acclaimed record man since the dawn of the industry. I'd met many artists, writers, and producers who would've gladly named their next of kin "Clive" for the wonderful ways he transformed their careers. I was so jealous of them. I dreamed of the moment I'd finally cross his radar. Then one day, after the aforementioned answering machine song made a little noise, I finally got summoned to the throne.

It was early in the new millennium, and Clive had just launched a brand-new label, J Records, in grand form by taking over an entire floor of the Waldorf Astoria as temporary offices. And that's where I was headed. I took the N train up to Fifty-Seventh Street and hopped off at the base of Central Park. It was arctic cold, and flurries were beginning to scatter across the backs of the carriage-harnessed horses. Though I felt a tremendous wave of trepidation, as I knew that my stuff wasn't up to snuff yet, I got so caught up in the postcard beauty of my surroundings that for once, I let my self-loathing and musical doubts take a back seat for a bit.

After a brief elevator ride at the Waldorf, I sat in the lobby for a good fifteen minutes or so before my wise old friend James Diener came out to greet me. James, who had just begun working in A&R at the label, had arranged the meeting based on all of the (still unearned) Pop Rox hype that somehow continued to exist in the industry after our first miscues. He gave me a quick overview: "You're gonna walk in Clive's office with five other A&R guys and myself. He's a very busy man. He'll ask you to play him some song demos. Keep it brief."

We strolled across the stunning hotel floor. Guest rooms had been transformed into opulent, sprawling offices. Finally we arrived at Clive's headquarters and James entered first. Clive was seated a good twenty-five yards away. The room had the most prime Park Avenue view. It was the biggest, most ornate space I'd ever seen. As I swiftly surveyed the digs, I wondered if billionaires like the Sultan of Brunei had previously held epic orgies in this same space. My math surmised that this spot could easily house a harem of fifty freaks.

Clive stood up, smiled, and reached across his mammoth desk. "Hi, Sam. Nice to finally meet you."

Holy shit, he knew my name! I was both starstruck and disarmed. The other A&R men in the room greeted me with pleasantries as well. I knew most of them from various meetings along the way. I had to say, this was a very nice bunch of humans. I was seated in the last seat in a semicircle of chairs directly across from Clive and his angularly positioned desk. We were separated by three feet at most. I had a plan of attack: Upon initial banter, I'd steer clear of shouting out his obvious accolades and instead praise some of his lesser media-celebrated successes. No Barry Manilow. No Whitney. I came with the Looking Glass classic "Brandy." From the jump, it seemed like a clever play, but unfortunately my nervous mouth kicked in. I simply couldn't shut up about the tune. Singer Elliot Lurie's rich, soulful vocal. The killer horn track. It was as if my verbal assault rifle had excitedly sprayed so much ammunition that the gun jammed. Clive was very sweet and seemed somewhat engaged in my blabbering, but I did begin to catch a couple of yawns. As usual, I knew I was wearing out my welcome. Mercifully, James interceded.

"Sam, why don't you play Clive some of the new stuff you've been writing?"

Message heard loud and clear.

I handed Clive a CD, and he slowly popped it in. As the speakers began to release my song, I took in Clive's every fiber. He wore a brilliantly tailored shirt. An expensive watch. It was all larger than life. I thought about my future. Standing on the Grammy podium in a fitted Paul Smith tux, exchanging pleasantries with Clive as we accepted our respective Record of the Year awards. The mentor. The mentee. It was all within my grasp.

The verse kicked in.

Clive rested his head back and began to soak in my sounds.

The first chorus, he seemed pretty into it.

I think he smiled.

The second verse, he nodded along to the music.

By the end of the second chorus, Clive had nodded off.

Yes.

Nodded off.

How did I notice? Maybe it was the shuttered eyes. Or the bumpy snores that floated over my melodies. Or possibly the awkward glances that began shooting like meteors between the A&R hombres seated beside me.

Yes, I'd successfully put the legend to sleep.

The A&R cat sitting on the opposite end of the semicircle slowly rose from his seat and slid behind the desk. He gave Clive the most subtle of shoves and whispered in his ear. Clive's eyes whipped open and he whispered something back. Then he looked me in the eye and without missing a beat, said, "Good song. Not a hit."

For once, I was speechless.

Meeting adjourned.

The funny thing is, Clive was completely correct. I unearthed the demo recently, and it was truly a painful listen. It wasn't a hit. It was god awful. Had I been in his position, I certainly might've caught a few Zs listening to it.

As I exited the building, the snow was now dancing down at a ridiculous rate. There were no cabs in sight. I considered taking a crowded subway ride home, but decided I needed to breathe. I spent close to three hours walking from Fifty-Seventh Street to Cobble Hill, Brooklyn, in a mini-blizzard, playing a losing game of backgammon with my fragile psyche.

I still had a long way to go.

## CHAPTER 14

# The Biggest Loser

Last month, I was midway through a Nashville dinner party with a crew of songwriter comrades when we began discussing the mistakes and missteps of our respective musical youths. It was a pretty funny batch of narratives across the board, but as the night wore on, it began to feel like a pissing contest of self-deprecation. Now, I didn't want to be that guy, but my tequila-fueled competitive streak kicked in and, to quote Donald Glover, "I had to stunt on those hoes."

You see, in the first decade of my career, no one could top my stack of bad breaks. For that one inglorious moment of time, I was the music industry's undisputed biggest loser. Since I wasn't leaving this dinner without a trophy, beyond my stalled rap career, Sabrina Sang, and Tarsha Vega, I knew I had to offer up a few (or a slew) more examples of world-record blowouts to clear my good name.

I kicked it off with Owen's Ghost, a trio of amigos I'd attended high school with. We'd been out of that last classroom for ten years or so when I took Jen to see them play in my hometown bar. I watched, hawk-like, as the local girls in attendance drunkenly sang along to their hometown anthem, "Tequila Sheila," while crowding the base of the stage. My old pal Dan Woods was the lead singer and, man, Dan had come so far from his early days playing bass behind my inferior self at the Battle of the Bands. This dude deserved better. The band's guitarist, Aaron Accetta, worked in tech support for a software company in White Plains. I believe their drummer was an accountant. Music had shifted into a weekend-warrior gig for all three. Duke and I began working with them a little, but we had one major issue: Their look was kinda suspect. Blessedly, Jen (now working sixty-hour hell weeks at *Vogue*) and her generous roommate, Kim, agreed to style the guys for a last-minute photo shoot.

From what I recall of that morning, the shoot started out fine, but somewhere around lunch, trouble arose (again). The drummer, whose hair line was rapidly receding, like mine, refused to wear a hat. Adamantly refused. Jen dialed me in despair. There was no negotiating with this kid. Suddenly, he vanished into the bathroom.

When he returned a few minutes later, he stormed through the door with the last of his thinning locks now dyed a color of swimming pool blue. It was a one-man protest against head coverings. Unfortunately, he was also wearing a blue shirt. Now he was beginning to resemble a lost Smurf. He really was a nice fella, but we had varying visions and parted ways the next day. We renamed the now-duo JBender, after Judd Nelson's emotional thug in *The Breakfast Club*, and began crafting a throwback '60s vibe in the Sugar Ray, Smash Mouth, and Fastball lane. From the jump, it was a pretty sweet concoction. Aaron was super on point with his pop changes, and Dan had his own uniquely super cool lyrical thing, so it was quite refreshing throwing down with the both of them. After a couple of weeks of intensive writing, we had a demo good to go. It only took a couple of months and we had two major label offers. We chose Columbia Records, but by the time we had finished recording, we began to get that awful feeling that JBender's debut was also bound for blackout. Yes, between a lack of preexisting fanbase and endless label overthinking about the single selection and correct radio format to launch the band, Columbia stalled and then subsequently pulled the plug on the project before it reached retail. Man, I can't express how awful I felt for my pals, and the shelving was way too déjà vu for my tastes, but I didn't completely despair, as I'd already begun another vision quest scheming the band that would become Bad Ronald.

Bad Ronald's name was derived from the 1970s after-school horror flick that scared the living shit out of me as a kid. There was no negotiating. I knew that had to be the moniker from inception. For the project, I wanted to create a hip-hop ensemble that threaded the needle between Sublime, the Beastie Boys (Rick Rubin returns), and the colossally underrated Pharcyde, whose *Bizarre Ride II to Pharcyde* debut had been pivotal for me as a sponge of all things jazzy hip-hop. I placed a Village Voice classified ad in search of MCs. After an exhaustive audition process, I settled on a quartet of White Owl, a rapper with impeccable bars; Deetalx, an NYU freshman DJ who could slice and dice with the best; Kaz Gamble, who I already knew as a Pro Tools engineer, but was young and game for anything; and Doug Ray, a SUNY Albany senior stoner with no post-graduation plan, who was like no one I'd ever met. Doug was unbelievably funny. He was like a rapping Andrew Dice Clay, but his deep baritone on the mic sounded like an eighty-year-old blues dude. He was a special kid. After a couple of months of demos, Bret began carting the band around to labels. It was an instant circus. After a slew of bids, we finally closed the deal with Warner Brothers Records and their super producer, VP David Kahne.

Two records firm.

For over a million dollars!

The record should've been a walk in the park, but then I made a highly questionable move. Kahne had produced the aforementioned Sublime and Sugar Ray, and I loved those records. Of equal importance, though, he had crafted my high school favorites by Romeo Void, Fishbone, and Translator—all major bangers on the soundtrack of my so-called personal teen-life. Now he was the head of A&R at Reprise Records, overseeing Bad Ronald's debut. I was such a big David Kahne groupie that, in an under-baked moment, I proposed the notion of his collaborating with Duke and myself on a few tracks. He was super into it. A week later, we were all posted up at the Standard Hotel on Sunset Boulevard, gearing up for a month of tracking with the boss. The best-laid plans of mice and men always go awry, right?

On that first night loading in our gear at Henson Studios (the home of both Charlie Chaplin and The Muppets—win), I knew my vision was fucked. In the process of bonding, Kahne played me his new musical muse, a prodigious jazz pianist who dabbled in avant-garde experiments. It was interesting, but it wasn't "What I Got." David also spun his score for a Twyla Tharp dance piece. It was stunning, but it wasn't "Every Morning." When I mentioned how excited I was to throw those Kahne Southern California blissed-out beach vibes on these tracks, he quickly replied, "I don't like repeating these things." He completely shot me down. And he ran the damn label! Duke and I spent days sketching out new Bad Ronald tunes in the Henson B room, while David dissected our work next door. I heard the dismantling through the door all day and night. It wasn't that it was all wack, though. Quite the opposite. He was creating some really cool soundscapes. It just wasn't anything remotely aligned with the vision in my head. I whispered my running, angry commentary to Duke and the band on the daily. After so many misses, I just couldn't afford this one to miss. I began to lose my shit. On one of those rocky evenings, Jen picked me up from the studio a bit early, and we had a much-needed Koreatown meal with a couple of old friends. When we returned to Henson later that night, Kaz and Duke were standing there, all blissed out. They looked like they'd just joined one of those Netflix documentary cults.

"Dude, we had the best hang with Kahne. We absolutely understand his direction for this stuff now. He's a genius!"

I'd been gone two fuckin' hours, and the boss had totally pulled a Bhagwan Shree Rajneesh out of his hat. I began to yell. I was completely out of control. Then I lost my breath and doubled over.

Soon I was strapped down in Cedars-Sinai hospital for the night. This was actually my first full-blown panic attack (it wouldn't be my last).

It was mortifying. I was lying on a gurney next to a comatose heroin fiend with bloody needle marks dancing down his exposed thighs.

The next day, Jen and I flew back to NYC while Bret begged David Kahne to let us finish the record alone on our own turf. Kahne was super cool about it. Looking back, I have mad respect for that. He easily could have hijacked it and bounced my ass. I certainly would've. We delivered the mastered record, and then something astounding happened. The Mark Klasfeld–helmed video for our single, "Let's Begin," got added to MTV. That first morning it debuted at 6 AM, and I began sobbing my eyes out. For once, I was finally in the game.

The video stayed in rotation for a solid month. Duke and I spent the eve of the album's release celebrating with the band at the Virgin Megastore in Union Square, where the cover—an Easy Rider–inspired, American-flag-decorated helmet—was displayed in a humongous five-foot-square poster along the front exterior window for the entire world to see. We took a zillion photos in front of it. We were truly the

September 11th, 2001. 12:30 AM at the Virgin Megastore with Duke Mushroom and Kaz Gamble celebrating Bad Ronald's release.

happiest kids in New York. The clock struck midnight, and we all hugged and agreed to continue raging in the morning.

That would be September 11, 2001.

I was awakened at 9 AM by a panicked call from Bret, but I could barely make out what he was saying.

"Look outside your window!" he kept screaming in an indecipherable tone.

I opened the curtains, and as the sun blared into my eyes, I could see the burning North Tower.

Then the second plane hit.

Bret lived two blocks away from the carnage and ended up scrambling on a fishing boat sans wallet to Jersey. After watching the towers fall from behind the Washington Square monument, Jen and I headed north to Union Square, where the white-soot-covered Wall Streeters began wandering aimlessly in search of their lost friends and relatives. This was all happening directly in front of the American-flag-adorned Bad Ronald cover poster. It was all so ominous and awful.

Amid the months of sadness that followed, I'm sure you can understand why the band, whose "Let's Begin" chorus went, "We're gonna light the weed. Tap the keg. Shoot the shit. Now let's begin," was yanked off MTV and dropped by the label within a matter of weeks. Those were delicate days. America wanted Norah Jones, not Bad Ronald. With all of that terror in the air, I experienced two straight years of panic attacks that thoroughly debilitated me. I refused to hop a single airplane flight. I was Michael Phelps swimming in a pool of lorazepam.

There were many more bitter pills to swallow.

Logan 7 was Duke Mushroom's electronic side project, which Chris Blackwell signed to Palm Pictures, his Island Records reboot. When we delivered the completed, slightly schizophrenic, album, the baffled label jumped the gun and pulled the plug. We were stunned. From what I've been told, it was the only project that the artist-friendly label ever actually shelved. Needless to say, that was quite a distinction.

Trace was a girl group featuring Kate Mara, a seventeen-year-old from my hometown (you might know her today as a big Hollywood actress and the older sister of Rooney). As we crafted their songs, Kate began inviting us to New York Giants football games to watch from the owner's box because, well, her family owned the damn team! That might've been the first moment I began to understand all the wonderful grifts of songwriting. Lots of free shit. Like the others that preceded it, though, Trace's record was iced when the label didn't hear a potential single in any of the tracks we presented. They were probably right. With the group's eventual dropping from the Warner Brothers roster, so went all my future invites to the owner's box as well. Game over.

Oval Opus was a terribly monikered rock quartet from Cincinnati who caught a whiff of interest. We wrote a pretty decent EP with them, but after a solid but not breathtaking showcase, all of the gatekeepers in attendance passed. Oval Opus was actually the first act that we were unable to secure a deal for during that four-year stretch. It was a spooky feeling. That being said, there was one big win that occurred via these kids. Their guitarist, Josh Edmondson, would eventually become one of my closest pals and collaborators.

Doug Ray formed a hip-hop duo, Doug and Bubs, featuring Doug and a 320-pound Arby's cleaning crew kid who specialized in a dance called "The Mop." It was an impressive visual across the board. I guess people the hula hoop, but no one bought The Mop. Then, a solo Doug morphed into Toothpick, a psychedelic acoustic-rap crooner. Can't knock the hustle, but with no significant major label interest, the Toothpick project eventually vaporized for good.

BONUS CUT

> Well, not completely. One morning I ran into Morgan Spurlock on Second Avenue. He looked like absolute shit. He told me that he was midway through a month of eating McDonald's exclusively, and he was filming the results. He wondered if Duke and I would be interested in writing a title song with him for his little Mickey D's film. It sounded like my brand of stupid. We brought in Toothpick to write it with us and perform it as well. Within a year, *Super Size Me* was nominated for Best Documentary at the Oscars. Though a very fleeting moment, it was pretty sweet.

The Cooler Kids were conceived during a songwriting collaboration between myself, Duke, and our brilliant friend Jill Cunniff of Luscious Jackson fame. We were having so much fun creating late-era disco jams that we decided to take it a step further. We began a search for a boy/girl duo to sing the tunes. For the male, I locked in Kaz Gamble, as I thought he deserved another look. For the female singer, we cast Sisely Treasure, a sweet and quirky eighteen-year-old Hollywood club kid. The project instantly got swooped up by a DreamWorks exec. I only got to meet that dude once in the entire recording process (very nice guy, for whatever it's worth). He rolled by the studio to listen to the finished record, but didn't offer up any commentary on the songs at all. The only actual commentary he offered up occurred when he looked down at my feet and exclaimed, "Fresh kicks, bro." Though my shoe game had always been pretty tight, it was a bad omen. Soon after, the record limped into retail. I only knew this because I found one 88-cent promo copy of it at Sounds Records the following week (déjà vu). Then, fittingly, DreamWorks Records was sold and folded into Interscope a month or so later. With no label, the Cooler Kids quickly melted. I'd love to consider this one a minor win, as we did have some Billboard Dance Chart success on the duo's first single, but fuck it, it still ended prematurely.

Finally, there was the incredibly gifted Michael Tolcher, a singer-songwriter from Atlanta. Michael arrived at our door via a really great session guitarist from Philadelphia named Gary Philips. We first used Gary on the Bad Ronald record and his jazzy chops were insane. Though Duke and I had never developed any act that we didn't write on, Michael became the one exception. His songs oozed with earthy optimism and soul. We immediately dove in on the demo and, upon a speedy completion, I ran down the block to James Diener's apartment to play it for him that evening. At that point, James had just launched Octone, a new J Records imprint (his first signing was the unknown but about-to-explode Maroon 5). On listen one, the songs intrigued him, but it was Michael's backstory that sealed the deal within minutes. You see, this kid had three cinema-worthy plot points in his young journey to date:

1. Michael's father was a chaplain in the Atlanta Federal Penitentiary, so on the Johnny Cash tip, he'd grown up playing for the inmates on Friday nights.
2. One prisoner in particular supposedly took an interest in Tolcher's talents and began shopping his demos from his cell. That fella was Mutulu Shakur, Tupac's stepfather.
3. Just a few years earlier, Michael had been a track and field star at the powerhouse Georgia Tech alongside a few future Olympians.

This kid was a winner. Diener immediately signed him.

**BONUS CUT**

As soon as we entered the Octone fold, James invited us to an intimate dinner with his other new signings, Gavin DeGraw and Maroon 5's Adam Levine. I remember marveling at the freakish showbiz charisma of both of those cats. Not to overstate the obvious, but Michael had his work cut out for him.

When we began tracking Michael's debut, it was readily apparent that he was the freest of spirits. He reminded me of Matthew McConaughey in a vat of mushrooms. He had a van full of Tibetan monks come down from upstate New York to bless Avatar Studios (the old Power Station) before we began recording. That was some different shit. We tracked in the Avatar A Room over a few weeks and had some incredible guests on the record, like The Roots's Questlove and the Allman Brothers's Warren Haynes. Thinking back now, I wish I had more memories of the Tolcher recordings, but in all honesty, they were both sunny and uneventful. I do recall sitting in the studio's communal lounge with Duke, Gary, and a very freaked-out Elvis Costello, who was recording with his wife, Diana Krall, in the B Room, as we watched President Bush announce that we were invading Iraq. (Peace? Love? Understanding?)

Soon the recording wrapped and, through James's relentless push, Tolcher toured incessantly. With his fervent performances, he actually began building a solid fanbase. I think he sold about ninety thousand albums. That wasn't enormous at the time, but Octone had a "bump up" clause with Clive Davis and J Records stipulating that once that sales plateau had been reached, the J Records radio staff would take over the project and give it a real shot at airplay. I can't say it felt like the perfect storm, but something was actually happening. This was potentially the life raft for Pop Rox. The record to reverse our never-ending drown. Diener set up the huge phone call introduction between Michael and the entire J Records staff, including Clive Davis himself. To understate the importance of this conversation would be a crime.

This was everything.

We desperately needed Tolcher to charm the hell out of Clive and the rest of those esteemed, hard-to-impress radio cats. James mapped out the call to Michael and his management with a series of blueprints. The number one rule of thumb was that Tolcher had to pimp his incredible backstory. Oversell it, even. That would be the difference maker. Clive believed in stars and Michael needed to come off as both an engaging and fascinating character. Keep in mind, we were now competing with the sudden explosion of the *American Idol* machine, which was birthing a slew of potential stars under Clive's tutelage. To get any sort of similar shine, Michael had to have a near flawless delivery.

On the day of the call, Bret and I sat beside our studio phone, ready to dial in and eavesdrop. Finally, at 3 PM, we silently hopped on with our collective nerves racing. James kicked off the convo with a beautiful introduction to Michael. It was a layup. Suddenly, Clive spoke. Chills.

CLIVE DAVIS
So, Michael, James tells us you have a very interesting backstory. Would you care to share it with us?

MICHAEL TOLCHER
Umm . . .

CLIVE DAVIS
You're from Atlanta?

MICHAEL TOLCHER
Umm . . . yup.

CLIVE DAVIS
Can you tell us more?

MICHAEL TOLCHER
Umm . . . Well . . . I'm a singer-songwriter, and I love playing shows for people and making them smile.

CLIVE DAVIS
That's great, but you also have a connection to Tupac Shakur, right?

## MICHAEL TOLCHER
### Ummm . . . yeah . . . well, kind of . . .

This was quite possibly the most flaccid conversation I'd ever heard. It took only a few minutes for the chat to disintegrate, and with that, Michael's brief career on J Records kinda flamed out before it ever began. It was a dreadful day. I was so furious about the blown opportunity that I punched the bathroom air dryer down the hall, and my hand blew up like a bonfire. Still, it was hard to hold any of it against Michael. He was such a decent and talented kid, but he just wasn't made for the major-label machine. He hated whoring himself out. Can you blame him? It's all pretty gross. That being said, I'm still a fan and will always cheer on his continuing body of work.

**BONUS CUT**

If you're an aspiring artist, and you have an aversion to selling your soul, this is quite possibly the greatest time ever to enter the music industry. You don't need to "play the game" anymore. Social media has completely leveled it out. If you create your own fanbase and culture, labels will inevitably bow to your every whim. Stay wild, stay weird, and though it's imperative to stay respectful to the gatekeepers, they no longer hold the same power or influence. The musical landscape is yours. Paint it as you like.

It was now 11 PM in Nashville. I felt like Albert Brooks in *Defending Your Life.* Last call had come and gone, and the busboys were anxiously awaiting our departure. I hedged my bets and rested my defense. As the table went silent, one of the writers sitting across from me suddenly threw her napkin down, began an '80s movie slow clap, and shouted the verdict out for all to hear.

"Wow! Honey, I'm impressed. You really were a huge loser!"

She didn't even know the half of it. Though I certainly had more record disasters I could have entered into evidence, the fact that I could look back and chuckle at that cursed decade without bawling spoke volumes about the undead protégés still roaming my musical heart. (For what it's worth, my therapist also believed it was quite helpful for me.) The truth is, even today, I still stand behind each and every one of those acts and records. I truly loved all of 'em! Most importantly, though, having the luxury of time to analyze and over-analyze the role I played in their negative outcomes was the greatest of blessings. In the years that followed, I rarely repeated my own blunders again.

**BONUS CUT**

Last fall, my old pal Matt Aberle was music supervising a film called *He's All That* and asked me to write a parody tune for it. Twenty years prior, he'd signed and A&Rd the Bad Ronald debut. I demoed the *He's All That* song myself and it swiftly got approved, so I found two of my favorite MCs to cut the final vocal. When Matt heard the final product, he instantly flipped and asked me who the rappers were. He thought the voices sounded eerily familiar. I replied that it was just a duo of up-and-coming kids I was developing. On the sneak tip, though, I had actually brought back Bad Ronald's Kaz Gamble and Doug Ray (now a corporate lawyer!) to rap on the track. When it was finally time to submit credits for the soundtrack, Matt called me in a fit of hysterics. The moment he saw their names credited as the artists, he seriously lost his shit. Bad Ronald had indeed bumrushed Hollywood two decades down the road. I'd like to think it was a sweet moment of redemption for the entire Pop Rox crew. Don't ever let the passage of time deaden the dream. You never know what's in store.

## CHAPTER 15

# The JFK List

I n 2001, Duke and I signed our first US publishing deals with Dream-Works Music Publishing. These were big, still unearned checks. I immediately put my newfound ducats toward an apartment on Broadway. This was a textbook example of "jumping the gun." A couple of months (and 9/11) later, we were in a million-dollar black hole at DreamWorks. While the entire world shut down, our relentlessly loyal DreamWorks creative executive, Michael Badami, kept pounding the phones with his Alex P. Keaton enthusiasm. He knew our stock was plummeting like Madoff-victim accounts, but was doing anything he could to keep us in the game. Working in tandem with Carianne Brown, an incredible young television and film music plugger at the company (now cochair and chief operating officer of Warner Chappell Music), he was able to land us a bunch of song placements in lower-rung movies—many of the straight-to-cable variety. Though exciting to hear our songs on the (smaller) screen, sadly those licenses barely made a dent in our recoupment. We even had a couple of UK Top 20 charters, but alas, nothing that really moved the needle.

So we hit rock bottom: "the JFK list."

"The JFK list" was a term I coined in those last days of Pop Rox. At that point, it was customary for labels to send artists to NYC for a week to write with the first-call "A and B list" writers—the surefire hitmakers who almost always guaranteed a competitive tune. Those sessions would hopefully result in a six-day onslaught of winners.

On day seven, it was time for the act to fly home. Now factor in an 11 AM hotel checkout. Since most artists typically preferred to take a night flight, this meant a solid five hours of nothing to fill. The labels, those frugal mind gamers, decided it would be in everyone's best interests to entice the artist to do one final session before takeoff. What this really meant was a nice warm place for baggage storage before the inevitable town car ride to JFK Airport, but it was sold to all as, "Take one more stab with these up-and-comers. They're not important yet. But they're awfully nice fellas."

We were those JFK-list fellas.

You can imagine the detectable hint of disdain we received from each burned-out artist who arrived, sans joy, much preferring a day of SoHo shopping over wasting a write with us. We threw down with twenty or thirty lower-priority acts during this period. None of those resulting tunes ever saw the light of day. These were songs in the key of death.

The absolute lowlight had to be the afternoon we spent with Trev, the lead singer of a Canadian boy band. I'd really dug his group's single from a couple of years prior. It sounded like a late-era George Michael tune—bouncy pop and R&B. When they didn't have a proper follow-up, their stock had begun to plummet. The label was on a last-ditch search for a radio monster.

On the day in question, Trev skulked into our studio and dropped his bags on our floor. This was not the happy kid I'd seen interviewed on MTV's *TRL* a year earlier. He'd now gone full Nickelback with his hair and spoke with a muted intensity. He wasn't unpleasant or anything, but it was was pretty obvious from minute one that the radio was no longer of interest to this guy. He certainly had zero interest in the session.

When I asked him what he wanted to shoot for that day, he began a long, somewhat fervent tale about his WWII-survivor neighbor, who he'd grown close with. He wanted to write a song as a tribute to that heroic gent and the "Greatest Generation" in general.

Hmm . . . Okay.

Trev grabbed one of our acoustics and began strumming. He started mumbling words and melodies with a pronounced Eddie

Vedder affect. There was definitely no "Careless Whisper" cascading off his lips. Then he turned his back on us and continued writing solo. He seemed completely intent on creating this opus without our involvement, other than the gratis use of our studio, while we sat there waiting for a biscuit of collaboration. Though Duke and I both thought we'd experienced it all at that point, we'd never been in such a precarious position. Whenever we'd attempt a musical suggestion, he'd seemingly ignore us and mumble louder. It felt like a bad *SNL* skit, and the comedy wore off pretty quickly for us. We terminated the session in the 180th minute or so and wished him a safe flight.

**BONUS CUT**

Just recently I heard Trev's lost pop gem on SiriusXM, and I googled the guy. It turns out his *Band of Brothers* anthem eventually saw the light of day, a solid decade-plus later, as a charity single. That's actually quite inspiring. Now I feel like a tremendous cock. In hindsight, I truly appreciate his heart big time. Sadly, that heart came at the wrong time for me and Duke. Our own band of brothers just desperately needed a hit.

After a while, the Pop Rox runway went eerily empty, and the end was obviously near. Jen, Duke, and I drove to a friend's Washington wedding during the DC Sniper panic, and I remember that as I hopped out of my car to fill up my gas tank somewhere on the edge of Maryland, in the most nervous of furies, my mind was also guiltily racing, attempting to scheme up whatever was next musically for myself. I knew I wasn't alone. I could sense Duke's conviction slipping as well. He was always the eternal optimist in our duo, but those endless record cruelties had finally crushed his indomitable spirit as well. From the moment we first linked up, his primary musical passion was for worldbeat-leaning stuff, which I'd never really let him address in our songwriting. As our docket dejectedly freed up, he began to chase it more aggressively. He moved out of the East Village and immersed himself in lower Harlem, where he began to create brilliant Portuguese and Ethiopian soundscapes. He'd found a new arrow. As both a friend and brother concerned about my fiscal sanity, Duke advised me to walk away from the studio lease and just keep a smaller setup in my apartment. It was a logical conceit, but I just couldn't do it. I'd left my living room behind seven years earlier. The studio was my sole identity at that point. I needed to make it work, so I decided to hemorrhage the entire studio knot solo and scour the streets for a new tenant to split the costs.

Over the next twelve months, Duke and I began to check in with each other less.

Weekly became monthly.

Then Pop Rox faded away for good.

## CHAPTER 16

# Decade of Musical Ashes

**B**efore I dig in further, I think it's important to shout-out my gramma Hilda. As I climbed, fell, and ate song dust in the city throughout my twenties, she was always there waiting with a hug, moral support, and a pretty decent home-cooked meal. She had a gin-dry sense of humor and the

Hilda and me.

slyest of winks in her eye. She truly believed in me and my friends' human potential, no matter how delusional the exploit.

I was smack-dab in the midst of this most frustrating of record stretches when Hilda began spiraling health-wise. I can't lie, it felt a bit dire, but I did try to avoid dwelling on all of the gloom and kept it semi-positive in my head. Then one morning, I got the nurse's frantic call to rush to Hilda's uptown apartment. As I edgily sat jam-packed on the 6 train, I had no idea what was in store.

Upon arrival, Hilda motioned me over to her bed and outstretched her weary arms. I leaned toward her, and she pulled me in, gripping me harder than anyone had ever before. Shaking and struggling to speak through gritted teeth, she told me that she loved me over and over. This went on for thirty seconds or so. The nurse tried to calm me down. She said, "It's okay. She's okay. She's moving on."

Then Gramma Hilda died in my arms.

I couldn't stop crying. It was so incredibly intense. It truly felt like she transferred some magical life force into me, but alas, that would not be the final body blow.

After she passed and was cremated, Hilda's remains sat languishing in my parents' living room cabinet for a year while we tried to agree on a fitting final resting place. This was par for the course for a bizarre, indecisive family who kept pet ashes boxed in closets for years on end. But then on a whim, my folks summoned us over to the house, as they'd finally decided to spread Hilda's ashes around a tiny tree in the driveway.

We were all there—Mom, Dad, Jen, Ben, and my sister-in-law, Julie, and we attempted to make a real ceremonial event of it. Sure, I was a little freaked out, as I'd never released powdery remains into the air before, but I thought it might be a divine experience. Regrettably, though, none of us bothered to listen to Storm Field's Eyewitness News forecast, as we chose a thirty-mile-an-hour guster of an afternoon for our little ceremony.

After a few words of loving tribute, Mom tearily uncorked Hilda's ashes, but the gale-force winds immediately sprayed them everywhere. I mean EVERYWHERE. We were all caked in it!

Jen even caught a little Hilda in her mouth.

I still remember her spewing up the dust with tears of laughter and horror concurrently running down her face.

Me, Mom, Jen, Ben, Julie, and Pops.

As I walked back toward the house and stared up at the most ominous of black clouds, I could only selfishly wonder if this was all just God's sick metaphor for my decade of musical ashes thus far.

## CHAPTER 17

# Pop-Punk is Sooooo '05

W inston Churchill said, "Never give up on something that you can't go a day without thinking about." Well, after ten years of records that blew out like vines of old Christmas lights, I still refused to pack it in. Songwriting was so much more than a fleeting passion. It had become my only calling. In my fixated mind, all of those woeful outcomes were nothing more than a minor deterrent. I'd come so close to actually being "in the mix." Having had that contact high of proximity was the absolute fuckin' killer. It was just enough of an endorphin rush that it didn't feel delusional to press on, even as I knew I was running out of options. Mistakes could not be repeated. I had to stop eating those tainted fortune cookies.

In an attempt to get ahead of my newly astronomical studio rent and expenses, I began creating music for commercials and industrials (non-broadcast clips like human resources training films, manufacturing films, educational films, and so forth). Garnier. Maybelline. Whatever product that cut a check. Yes, I do know many super-talented musicians who make great livings doing this, and lord, I would never judge another person's path, but I knew this wasn't my passion. To me, it was a job and I felt like I was on the verge of asphyxiating in that creatively unfulfilling grind.

(Re)enter Gary Philips.

Gary, of Bad Ronald and Michael Tolcher fame, had been hired by Razor & Tie Records to take on the full-time task of producing the Kidz Bop series. For those who've avoided this top-selling phenomenon, Kidz Bop creates covers of Top 40 hits by using (usually heavily) Auto-Tuned kid singers performing G-rated redos that make the songs more appropriate for family fun. When Gary became aware of my rent issues, he stepped in like a shiny Autotune knight and offered me a side-hustle gig working under him as a drum programmer on Kidz Bop tracks. Every little bit helped, but man, it was a bit demoralizing. But it got sadder. To further supplement those gigs, I began creating ringtones for jam bands. Oh, I'm totally serious.

I MADE RINGTONES FOR JAM BANDS!

Yes, for a mere $40 a tune, I'd fidget in front of the Pro Tools rig for hours on end, editing twelve-minute meandering arrangements down to a solid fifteen seconds of phone worthiness. On a good day, I'd clock $280 for this time suck.

My creative spirit was bottoming out. I was devolving into the most miserable of human beings. I began to develop severe eczema that devoured the cuticles on each of my fingers. I was literally guzzling Valium with my cereal. At the same time, Jen and I had been talking about having a kid. These discussions were usually followed by a few minutes of silent trepidation as I envisioned a sour life spent rationalizing my almosts and should-have-beens at the dinner table to my spawn on a nightly basis every time the third glass of wine took hold. I'd most certainly have to quit drinking.

Then I got the call that changed my life, from Jonathan "JD" Daniel.

The aforementioned JD was an ex–power pop/hairband bassist turned manager who I'd casually run into at various showcases around town as we trolled the lower tier of the business. I dug him instantly on our first meeting. He had this amazing laid-back calm like Sam Elliott in *The Big Lebowski* as we discussed failure. He was the sharpest cat I'd met in the industry to date. He also seemed to be the only individual in the business who seemed to appreciate my work on aesthetic terms. This is no overstatement. People genuinely rooted for me, but most had lost all faith somewhere along the way. JD was quite the opposite. He saw the quirky heart in my failings and pushed me to continue to follow it. Almost a decade older, he was the wisest of sages, but mystifyingly with only a few big victories on the board himself. We started grabbing weekly coffees at Dean & DeLuca in SoHo, discussing all things music from Brenton Wood to the Bay City Rollers. At that point, I'd made some wonderful industry friends, but I knew very few like-minded souls who understood what I was actually shooting for.

So as I was putting the finishing touches on my third and (blessedly) final Kidz Bop bed of beats, JD hit me up and asked if we could meet at the Virgin Megastore to talk shop as soon as possible. An hour later, I met him at the Union Square location, where my 9/11 memories still resided. JD sat down and immediately launched into a TED Talk of sorts that still rings word for word in my ears. He kicked it off with a long explanation of the arc of '80s hair metal. How a genre that began so heavy and raw (e.g., Metallica, Slayer) slowly transitioned into "Unskinny Bop"—sugar-frosted gold. In JD's eyes, he was holding the cards to the next hair metal.

Pop-punk.

At that point, I wasn't really fucking with the genre. It's not that I was a purist, but none of it spoke to me like Hüsker Dü, The Buzzcocks, or The Replacements did as a kid. Beyond a couple standouts, most of the pop-punk stuff I caught on MTV at the time felt kinda whiny to my ears. But that day, JD handed me his iPod and turned on a playlist of his new roster of bands. I slapped on his headphones. Fall Out Boy. Midtown. The Academy Is. They were all real young, wild, and witty. They reminded me of everything I aspired to be in my journals at eighteen. Unfiltered and overwritten. Then JD launched into the pitch. "There's a kid named Pete Wentz, the bass player in Fall Out Boy. He's real special. He's got a Jay-Z/Rockafella Records mentality, so he's signed a bunch of bands in the scene to his indie label. Eventually, they're gonna need to write stronger songs. You're a song guy. You love the craft. You love developing bands. This is where you could step in." I didn't even give him a second to reconsider.

"Done!"

There was only one problem. To foot the studio bills, I had to continue to take all these scrappy gigs that monopolized my time. JD immediately admonished this line of desperation. "I'll find you someone to share your space. Just stop taking these chickenshit jobs and go for this thing 24/7."

And that's exactly what happened. JD connected me with another Greenwich Village songwriter who had just been booted from his studio and desperately needed a new room.

His name was Dave "Sluggo" Katz.

Sluggo moved in a week later, and we reconfigured the setup so we worked in adjacent hubs separated by a glass partition. At first we rarely interacted. He was quite an enigma. He seemed to waste the days playing video games, sipping cocktails, and chasing any and every inappropriate internet time suck. No, he was not sixteen. He was a grown-ass man in his mid-forties. I guess this was par for the course, as most of us songwriters are completely stunted misfits.

One evening, out of pure curiosity, I walked into Sluggo's room, sat down on the grubby-ass couch, and went blunt.

"Okay, Sluggo, question: So what the fuck do you do all day?"

He responded with the slyest of smiles and slowly pulled out a little boom box from behind the couch. Then he handed me a CD that read "Stockholm." He explained that he'd spent the previous six months learning the Swedish songwriting technique called the melodic math (obviously in between Vivid Video and *Call of Duty 2* breaks). In this formula, lyrics were never the driver of the song. They were there simply to support the melody. These chart-dominating Swedes, led by the late Denniz Pop and his protégé, Max Martin, had specific metric rules for creating melodic perfection. If a line had a certain number of syllables, the next one had to mirror it. It was all about tight repetition. Sluggo spoke so authoritatively and passionately about this melodic math that I knew he had to be onto something. At the time, Sluggo's pal and musical partner was a guy named Lukasz Gottwald. He played guitar in the *SNL* band. He was also freakishly gifted. Together, Sluggo and Lukasz developed a seventeen-year-old R&B singer from Brooklyn named Jeannie Ortega and signed her to

Disney's Hollywood Records. They spent months writing and recording her debut. It was the slowest, most laborious process I'd ever witnessed. When they finally delivered Jeannie's record to Disney, the duo swiftly got booted from the project. I'd never seen that happen before. Like Pop Rox, they were the act's production company, so I thought they were deservedly insulated. Strangely, though, they were completely neutered. A month later, Lukasz met Max Martin at *SNL*. Then he became Dr. Luke.

Now he has a star on the Hollywood Walk of Fame.

I've gotta say, that was definitely a tremendous choke in the house of the Mouse.

As Sluggo and I began collaborating here and there, my pub deal with DreamWorks was fluttering out just as the Hollywood power trio of Spielberg, Katzenberg, and Geffen decided to divest the business. DreamWorks Music Publishing was rushed to sale. Since he knew the doors would soon be shutting, my saintlike publisher, Badami, attempted to get me one last long shot of an advance. Wisely, the higher powers declined. Duke and I were just collectively too deep in the hole to warrant any more dollars lobbed in either of our directions. The sale dragged on, while I waited and prayed that the transition would mean a new owner who might just toss me in the blue bin for someone else's recycling.

It was 12:30 AM, and I was lying in bed with my now pregnant wife, nodding off to a *Blind Date* rerun, when the phone rang. Calls at that witching hour usually meant two things: family health emergencies or wrong numbers for a dude named Hector, courtesy of some furious chick who screamed her vowels into absolute distortion.

"Dude."

It was Badami.

"Are you sitting down?"

"Um, no, I'm in bed. Who died?"

"Nobody died. Relax. Okay, so this is gonna sound crazy! I got a call today. This guy noticed the name Sam Hollander on the Dream-Works roster and was curious if this was the same kid who he'd attended elementary school with in Chappaqua years ago."

I tried to interrupt.

"Shut up! Let me keep going. I told him that you did in fact grow up in Chappaqua."

I tried to interrupt again.

"SHUT UP!" He continued, "Does the name Joe Samberg ring a bell?"

"Joey Samberg? Of course. Wow. I haven't seen that guy since a fight at the end of high school. That's so strange. Why'd he call?"

Badami screamed, "BECAUSE HE JUST BOUGHT DREAM-WORKS!!!"

I damn near dropped the phone.

Joey Samberg. The tallest dude in fourth grade. We grew up on the same street. Joey and I were always super cool with each other. Then I moved to the next town to attend Fox Lane—the rival high school. Fox Lane and Horace Greeley were sports rivals. This resulted in the occasional brawl. One night toward the end of my senior year, one of these ruckuses erupted behind the town diner. A bunch of misfits from each high school jumped in and squared off. A bit of blood ensued. Joe Samberg was standing directly across from me. We locked eyes. Then we both smiled and walked away from the scrum, catching up for a spell as the fists flew. I guess the Hebrews know when to say "when."

That was the last time I saw him.

Fast-forward to late 2004, and Joe's own hedge fund, JDS, had purchased DreamWorks Music Publishing for a reported $40 million!

Within twenty-four hours of the Badami conversation, I was sitting across from Joe at the Oyster Bar in Grand Central Station, reminiscing about the good ol' days. Then he got down to brass tacks.

"Sam, this is so amazing. I was talking to my wife about it this morning. I told her, 'Sam Hollander was always such a great kid.' I can't believe we'll be working together."

"Well, Joe, there's nothing that would be more amazing, but I'm about to be a free agent, and I think there's lots of heat out there for me." (Insert poker face.) I nailed the delivery. He seemed intrigued.

"Well, what would it take for you to stay on with us?" he asked. "What if we threw in a new deal plus a separate joint venture with us as well—a fund to sign young writers and develop them underneath you?"

The response took a solid sixteenth of a second.

"That sounds incredible. Let's make it happen!"

And there you have it. Soon, I was financially set up, just as JD had envisioned. No more Garnier. No more Kidz Bop. No more Jam band ringtones! I ran over to JD's office and told him that I was now more than ready to tackle any act he had. I just needed a shot. He sent me a link to the newest group they'd just begun managing: Geneva, New York's, own Gym Class Heroes. From the first bar, they entirely rearranged my molecules. Their MC, a kid named Travie McCoy, was everything I wished I could've been as an artist. Super cool looking. Amazing verbal dexterity. He had an IDGAF air about him that I adored. Gym Class were one of the pioneers of emo-rap. I begged JD to give me the record. He said I'd have to convince his partner, Bob McLynn.

Now, Bob liked beer. I knew this. I brought a twelve-pack over to his house under the pretext of watching the Steelers play on Monday night, but covertly, I'd like to believe, I spent the entire game working him over on making this album. Eventually I wore his ass down. He agreed to give me the gig. The budget was $27,000 all in. Now this indeed was some scrappiness. I'd never made an album for such a shitty sum. I'd also never made a successful album, so I figured, who the fuck was I to complain?

**BONUS CUT**

I often read posts and blogs from irate young music interns about "making sure you get paid your worth" fiscally as you climb the proverbial music business ladder. Though I do respect this sentiment, I also believe it's imperative to take any opening you can get, even when it's beneath your pay grade. Sometimes you just need to assess the bigger picture. In the case of Gym Class Heroes, this was probably my last shot to stay in the game. If I had haggled, I NEVER would have gotten the gig. The nothingness of the budget also meant complete creative freedom, which was a huge carrot. That was probably the biggest draw for me.

Four nights before the band touched down in the city to begin recording, my daughter, Joey, was born. It was the greatest feeling of my life. After years of blunders, I had finally done something right. I felt very guilty rationalizing to my beyond-patient wife that I needed to spend the next four weeks going 24/7 on a record whose advance would barely pay our diaper fund, but blessedly, she seemed to understand. It was "manifest this shit," now or never.

My first task was taking the group's clever "Cupid's Chokehold," a clever interpolation of Supertramp's "Breakfast in America," and re-producing it. It took me two weeks of trial and error to get it right. Though I'd previously logged years behind the Pro Tools rig, my skills as a programmer and engineer were now less competitive in the ever-changing world of tech. On Cupid's and the subsequent album, though, I was forced to do tons of programming and engineering. It wasn't playing to my strengths, but that's all I could afford on the gig. That being said, I remember thinking, "Wow, I actually kinda murdered this!" Sluggo hopped on board to helm the remainder of the record with me. He was quite helpful with dialing in the song arrangements and vibe. I loved throwing down with him. Even though I was clocking in a modest two to four hours of sleep a night due to a colicky newborn, every day felt like we were really onto something. And Travie McCoy? We had a very strong bond. He adored old-school shit. I turned him on to a crate of rare groove, new wave, and obscure R&B. We'd riff on it for hours on end. He was such a gifted kid. I don't recall ever having as much fun in the studio up to that point. As the record progressed, JD asked me if I was open to bringing in Fall Out Boy vocalist Patrick Stump to collaborate with us on a few songs. I wasn't against it per se, but I knew he sensed the apprehension in my measured response. "Let me give you one good piece of advice," he said. "These kids are real talented. Their frame of reference is insane. Most importantly, they understand what works in the scene. Don't sleep on them. They'll totally elevate your game tenfold."

BONUS CUT

JD was 100 percent correct. The kids were (and are) all right. Now more than ever. Toss your ego to the side and let them take you to school. The younger ones are infinitely more aware of the musical trends and believability in general. Instead of overanalyzing it, they live it.

Patrick Stump most definitely lived it. He had peerless chops. He might've been the most talented twenty-year-old I'd ever encountered. He wrote brilliant melodies and was a beat-making whiz. The Gym Class Heroes record was beginning to take an amazing shape.

Then a pile of evil Percocets took over.

Travie was so out of his head that he came down with writer's block on the last song. Man, it was just the worst. I pushed. I prodded. I begged. I even spitballed verse ideas. He wasn't having any of it. He just sat slumped on the studio floor with his eyes withdrawn and his headphones pounding. I was beyond frustrated. I called up an old friend, Steve Greenberg, who'd just been named the president of Columbia Records, and asked him if he had any lower-tier artist lying around that Sluggo and I could write with during those next few days as we waited for Travie to return from his lunar walk. We desperately needed an energy flip in the room. Steve thought about it for a second and then replied, "Do you know Katy Perry?"

Katy Perry. I knew the name, as she'd been kicking around for a spell. In the industry's eyes, she was already bordering on "damaged goods" by the ripe old age of twenty-three due to three failed record deals. The second Sluggo and I met her, however, we were all about her. She was raw, bold, and super lyrical, with her own funny perspective. We spent a couple of days writing together, and the resulting tune was kind of a banger. As she packed up to peace out, she whispered in my ear, "Who's the hot rapper guy on the floor and why is he avoiding me?" Travie didn't know it, but he had just redefined hard to get. No, he wasn't being aloof. He was just so deep in a chemically detached stupor that he didn't even notice her. Miraculously, though, we were able to drag Travie out with us that evening. Within a mere matter of minutes, he and Katy became somewhat cosmically aligned.

"The Queen and I," the first single on the Gym Class Heroes' *As Cruel As School Children* record, dropped late that August. It was actually the first song I'd ever co-written that spun in rotation on my hometown Z100! That was nuts. It made a little noise, but as the tune began to disappear, a DJ in Milwaukee began spinning "Cupid's Chokehold," and it blew up big time. It was a monster. It climbed the charts for months until it became the number one song on Top 40 radio!

I felt like I was watching a dream.

When I moved to the city at eighteen, I stood on the periphery as Blues Traveler and the Spin Doctors (Jaik Miller's pals) got record deals and owned the radio before their twenty-first birthdays. I witnessed Maxwell's ascension firsthand, from a teenage busboy at the coffee shop in Union Square to the heights of R&B superstardom. In my head, everyone had won young except for me. Now the longest drought on record had finally been lifted. You see, for a decade plus, all I really wanted was just one miraculous hit that my mom would hear every time she set foot in a TJ Maxx. I considered that "making it." But endless years of dreadful failures had produced more than resolve. It birthed my own personal Nikola Tesla–like stack of musical goals that I scrawled on Post-it notes that were littered across my studio coffee table. If I could just break through the door with one smash, I genuinely convinced myself I could have many more.

And Katy?

Right after Columbia Records unceremoniously dumped Steve Greenberg, Katy ended up getting ejected from the label as well. Just when it appeared she was done for good, though, she got signed to her fourth deal seemingly overnight: Virgin Records. Since I'd laced her young A&R, Chris Anokute, with a gratis demo a few years earlier when he just was starting out in the business, he did me a real solid. He successfully campaigned and got our Katy tune, "If You Can Afford Me," on her debut, *One of the Boys*. It was an amazing break for us because Katy Perry became KATY PERRY!

A few years later, on VH1's *Behind the Music*, I was asked to discuss the story of the day Travie met Katy. If you look closely, you can see mad layers of sweat starting to dance across my caked-up forehead.

As I type this, *As Cruel As School Children* has just turned sixteen years old. Same with my kid. Watching this fantastic specimen grow has been the

Gym Class Heroes Gold Record party with Pete Wentz, Travie McCoy, John Janick, Craig Kallman, and Julie Greenwald.

most life-fulfilling shit ever. We have a very similar fiery wiring. On those occasional days of frustration when she vents about some random tenth-grade drama, I always make a point of capping the pot before she's reached a boiling point of no return. It just takes three simple words: "Remember Joe Samberg." Keep it cool with everyone you meet. They might just boomerang back into your life someday.

## BONUS CUT

Tyga was an unknown when Travie met him at a tattoo parlor on Melrose. Travie thought he was special and asked me to write some tunes with the kid. As I formulated some hooks, I let Tyga and his pal/hype man, GaTa, use my B room to dabble. They were both sweet fellas. On many nights, I'd walk by and hear these guys rap battling kids in Nebraska on Skype. Midwestern Skype rap battles were a new frontier to me. Nevertheless, we got along great, messed around with a few ideas together, and when I laid down a decent enough beat and wrote a bouncy hook with Tyga's manager, Anthony Martini, we recorded the tune. It was called "Coconut Juice." Bob McLynn dug it and picked it to be Tyga's first single. MTV played the "Coconut Juice" video on loop for a spell, the song charted, and Tyga performed it on *Jimmy Kimmel Live!* Though the song evaporated pretty quickly, Travie and

Bob held fast to their belief in Tyga, so they brought him to Las Vegas to perform with Gym Class Heroes, Fall Out Boy, and special guests Rihanna and Weezy at the MTV Music Awards (where Gym Class Heroes won Best New Artist!). That moment turned out to be a game changer for the kid. Tyga was incredible. He stepped up and absolutely crushed it on the biggest possible stage. At the afterparty, a now-also-mightily-impressed Wayne seemed to pull a "Can I steal you for a second?" maneuver straight out of *The Bachelorette*, and Tyga hopped aboard the Young Money bus and blew the fuck up. He also parted ways with GaTa. GaTa hightailed it back to LA, where for years he struggled to get his shine. Then one day Anthony Martini resurfaced with a new MC he he had signed, a funny kid named David Burd. He asked GaTa to take on the hype man role for his live shows. When

David Burd's alter ego, Lil Dicky, fully entered the pop consciousness with his hit TV show *Dave*, guess who was cast in the role of his best friend? Yup, after a decade of toiling, GaTa became a burgeoning star himself.

Tyga and myself (no mention of "Coconut Juice").

## CHAPTER 18

# The Faculty

I was in the midst of a summer vacation at my wonderful in-laws Tony and Kathy's Cape Cod spot when I plopped down on a bench in front of the town library. As I settled in, I noticed a small, fading memorial plaque affixed to the back of the seat. The words read, "Joe Raposo,

Joe Raposo.

who taught America's children to sing. Dedicated July 4, 1996."

Chills danced up and down my arms.

As a song nerd, I considered Joe Raposo to be one of my supreme writing heroes. Thanks to his prowess, back when I was a little dude I nonstop hummed the *Sesame Street* theme, moistened my eyes to the Carpenters' cover of "Sing," and whistled the *Three's Company* theme as I endlessly mimicked John Ritter's opening-credit bike fail. Joe wrote all of those classics, plus a few more (Sinatra's "Winners"). On the surface, his lyrics might've read a bit simple, but the complex chords and arrangements that supported them made for some seriously sophisticated shit. This man was truly a master.

As I sat there on that bench getting mad nostalgic about his influence, I began to ponder how wonderful it would've been if I'd had a chance to study under his tutelage (sadly, he died of lymphoma at fifty-one). That sent me down a lengthy path, as I began viewing my career through a lens of academia. Certainly Joe would've been one of my dream professors of song. Lennon and McCartney were no-brainers. Nile Rodgers was obviously a given. Who else would've made the cut? It was a ton of push and pull in my head, but I landed on the following batch of writers and writing teams. I'd like to believe my song voice is some strange combination of their brilliant lessons.

## BARRY GIBB

Barry wrote about street scenes and survival and dominated the globe. Sometimes his words kissed paranoia. I loved the juxtaposition of those themes against the funky bliss. Sweet + sour has always been my go-to. Barry's meticulously sculpted melodies completely transcended eras. He gets extra credit for crafting disco-less classics for the likes of Barbara Streisand, Diana Ross, Dolly Parton, and Kenny Rogers.

## BERT BERNS

Representing the Boogie Down Bronx, Berns knew he was on the clock from birth courtesy of a damaged heart. But before his untimely passing, he had an unparalleled eight-year run writing a slew of '60s Afro-Cuban R&B-influenced chart-toppers like "Twist and Shout," "Piece of My Heart," and "Hang on Sloopy," as well as producing "Under the Boardwalk" and "Brown Eyed Girl." The bulk of his tunes still slay today.

## BOB MOULD

Sure, Michael Stipe, Morrissey, Ian McCulloch, and Elvis Costello dominated my high school mixtapes, but it was the words of Hüsker Dü's Bob Mould that knocked the air out of my gut. Balancing raging hardcore and melodic brilliance with vulnerability and the disaffection of youth, Mould and his pen inspired most of my early salty lyrical takes.

## THE BOSS

The first time I heard "Does This Bus Stop at 82nd Street?" I was floored by the wordplay. Just the "Broadway Mary, Joan Fontaine" shout-out alone. Sure, his word seeds were birthed in Dylan's garden, but the rhyme schemes and red, white, and bruised lyrics spoke to me on a much more personal tip than the bulk of Blind Boy Grunt.

## CHINNICHAP AND HOLLY KNIGHT

Initially it was the killer duo of Mike Chapman and Nikki Chinn who created a slew of absurdly titled rock classics ("Little Willy," "Tiger Feet," "Ballroom Blitz") that totally opened my eyes to the notion of unbridled lyrical insanity. Then Chinn split and Chapman threw the badass Holly Knight in the mix. Holly's explosive hooks completely redefined '80s bombastic anthems. From "The Warrior" and "Love Is a Battlefield" to "Simply the Best" and "Obsession," I can't think of another pop writer who better soundtracked my mid-'80s summers.

## DONALD FAGEN

Fagen's wry and detached bite inspired some of my favorite sardonic lyrics ever. His Steely Dan collaborations with Walter Becker had that ice-cold, winking charm that slayed me from the jump, but it was actually his solo debut, *The Nightfly*, chock-full of nostalgic suburban-kid optimism and escapism, that really connected all the dots in my head.

## FREDDIE PERRIN

Freddie Perrin. Kids don't even know how bad this man was. From "ABC," "I Will Survive," and "Heaven Must Be Missing an Angel" to "Shake Your Groove Thing," "Reunited," and "Makin' It," this Motown vet absolutely crushed the Me Decade. Total melodic master with a tackle box full of hooks.

## GAMBLE AND HUFF

The apex of dope. Musically their take on the Wall of Sound (Huff actually played piano on Spector sessions early on) produced the jazziest of soul vibes, and Kenny Gamble's lyrical voice was on some other shit. Like Marvin Gaye, he was a verbal activist envisioning a world of equity and a timeless romantic to boot. I still marvel at the perfection of Philly's finest.

## JIM CROCE

Jim Croce was that rare writer who could craft both up-tempo, rollicking sing-along choruses and staggeringly beautiful ballads. That kind of versatility is tough to fuck with. I loved the characters he created. They painted the grittiest vivid pictures in your head. Though he only recorded a few studio albums before his tragic plane crash, the fact that his legacy has been somewhat glossed over totally crushes me. An absolute master of craft.

## NATIVE TONGUES

Though there are many MCs who could crack this list, musically I related to the Native Tongues' A Tribe Called Quest, Jungle Brothers, and De La Soul like nothing previous. Each had their own distinct boho thing, but Q-Tip's cliché-free, deliciously playful, eccentric rhymes were the gateway drug for me as a writer. I seriously doubt there'd be a Kanye without "Verses from the Abstract."

## PAUL WILLIAMS

Sure, I'm biased, as he's an all-around spectacular soul, but Paul's songs were always the warmest blanket of my youth. "We've Only Just Begun," "The Love Boat," "Rainbow Connection," and "You Give a Little Love," among many others. As a wordsmith, Paul always wore his uncynical heart on his lyrical sleeve. I've usually written from a more closed-off space, so whenever I need to dial up the emotional spectrum, Paul's my go-to listen.

## STOCK AITKEN WATERMAN

This trio of gods scored more than a hundred UK Top 40 hits! They had such a distinct high-energy synth-pop thing musically that you could sniff their tunes straight off the speakers. Though "Never Gonna Give You Up" probably has the widest reach, "This Time I Know It's For Real," "Together Forever," and Bananarama's "Venus" cover are all timeless gold.

## CAROLE KING AND GERRY GOFFIN

This formidable tandem were the Brill Building–era GOATS.
I could make a strong argument for my pal Jeff Barry and Elle
Greenwich (or Barry Mann and Cynthia Weil) as well, but at the
end of the songbook, Goffin and King were kinda untouchable.
Carole's melodic genius. Gerry's lyrical brilliance. Their songs
expressed what every '60s kid was feeling within but was unable to
articulate—the weird and wild roller coaster of teen love.

My own creative relationship with Carole began during the
Tarsha Vega sessions when I was searching for an iconic cameo.
The label suggested India.Arie, Erykah Badu, and other neo-soul
notables of the era. I was hoping to land someone a bit more
classic. Jen had caught *Blood Brothers* on Broadway a few years
before and casually mentioned how stunning Carole's voice still
was. Though somewhat of a Hail Mary, I thought it would make
for a fascinating pairing. I asked RCA if they had any connects, and
as luck would have it, our A&R at the label, Brian Malouf, had a
relationship with her management. Brian sent Carole the Tarsha
demos, and she seemed to flip. She arrived in NYC beyond thrilled
to write with this young, lyrical rap chick. Then Tarsha clarified
that the words were mine. I sensed Carole loved that reveal. From
the first day we collaborated, she was so grounded and open—
every day riding the 1 train down from Morningside Heights.
Carole, Duke, and I wrote a bunch of sweet songs together in
blocks. It was like attending a master class, and she was the perfect
professor. During that stretch with Carole, she began crafting her
first solo record in years and asked us to write a tune with her for
it. Somehow, throwing down amongst the likes of David Foster,
Babyface, and a who's who of song icons, our collaboration "Love
Makes the World" ended up as the album's first single and title
track. That was huge for our morale. The tune was used in a big
national Gap ad as well. She even asked us to cameo in the music
video and shouted me and Duke out at concerts and interviews
after. She was 100 percent humility. Pure class. She set the highest
of bars that only a few have equaled (but none have surpassed).

Wait, I forgot Stevie Wonder . . . And Jeff Lynne! What the hell was I thinking? Hal David! He could be Top 3! Rod Temperton! Shit, this list could go on for pages on end. Maurice White!!! At the end of the day, there had to be at least forty master educators that I debated on that bench, so if you're one of the neglected, please take no

Writing with Carole King, Paul Williams, and Duke Mushroom.

offense. For the record, I've studied all of these folks' catalogs to such an obscene extent that, at this point, I'm worthy of some sort of cap and gown. Or at least a University of the Pacific honorary degree?

## CHAPTER 19

# Boston Strong

One evening, right around the time that Gym Class Heroes reversed my decade and a half of fizzles and buckles, I had dinner with the great Paul Williams. This legend has won a Grammy, Golden Globe, and an Oscar, and was inducted into the Songwriters Hall of Fame. And amazingly enough, this esteemed member of my "faculty" is also my close pal.

**BONUS CUT**

As a complete unknown in 1999, I bought a $25 ticket to watch a bunch of NYC music dignitaries perform a homage to Paul's songbook at a bimonthly showcase called Loser's Lounge. Though I'd never met him or even been in the same room, I'd always felt an inexplicable connection with him. When I arrived, I was stunned to see that he was actually sitting in the front row that night. He was mobbed after the show, so I only paid tribute from afar. Just one year later, Carole brought Paul in to write a song with herself, Duke Mushroom, and me. That's the magic of the music business. You never know who's on deck.

So Paul and I were halfway through our dinner at El Floridita in Hollywood, and I was doing my usual full-on grilling him on every aspect of his writing process, when he made a brief aside that stuck with me. Paul said the secret to his hit songs was that they were, for the most part, "codependent anthems"—full of that "you and me are gonna make it through, no matter the cost" lyrical sentiment. Historically, it was the kind of offhand remark that'd barely register with me. That night, however, those words hit me like a fuckin' hammer. From that meal forward, I focused less on the singular "I" in my tales and instead introduced a lot more "we," "us," and emotional reliance. As I spent my days applying the seeds of Paul's circular-relationship blueprint to the bulk of my lyrics, I continued to scour the streets in search of more talent to develop.

First I attempted to launch the solo debut of Rich Cronin, the lead singer of LFO—the late-'90s two-hit wonders with "Girl on TV" and the magnificent "Summer Girls." I've known a ton of characters, but Rich was truly a one-off. He was easily among the most deceptively charismatic guys I've ever met. He had brilliant comic timing, never rushing the reveal of a joke. He could hold court for hours on end, telling jaw-dropping stories about anything from his nutty youth in Boston to his crazier journey to Orlando in search of a piece of the pop pie.

Now at the time I began throwing down with Rich on his solo debut, he was furiously attempting to keep his name in the game. I know that sounds dramatic, but the music business can truly resemble a cruel type of dementia with its short-term memory issues. I guess we'd written three or four new tunes at this point, when one night Rich called me freaking out about an eighteen-year-old pop-punk from Andover, Massachusetts, named Martin Johnson, whose band, Lancaster, Rich suddenly decided to develop on a whim. It was a very Rich move. He was all over the place, so I was a bit frustrated, as it was painfully obvious his attention span for his own project was waning. He was also incoherent. Shitfaced. From what I could make out, he'd been hanging at some Orlando club where he met Eric Johnson, an heir to a $400 million Johnson & Johnson fortune, and the guy expressed interest in starting a label. Rich would be his partner—in charge of A&R.

It was a real whirlwind.

Within ten days, Rich subleased his Orlando condo and moved his belongings into Eric's sprawling mansion, overflowing with bad ideas and worse decisions. Then they flew up to Taunton, Massachusetts, to sign Lancaster to a "million-dollar" deal. On that trip, Eric also let Rich in on a little secret: he'd just been selected as the next leading man on ABC's *The Bachelor*. The show would be heading to Orlando to tape him. Rich was living ridiculously high on the hog.

At that point in my life, I was a full-on skeptic. My own missteps and cynicism gave me the innate ability to call bullshit on everything. I told Rich that it sounded real suspect. I can still hear his slightly manic response in that full-on Masshole accent. "I'm telling you, brah—this kid Eric is legit!"

Well, guess what?

This kid wasn't legit. His real name was Eric Simanton, and he was arrested a week or so later for passing fraudulent checks for over $1 million. He was no J & J heir. There was definitely no Bachelor. It was all a grift. Rich fishtailed back to Boston, completely confused and devastated. Lancaster's record deal went up in smoke. Martin was beyond pissed. He peaced out and decided to go for it solo. Soon Martin's exasperated manager (and former LFO tour manager), Mike Caputo, rushed him to NYC for a last ditched sit-down with me and Sluggo.

From the moment I met Lancaster's Martin Johnson, I knew that kid was special too. I was dead set on developing him. He was freakishly gifted. After an hour of feeling each other out, he excused himself to use the restroom. As he was walking toward the door, I asked him if I could check out his iPod.

"Go crazy," he said.

I did. And it was career-altering crack. Sure, he had all the prerequisite pop-punk and emo stuff on there, but he also had everything from REO Speedwagon to the *Rent* soundtrack. He loved all the stuff that we'd thrown out. When I was sixteen, I openly professed my musical admiration for Debbie Gibson's "Only in My Dreams," and I almost caught a brick in the eye from my (only) indie rock–obsessed pals. Martin taught me that everything was now game. All music was music. The genres had finally melted.

Sluggo and I were on our third day of throwing down with Martin when we collectively wrote a tune that would change everything for me as a songwriter. It was called "The Great Escape," and it was our attempt at a codependent/escapist anthem that celebrated the limitless possibility of youth. Basically the sum of a bunch of Paul Williams tricks! We shopped Martin's resulting demo all over town. Everyone passed. Literally everyone. A disbelieving Hollywood Records executive went a step further. After a face-to-face acoustic showcase on our couch, he chuckled at Martin and whispered to us in a not-so-hushed tone, "Good luck with Johnny Bravo, guys" (a reference to Greg Brady's contrived rock 'n' roll alter ego on *The Brady Bunch*). Finally, my friend Steve Yegelwel, one of the true great guys and best pop-rock ears in this game, gave us the shot. After much haggling, we all agreed on a new name for the project—Boys Like Girls.

Just as Sluggo and I began diving in deeper with Martin, Rich Cronin started to lose interest in his own solo debut and decided to pair with Bad Ronald's Doug Ray on a brand-new project. Their producer was Gary Philips, my old session-guitarist-turned-Kidz-Bop-boss. This business is truly musical deck chairs on the *Titanic*. We all just orbit each other hoping to avoid the inevitable icebergs. One night while they were recording their demo, Jen and I caught a meal with Rich at John's on Twelfth Street in New York City (our own personal Cheers), where Rich revealed some slightly horrifying tale that involved a mother and a daughter in the back of the LFO tour bus parked at Disneyland. Though disgusted, Jen absorbed the gruesomeness and immediately came up with the best idea ever: a reality show that consisted of a bunch of ex–boy band guys forming a new supergroup.

"A Manband?" I replied.

And we were off.

I pitched Manband to my old pal Kennedy, no longer rapping or making booty music videos, as he'd graduated to a career as a highly in-demand commercial director. He filmed a hilarious pilot starring Rich, Chris Kirkpatrick (NSYNC), Jeff Timmons (98 Degrees), and Bryan Abrams (Color Me Badd). We shopped it to JBender lead vocalist Dan Woods, who was now a TV executive at TBS (when I think about all of these intersecting paths, it still boggles my mind). Dan sent it over to a friend at VH1, and the series sold. Eight episodes! I learned so much about the inner workings of reality TV in the process. Though the concept was killer, the execution was ultra wack. The pilot that Kennedy had shot was pure, unfiltered mayhem. The finished product, now co-opted by an L.A. production company, was sanitized garbage. The funny was gone. But that was by no means the worst of it.

Rich Cronin was suddenly real sick.

He'd been diagnosed with acute myelogenous leukemia months before taping, and he struggled to make it through the grueling six-week shoot. It was just gut-wrenching. This occurred just as "The Great Escape" was released and blew up overnight. Honestly, it was all just the biggest mindfuck. Boys Like Girls would go on to have six Top 40 hits. Tragically, Rich would pass away in the midst of it. I could go on and on about this brilliant kid, but at the end of the day, words will never really do Rich justice. I can sincerely say, however, with no hyperbole, that his book would've been a much funnier and charming read than mine.

**BONUS CUT**

Mike Caputo ran a pop-star-making factory in Boston. Truthfully, he was one of the best talent scouts I'd ever encountered. I still find it strange that he was never swooped up by a label. That being said, Mike definitely dribbled outside of the paint, and I'm not sure he could've existed within the corporate-stickler environment.

One of Mike's young prodigies at the time was an awkwardly monikered kid named Lu Ballz, who actually lived in Mike's basement. Mike ran a veritable boot camp down there, so on many days Lu was tasked with making beats for eighteen hours on end. He was definitely at the base of the mountain, but he was quite talented. Lu did the bulk of his programming in the then somewhat entry-level software

FruityLoops, but we were so impressed by his beats that we had him coproduce a few tunes with us.

As time went on and I moved to L.A., I didn't check with Lu that often, so I knew little of his exploits. One day, I heard the kid had finally moved west, but was now working with some new young manager. Like Caputo, I guess this manager guy had his own roster of up-and-comers and paired Lu with one of them—a kid named Austin Post. Soon, Austin Post was rechristened Post Malone, and Lu Ballz reverted to his government name, Louis Bell.

Last year, Louis Bell was the biggest writer/producer in the music business.

If you see him, tell him I'm totally available to mop his studio floors.

## CHAPTER 20

# Mighty Seven

I n early 2006, Bret and I began scouring the city for a smaller studio space, as a rent hike on our previous spot had finally priced us all out of the building. At the very same time, JD, Bob, and their rapidly expanding Crush Management were also on the hunt for new digs. Throw in the up-and-coming video director Alan Ferguson, and on a whim we all decided to pool our dollars and rent an old, dilapidated loft on East Eleventh Street.

Thus, an island of misfit toys collectively united.

The universe works in the wackiest of ways. On the day we finally stumbled on the listing, the landlord looked real familiar. Turned out my mom used to buy antiques from this guy in the late '70s, and as a little kid I had actually tagged along with her and played in this exact building.

A lifetime later, now I was setting up shop on the Mighty Seventh Floor.

Since the rest of the musty building was used for furniture storage, to say that this place was on the bougie tip would be an incredible overstatement. The awful elevator shook its way up the sky, frequently stopping with a jolt and occasionally free-falling a floor or two on every hell ride. The stairwells were equally eerie. I can't even bring myself to ponder the potential asbestos looming everywhere. This, my friends, was the definition of a pit.

When we moved in, Crush took the front part of the loft. Alan and Bret set up offices in the middle. Sluggo and I grabbed the two studios in the back. The overall decor definitely put the shabby in shabby chic. My completely disjointed beachfront wallpaper that seemed like an inspired idea at that moment. Blown-up magazine covers in mismatched frames and sizes. Dusty gold records. Deceased bottles of wine. Gaggles of late-night mice.

With so many quirky characters involved, the transition could've been even uglier, but for the most part, beyond the crack-house aesthetics, it was all somewhat effortless. Three different camps with tons of symbiotic spillover. Crush introduced me to Gym Class Heroes and Panic! at the Disco. I linked Crush with Train. In time, Alan would direct *TRL*-topping and VMA-winning videos for all of us.

Over the next seven years, we hunkered down together creating art that we all hoped would enter the mass consciousness. We competed with ourselves, and each other, to an extent, to break down the industry gatekeepers and push our respective visions and agendas through. Everyone from Sia to SZA did time in the spot before they properly entered the zeitgeist. Even Beyoncé made a cameo appearance. Beyond all of the songs and videos that originated within those walls, so many spin-off careers were birthed that dominate the industry today. More importantly, I made some of my greatest lifelong friendships up in that spot as well.

As I sit here reflecting on it, it really dawns on me how wonderful and unique that stretch was. The music was brash. The haircuts were funny. The possibilities were endless. The relationships eternal. I'm only hoping that we can all re-create it again someday.

Working late night on the Mighty Seventh Floor.

### CHAPTER 21

# Making the Hit

I absorbed a few mentalism bits from the playbook of the late Lou Pearlman. Not from the wretch of a human who landed a twenty-five-year prison sentence for masterminding a half-billion-dollar airline Ponzi scheme, but the wretch of a human that assembled boy bands with military-like precision.

When the Backstreet Boys had early success in Germany, Lou immediately replicated them with NSYNC. When NSYNC connected, he launched LFO and O-Town. He had an assembly-line mind. He understood timing. I admired that. Striking before the narrowest of windows closed. It sounds soulless, but I was immediately transfixed by Lou's relentless machinations and found them fascinating and somewhat intoxicating in that Berry Gordy way as he ushered in a wave of frosted-hair pop. You see, Lou protected his interests. He knew that by instilling innate jealousy and competitive fire between his acts, he could raise the musical stakes. I know that sounds incredibly dark, but he was totally astute. Each of his bands attempted to outdo the others in every aspect of their careers, when others might devolve into complacency. In doing so, Lou's groups were all part of a pop revolution that, had he not made such greedy maneuvers, probably would've remained in his controlling hands.

**BONUS CUT**

I've been incredibly blessed to taste some success with artists on the earlier ends of careers when they were still wide-eyed and open to collaborate. They didn't know me well enough to doubt me yet, so I still maintained a little mystique in the dynamic. I've also had wins with bands on their fourth or fifth records, after they'd experienced both success and ego-deflating flops and were now hungrier and more collaborative than ever. It was the follow-up record to a hit that was the most arduous experience for all. It was rarely a pleasant scene for either side. The artist wanted to work with bigger, more credible names. The writer/producer wanted to maintain some semblance of directional control. The result was inevitably a shitshow. I remember when *As Cruel As School Children* blew up, Travie endlessly reassured me that we'd be making the follow-up together. Then one day he rolled by the studio and played me a slew of tunes he'd done in Miami with bigger hip-hop cats. He'd completely moved on. I was bummed, but I couldn't blame him.

That's why in the very moment that Boys Like Girls exploded and Martin (wisely) began plotting collaborations with others outside of our fold, I knew Sluggo and I swiftly needed to find the NSYNC to Boys Like Girls's Backstreet Boys. At the time, Pure Volume, Absolute Punk, and, most importantly, Myspace were the websites where the future resided. This was where unknown bands posted their demos and links, and page upon page of critical love or hate would follow. It was the official beginning of democratic A&R guided by the ones who truly mattered anyway—the kids themselves. For songwriters and producers, it was the most incredible resource ever for talent scouting and scouring. We discovered the bulk of our acts via these sites.

One day in late '06, while biding time on another endless conference call, Bret began refreshing his bookmarked Pure Volume page over and over as an anxious antidote to the morning boredom. Then an ad popped up that caught his eye. It was a band called Desoto.

The singer had huge, beastly ginger-red hair that resembled that evil Syndrome kid from *The Incredibles*. Bret hit the link and opened their MySpace page. Then we all listened. Their tunes were kinda whatever. They'd absorbed elements of each of the pop-punk stars of the moment, including our own Martin Johnson, but they didn't really have their own unique thing. The kid had a solid voice, though. Bret casually messaged them and got an eager response from said vocalist, Travis Clark, within the hour.

I really dug Travis from the jump. He was an ambitious, super respectful kid living in Orlando, who, at twenty-one, was watching his dream slowly fade into the Epcot ether. He told us that he'd actually borrowed $200 from his old man to place the ad on the Pure Volume page that very same week in a last-ditch effort to get heard. I grilled Travis with all of my typical vetting questions. Was he in school? How much local gigging had Desoto done? Any touring outside of Orlando? Was he open to co-writing? Was he open to a name change? Then Bret threw down the gauntlet. "If you and your boys are willing to get yourselves up to NYC next week, Sam and Sluggo are down to write a couple of songs with you, and we can test out the vibe."

That's all it took.

These Desoto kids loaded up their crumbling sprinter van and drove dead on to New York. Twenty-two hours straight. When they arrived, we put them up in our five-star accommodations: our studio's equally crumbling, grubby, stain-coated couches. This was the beginning of December, and there was no heat in the building after 7 PM. Also, a colony of sooty mice ruled the roost. Unflustered, the band ended up crashing the entire month.

Travis, Sluggo, and I got on with writing a stack of inspired tunes. We'd dig in for a spell every morning, and then Sluggo and I would go off and write with whomever we were booked with that afternoon while Travis continued to workshop the morning's ideas. We'd reconvene in the early evening for another round with all of the Desoto boys hanging hard for moral support in the frigid cold. We loved every second of it. They were an incredible crew of humans. They just needed a name.

At the time, there were 135 Desotos on MySpace alone. It was a boring handle, and it wasn't even available. Since I kept, and still keep, a dinner-menu-sized list of unused monikers that I add on to when inspiration strikes, I shuttled my favorites over to the quartet. They hated each and every one of them. That was so Florida of them. They returned the serve with their own list of favorites. All of which were . . . disgraceful.

We were at an impasse.

I was walking down Fifth Avenue a few days before Christmas, soaking in all the holiday mirth and splendor, when I got a call from Hunter, the guitarist.

"Hey, dude. So. Um. We've made a name decision as a band. And we really want you to greenlight it."

Hit me.

"Um. It means a lot to us. It's who we are, bro."

Blah blah. Hit me.

"Okay, you ready?"

The suspense is killing me. Snore.

"Check Yes, Juliet."

Huh?

"Check Yes, Juliet?"

Could this name suck worse? It sounded like it came from a shitty pop-punk band name generator. Check Yes, Juliet—the band—was just not gonna happen. We resumed writing and prerecording with the still nameless quartet in early January, and we finally came up with the perfect hybrid of a moniker from multiple selections—We the Kings. Everyone involved knew it was a record-deal-worthy tag from the jump. Some names just have that effect (the Sex Pistols, anyone?). And like clockwork, my pals Steve Yegelwel and Steve Greenberg signed this band to their freshly relaunched label, S-Curve Records, immediately. The team was back together. We had an entire album written, tracked, and ready to go. We just had one tiny problem.

We didn't have a "Great Escape."

And Sluggo and I both knew it.

We tried spitballing a ton of ideas, and nothing felt big enough.

Then one morning we got an unusually early start, and Sluggo and Travis summoned a superb melody that was especially singsong-y. It felt like a nursery rhyme from the gods. I was about to start kicking a lyric around when it dawned on me that I'd neglected my usual coffee routine at the Astor Place Mud Truck. That spot was my caffeine hub on the daily for years. I trudged outside into that drizzly, raw air and stood in line when I began unconsciously scatting words to that melody. "Check yes, Juliet, are you with me, rain is falling down on the sidewalk."

How do these things happen? These strange bits of inexplicable, wordy happenstance when lines suddenly feel like they are implanted into the mouth from a Johnny Mnemonic brain hack? It's impossible to quantify, but the right song really will tell you what to do. When it does, it's rub-your-belly, lotto-ticket, divine intervention.

I dashed back to Eleventh Street, spilling my coffee everywhere while simultaneously attempting to one-hand-type words into my Blackberry. By the time I dashed through the door, it was on. The song was off to the races.

A month or so later, I flew down to Orlando for the newly minted We the Kings' first hometown show. After two fun-filled days toiling around "The Happiest Place on Earth" with my fam, I had a few hours to kill before the group's hometown relaunch, so I spontaneously decided to reach out to my old high school pal, Aaron Accetta, formerly of the ill-fated JBender, who was now residing in Orlando as well. His job? The salaried in-house house producer for . . . drumroll, please . . .

Lou Pearlman.

On paper, this was a huge break for Aaron. It was his first real paid music-production gig. Be careful what you wish for. By this point, Lou and his company, Transcontinental Records, were an ugly shadow of themselves. All of the moneymaking acts on the roster had flown the coop in a series of litigious actions. Now they'd been primarily replaced by a rotating cast of attractive Chippendale dancers and private limousine drivers that Lou hoped to "turn" into aspiring pop stars.

This couldn't have been fun. Aaron spent every hour alternately trying to mold these not-so-ready-for-prime-time kids into something viable, while continuing to produce the last of Lou's remaining stable of boy band castoffs. It was all kind of a jerkoff, since there never seemed to be a plan of attack for any of it. That night when we spoke, Aaron seemed, for a fairly laid-back cat, strangely anxious. He asked me to run by the studio as soon as possible. I told him it might be tough, given We the Kings's early set. But he wasn't taking no for an answer.

When I arrived a few hours later, there were a bunch of menacing black vans surrounding the building. That was weird. I knocked on the door, and a now quite paranoid Aaron answered, rushed me in, and gave me a whirlwind of a tour of the crumbling boy band kingdom. It was still all tacky excess, but the sheen had clearly faded. Then he led me into Lou Pearlman's office, where he proceeded to lock the door and sit behind the desk.

"I don't know what to do, man. Lou owes me a ton of cash. I'm freaking out!"

I looked at him, puzzled.

"You didn't see the news today?" he continued. "He's on the run. They think he fled the country! Those vans outside are the feds!"

Yes, as we'd later learn, Lou had embezzled half a billion dollars from 1,700 unsuspecting investors. As the antsy Aaron continued, I surveyed the digs and noticed a cardboard box with Lou's girthy face on the sticker gleaming like an Elf on the Shelf.

"What is that?" I interrupted.

"That's the prototype for his Lou Pearlman Making the Hit recording system. It's a bunch of DVDs full of behind-the-scenes tips for success. He's planning to sell these things everywhere."

We both began laughing uncontrollably. I asked Aaron if I could hold it. He generously handed it to me. I began rubbing Lou's head.

"Lou, I don't wanna seem greedy, but I could use another hit!"

Then I closed my eyes and slipped that shit under my jacket.

Aaron seemed perplexed. "There's about $500,000 worth of gear in this spot, and it's all gonna end up in some government locker, tied up till it's no longer relevant or usable, and the only thing you wanna grab is this piece of junk? Sam, this guy owes me thousands of dollars!" He raged on. But I didn't hear any of it. I now had my very own Lou Pearlman Making the Hit home recording system. The world was mine.

I slowly slid out the front door and raced off to the We the Kings gig, simultaneously checking for the feds in the rearview. As I hit a bit of Orlando traffic, I wondered what the potential punishment would be for stealing this wondrous $10 scam souvenir that I so coveted.

An hour later I witnessed "Check Yes, Juliet" performed live for the first time, and I knew it was a smash from the intro alone: the crowd was jumping up and down like disciples of the Polyphonic Spree. Within a few months, the song blew up. It was all over the radio that entire summer. It was my third platinum hit that year. I can close my eyes and flash back to the first time I heard it on the radio as it blasted my roof off while I crossed the George Washington Bridge under the sweetest sunset. The tune's still one of my favorites. And though it's somewhat uncouth to state this, I do believe that I owe a decent por-

tion of We The Kings' success to that Lou Pearlman Making the Hit belly rub and the framework that the bubblegum-impresario convict created. As a means of respect, I still keep that "Check Yes, Juliet" plaque hung in a corner of the studio, bowing directly down toward my Lou Pearlman Making the Hit box.

Lou Pearlman's "Making The Hit" box.

**BONUS CUT**

Don't worry about Aaron. A few years later, he partnered with an equally great writer named Shep Goodman, and together they wrote the American Authors smash "The Best Day of My Life." It was one of the biggest radio tunes of the decade. Making the Hit was obviously responsible.

### CHAPTER 22

# Uncle John's Band[1]

**W**hen I was a kid, my uncle John always held court at the holiday dinner table, receiving endless praise from the relatives gathered around on his latest book or contribution to *The Paris Review*.

There was plenty to celebrate.

From the publication of his first collection, "A Crackling of Thorns," which won the 1958 Yale Younger Poets Prize, my uncle published dozens of volumes of verse and numerous works of criticism. He received most of the big awards a poet could receive: the Levenson Prize, the Bollingen Prize, the Mina P. Shaughnessy Prize, as well as fellowships from the MacArthur Foundation and the Guggenheim Foundation. I didn't appreciate any of this at the time. On the surface, we had nothing in common. Yes, I knew that he once ran with Ginsberg, but his world of poetic forms meant little to me. I wanted to roll with MTV and Martha Quinn.

My uncle was forever an imposing figure. While I was struggling to pen Baha Men records (no, not even "Who Let the Dogs Out"), he was one of the preeminent poet-critics of his generation. We barely understood each other. At family gatherings, while John regaled the

---

1 This chapter appeared previously in the *New York Times*. Sam Hollander, "John Hollander: My Uncle, the Poet and the Pop Star," *New York Times*, December 21, 2013. https://www.nytimes.com/news/the-lives-they-lived/2013/12/21/john-hollander/.

room on verse and allegory, I mostly tuned him out. Some of my most powerful impressions of him were formed in strange, unexpected ways.

There was a Pizza Hut waiter upstate who took my credit card and, after inquiring about the connection (not the sort of dialogue you expect with your Spicy Sicilian), actually screamed profanities about my uncle and his poetic elitism. There was also the slightly intoxicated ride late one night on the F train when I looked up to see one of Uncle John's poems in the empty subway car (part of the Poetry in Motion series).

It was a beautiful, humbling moment.

That night inspired me to finally crack open his critically lauded *Powers of Thirteen*, which had been gathering layers of dust under a pile of 45s. It required patience and attention. It was touching and witty. I never reached out to him to tell him.

I was too busy chasing something big myself.

Eventually, the miraculous happened. I wrote a hit. Then another. At this point, my uncle and I rarely spoke, and by the time I finally made something of myself in song, we had lost touch altogether. So you can imagine my surprise at hearing Uncle John's baritone bellowing through my phone a few years later.

"Hello, Sam. It's your uncle John. I received an email that I'd love to run by you. May I read it to you?"

Absolutely, I told him, and he continued: "Dear Professor Hollander. I'm a huge fan of your work. My name is Don Henley. I've set one of your poems, 'An Old-Fashioned Song,' to music, and recorded it with my band, the Eagles."

Then he paused and said, "Sam, who are these Eagles?"

WTF?!

Uncle John's resulting collaboration with the Eagles—a song eventually titled "No More Walks in the Wood"—was released on a new Eagles album in late 2007 that went directly to Walmart stores, shining brightly on the racks next to Jay-Z and Britney Spears. Within a few months, it sold several million copies. My uncle John was seventy-eight and featured on the number one record in America. When he died, the Eagles song understandably did not appear in his obituaries. It wasn't mentioned in the many speeches, memorials, or tributes, lost amid a sea of literary achievements. To me, though, it was enormous. There I was, standing beneath John's shadow even as a songwriter, yet somehow we were finally connected. I hope that someday I will inherit his platinum plaque for my studio wall.

Uncle John Hollander,
mini-me, Dad.

## CHAPTER 23

# Jazz Hands

I t took six years of pestering people for me to finally get a crack
at writing with Jason Mraz. Campaigning for that long-awaited
collaboration required intermittent bouts of pleading and pesky
manipulations of the beleaguered folks at Atlantic Records. Eventually the exhausted gatekeepers acquiesced and granted myself and
Sluggo two days with the soft rock god.

They had one simple request: Write a hit.

You see, when dealing with self-contained singer-songwriters like
Mraz, you really have just one shot at cracking the record . . . a single
or bust. In most cases, artists of Mraz's ilk fight to write the bulk of
their artsier/more intimate numbers on their own, and those resulting songs usually end up comprising the body of an album. That
only leaves a couple of potential spots for co-writers aiming for radio
glory. Now, Mraz's case is a bit more nuanced by the fact that he
composed his biggest pop hit to date, "I'm Yours," on his own with
no collaborators. It was a ginormous cut. The song ended up logging
seventy-six weeks on the Billboard Hot 100, breaking the record for
most weeks spent on the chart. It also put Mraz in the driver's seat
for the follow-up. Yes, for this go-round at least, he would not have
to face the dreaded A&R "song collector"!

BONUS CUT

While many A&R folks might set a goal of twenty song demos or so before a single is picked from the pile, the song collector will force the artist to write with every potential hit-making fool in the industry, while also accumulating a stack of outside "pitch songs" (tunes composed specifically to be lobbed at an A&R person, publisher, or artist directly with the goal of getting "placed" on a record). This can lead to around a hundred-plus tunes up for consideration. I can't speak for others, and I'm obviously biased as fuck, but for me this is both writer and artist's worst-case scenario. For the writer, the chances of sliding on a song collector's records are incredibly rare, like spotting a triple rainbow in your lifetime. For the artist, it's exhausting, and It starts to reduce the art to a soul-sucking numbers game.

Now, from my first "Curbside Prophet" listen on an Aware Records sampler, I was immediately drawn to Mraz. It was so obvious that we shared many of the same musical influences. So much so that I felt we might just be song twinsies. Sluggo? It was a little less his thing. He was always a bit more pop-focused at the core. He was definitely rattled by my affinity for the Holy Trinity of Kenny Loggins, Michael McDonald, and Christopher Cross.

When Mraz arrived in NYC and settled into our couch, he was quite guarded. We muscled through a solid hour of small talk involving his coffee farm in the hills of San Diego but received monosyllabic responses at best. It was pretty evident that he didn't want to be in our room, or any room for that matter. It just felt like he wanted to be stoned out of his damn mind in the Southern California beach haze, making chocolate avocado sandwiches, and strumming softly in utter bliss.

Can you really blame him?

Sluggo was swiftly losing interest. I, however, was desperate to make it work, so I went all in. From Gilberto Gil to Grover Washington Jr. to the Sanford-Townsend Band, I kicked a ton of '70s mellow and jazzy symbiotic music knowledge back and forth with Jason. Minute by minute (see what I did there), it seemed that I'd broken past the uncomfortable pauses of this musical first date.

"So what kind of tune are you feeling?" an increasingly checked-out Sluggo inquired.

Mraz pensively paused and glanced down at his guitar.

Slowly, he began to strum lounge-like jazz chords over and over.

Just some slow, *Love Boat* lido deck–type shit.

I was obviously stoked.

Sluggo gave me death stares.

Note to self: When writing with Jason Mraz, it's probably best to leave whatever floats my yacht back at the marina.

You see, by motor-mouthing my late-night stoney '70s leanings to this cat, I'd awoken the mellow, jazz chord giant and totally slit our own throats in the process. It was painfully obvious that we would never create anything pop-radio friendly that day. Just a vibey album track at best.

I knew I'd choked it.

I tried to rectify it.

I spent two desperate days attempting to subtly push Mraz over to the pop side, but there was no turning back. The fruits of this collaboration would never result in the new infinity swimming pool of my dreams.

As we wrapped up the second day, I emailed our demo to the label, who were rightfully less than impressed, as the tune didn't feel the slightest bit "radio."

The jig was officially up.

That night, Mraz, Sluggo, Bret, and I all shared a couple of bottles of wine on our friend Mike McKoy's roof, where Jason continued his coffee-farming discourse. He seemed much happier outside of the studio confines. I actually found him to be quite interesting and a really sweet guy. Then he vanished into the night.

As a pop songwriter, your influences and taste define the body of your work. On magic days, you pull from various bits of your musical DNA and create something epic. My friend Rivers Cuomo of Weezer combined the Beach Boys, Slayer, and Nirvana in his writing and changed the radio. In those early days, if he'd tossed Luther Vandross into that blender, the resulting smoothie might not have tasted the same (I probably would've loved it, though!). I've seen so many writers fail based on the mishmash of their inner jukebox. It's all about altering your inner determinants until the amalgamation is uniquely yours.

Even then, once your hybrid has birthed a sound that's definitively both you and radio ready, you're still often faced with the harsh reality that there are just certain artists who you'll never win with. That doesn't mean they're not the most wonderful peeps or that you're a shitty writer. Sometimes, it just comes down to this inexplicable energy that prohibits any possible victory. I think I've written four songs with Jason Mraz to date. Sadly, they all died on the vine. Also, at least seven songs with the very sweet Australian pop kids 5 Seconds of Summer. None of those have ever seen the light of day either. I take no offense whatsoever. It's an imperfect science. At the end of the day, I'm just thankful for the opportunities.

## CHAPTER 24

# Riding on the Metro

O ne day I was riding the L train out to Brooklyn when I got overwhelmed by a strange realization: After all the years of futility, I'd finally permeated the big leagues. Man, it was such an inexplicable rush. I'm sure Sluggo had a similar revelation. By tossing a dash of Swedish-inspired melodies, quirky lyrical takes, and a bit of the pop punk kitchen sink in the noisy mix, we had become first-call guys. And that's when the panic really kicked back in. I knew we now had to grind harder than ever or risk getting kicked back down to the minors.

Step Brothers (myself and Dave "Sluggo" Katz).

To maintain our spot in this volatile game, we spent endless hours harnessing our sound. We became obsessed with decoding the DNA of hits—sometimes for reference, but often just so we could then unlearn all the shit we'd absorbed and go solely from the gut. I know that sounds a bit backward-ass, but by reverse-engineering whatever tune was connecting at the moment, we'd figure out why and how things were working. This would inevitably lead us back to our own lane with a few freshly paved new tricks. We'd blast a tune on loop, studying every crevice of the lyric, melody, and chord choices. Basically, the whole shebang: Did the verses deftly avoid a cut-and-paste feel and build to the perfect payoff? Did the pre-chorus elevate or shrink to steer clear of the chorus? How were the background vocals used in the hook? Was it an REM/Mike Mills–like counter-melody thing or some steroid-ed Mutt Lange harmony stacks? Was the second verse one half the length of the first? What was added instrumentally to hype up the bridge? Was there a post-chorus or gang-vocal moment? So many probes. The more we decrypted tunes, the more we were able to add our own fresh take.

BONUS CUT

We even experimented with different song forms, like *AABA*. I think it was Carole King who initially inspired me and Duke Mushroom to mess with that old-school song form. Back in the first half of the twentieth century, AABA, also known as the *32-bar* form, was the primary style of popular music writing. In AABA, the A sections were the verses—each usually ending in a payoff refrain line—and the B section was the bridge. An example of this would be Carole and Gerry Goffin's classic "Will You Still Love Me Tomorrow." Though the AABA form occasionally rears its head in songwriting today, it's definitely more exception than rule at this point. For aspiring writers, though, it's a great technique to play around with because you really have to dial in the real estate of the verse to make that lyrical climax work.

As we continued our song exploration, a flood of artists rushed through our studio doors. For a while, every day was exciting. We were the first writers to collaborate with prog-metal czar Claudio Sanchez of Coheed and Cambria. When he pulled up that first afternoon, he looked absolutely petrified. He excused himself and slumped out to our fire escape to smoke a cigarette. I think it was his first smoke in two years. I guess the co-writing thing scared his ass back to menthol. To soothe the vibe and save the session, I shouted out the exposed Klaus Nomi album cover tattoo on his calf. By that point, Klaus was primarily a music footnote for record-shop nerds like myself, so I thought he'd be impressed. I was correct. He was so floored by the fact that I was familiar with this obscure, groundbreaking operatic artist that it eradicated the tension, and in time, we actually ended up writing a minor Coheed radio hit. Another killer moment was launching Cobra Starship with our buddy Gabe Saporta, when we cowrote and produced the title track for the cult classic *Snakes on a Plane*, as well as the band's subsequent debut. Let's see, there was also a freshly minted Neon Trees, teenage All Time Low, and the should've-been-way-bigger The Academy Is. Sluggo and I did some of our best work with this batch, but as time went on and we continued to grind like maniacs, we both began to get burned out by the process. We rarely turned down work because we were so scared of our moment of relevance waning. It was utter chaos. We were also frantically developing our own next wave of homegrown acts.

One of these was Metro Station.

Metro Station was a newly formed, L.A.-based, electro-pop quartet, whose two-headed lead vocal tandem were the older brothers of *Hannah Montana*'s Miley Cyrus and Mitchell Musso. Their self-made Myspace page demos were incredible. Columbia swooped them up instantly. Bret was brought in to manage.

The day after Metro Station landed in NYC to begin workshopping with us, Sluggo and I rolled uptown to meet the kids for a quick introduction at a grungy rehearsal room buried deep in the Garment District called Smash Studios. I've definitely lost count of how many bands I shedded or showcased at that grimy little spot. On the surface, it had next to zero aesthetically redeemable charms. It usually smelled like a toxic blend of puke and dusty foam cushioning, but it was a go-to for musical dues-paying in a city sorely lacking affordable rehearsal space. When we walked through the Smash Studios door, the keyboardist and the drummer jumped off the couch and eagerly shook our hands. Super respectful and enthused.

This was gonna be a blast.

The two frontmen (really, front kids), on the other hand, seemed to be complete dicks. Sulky, spoiled Hollywood spawn who couldn't have been less interested in our presence. They just laid down on the floor, texting whomever, completely ignoring us.

This was gonna suck.

After thirty minutes of fruitless attempts to permeate their respective pouting shells, I finally threw in the towel, wished them the best of luck, and stormed out. I called Bret and told him to hit the label and tell 'em they could keep their check. Sluggo stood there, furious, and screamed at me in the street. Between two kids in private schools plus rent and other living expenses, he couldn't afford to fling away Sony money. It got pretty heated. In the end, Sluggo was right, though. I was being a selfish, whiny bitch. I had to simmer down.

The next day, the band came down to the studio and delivered a mea culpa that felt completely crafted by Bret, or a brilliant publicist, but it did do the trick. I apologized as well. We all hugged and began digging in musically. The tension immediately lifted. We spent a couple of months crafting their debut. Metro Station were awesomely raw. Mason Musso had a ridiculous voice, and, man, he was quite a gifted writer for his age. And Trace Cyrus just dripped of MTV's *TRL* swagger.

**BONUS CUT**

It kinda blows that the Gen Z kids—mine included—will never get to experience the fan excitement and raw energy of MTV's *Total Request Live* (*TRL*). It didn't matter if you were viewing from your couch or lucky enough to loiter in the Times Square studio, it was the absolute zenith of the pop universe. As a songwriter, it was an imperative watch for me, as all of those visuals of youth culture inevitably inspired my pen. Having been raised on a diet of *American Bandstand*, *Solid Gold*, *Video Music Box*, *Dance Party USA*, and *Soul Train* before it, I'm still quite nostalgic for that kind of thing.

It's also worth noting that both Mason and Trace spent an inordinate amount of time coiffing their respective swoosh haircuts with endless coats of hairspray. JD's prognostications from five years previous were correct. We'd finally hit the spandex space-time continuum.

Hair bands were back in business! Warrant, Winger, White Lion . . . Metro Station.

As we were wrapping up their debut, it seemed that we had at least two or three singles ready to go, but Bret became super focused on one cut that was flying under the collective radar. It was called "Shake It," and he couldn't stop pounding me to finish it. So, one slow day, finally drained by Bret's nudging, I grabbed the Pro Tools files for the "Shake It" song, locked myself in our shithole of a B room, and made a conscious effort to do some actual programming again. By that point, I'd totally stopped making beats altogether. I was so busy writing toplines and overseeing production on multiple cuts and records at a time that I couldn't summon a second to sit down and chop up sounds the way I did on everything up to and through Gym Class Heroes. In hindsight, I think the success of the *As Cruel As School Children* record had been enough for me. It was a vindication on so many levels, but the beat-making side of me, the one that couldn't get arrested in hip-hop, truly felt like the sweetest retribution of all. Now here I was, sweating next to an ancient heater that was spitting germ-inducing dry heat directly into my fraying sinuses as I struggled to learn the latest software all the kids were using. It was called Reason, and I was already 2000 and late to the table. Man, this sequencer was so user-friendly. All you had to do was insert the song tempo and scroll through loops in real time. I'd started out chopping up beats and samples in the most primitive form. Eventually, I graduated to Pro Tools, where I learned to cut, paste, and create on the grid itself. That was the extent of my programming knowledge, so the simplicity of the Reason software was just insane. That day, I started layering Reason drum and percussion loops into "Shake It" with the notion of creating a bombastic post-chorus event. Throughout that afternoon, I smoked a couple of Js solo, and in my stoney state, I proceeded to lay down twelve percussive drum loops on top of each other. Twelve loops! As a producer, this was not a good look. I completely drowned out the hook in my sonic lunacy, but in my blunted ears, it sounded fresh as fuck. I wanted the payoff to feel like a Bahamian Junkanoo street fest.

BONUS CUT

Junkanoo was a street parade I first experienced early in my career working on the ill-fated follow-up to the Baha Men's "Who Let the Dogs Out." Back in the Pop Rox days, I spent a week in Nassau working with the suddenly one-colossal-hit wonders. We wrote a little tune called "Move It Like This," and it became a (somewhat forgettable) Top 20 UK pop hit. More importantly to this tale, it permeated the Disney Channel on loop, where it influenced the Metro Station kids. Also, I must mention that one of the Baha Men guys jacked my headphones. If you catch them performing on a cruise ship or some shit, please ask the Baha poacher to kindly return my AKGs. Oh, and on our final day of recording, the group's patriarch furiously screamed at me, Duke Mushroom, and Mike Mangini for arriving five minutes late to the session with McDonald's Happy Meals in hand. We learned the hard way that the Baha Men had a zero-tolerance policy for the tardy and the Big Mac.

Okay, so "Shake It" was now the most cluttered slice of mayhem ever. Then, for the proverbial icing on the cake, I had the Crushettes (Crush Management's fabulous Danielle, Ashley, Alix, and Taylor) lay down mob after mob of chaotic gang vocals. When I sent the files to Tom Lord-Alge, the prominent pop rock mixer of the era, he called me up somewhat concerned about my mental state. I'd like to believe I convinced him that there was indeed a method to my madness, but he must've hopped off the phone more than a bit alarmed. Then after a bunch of weed-whacking revisions, Tom delivered his mix of the tune to Rick Rubin (!), now running A&R at Columbia Records. I was blown away when Rick actually chimed in. His one note was that he wanted less organic instrumentation in the mix. I questioned that call, but he was spot on. The electronic leanings just sounded better on the record. The label seemed genuinely stoked about the song's prospects. Then they went with another single. Ordinarily, I would've been furious, but frankly speaking, I was ready to move on. I was past Metro Station. I was kinda over *all* of our projects, actually. Our records were beginning to resemble some Weird Al parody to me, and my musical spirit was craving something more challenging. Everything we did, from Boys Like Girls, We the Kings, and Metro Station, to Good Charlotte, Cartel, and All Time Low, existed within the pop-punk landscape, and that world, though wonderful and life changing, had become too creatively insular. I wanted to make a record that would bridge all musical skylines with that Flying Wallenda fearlessness. Every creative has this epiphany—the desperate need to be taken seriously. Now that I was playing in the big leagues, I wanted to do something "important."

And let the eye rolls commence . . .

---

I got a call from an attorney friend who asked me to meet her twenty-six-year-old client, Nikki Jean, a singer-songwriter from Philadelphia, who she was sure I'd dig. They popped by for a hang a couple of days later, on the day that our equally worn-down engineer, Sean Gould, sat at the computer backing up the Metro Station files for mastering.

Nikki was a true beauty. Wickedly smart and brilliantly poker faced. Behind her incredible smile, it was hard to tell where we stood. She came with some great hip-hop cosigns. She'd been featured on a Lupe Fiasco single. Questlove was a fan. When we met, she was fronting various offshoots of the Roots crew in Philly while holding it down at a bakery on the nine to five.

"So why do you wanna work with me?" I inquired.

I naturally assumed she wanted to make some Gym Class Heroes–ish hybrid, given that *As Cruel As Schoolchildren* was still selling boatloads of records.

"Because you worked with Carole King," Nikki replied.

This is why you never assume.

Though I was quite intrigued by Nikki's response, as I pondered it, I couldn't spell out where Nikki fit in the current industry landscape. Her musical tastes were so different from any of her contemporaries.

She'd been brought up listening to Jerome Kern and Irving Berlin. Tin Pan Alley and Brill Building. But she could dissect all of J Dilla's beats and Dilated Peoples' verses as well. Her song demos that she played me existed in somewhat of an urban adult contemporary space. I'd never met anyone like her. We shook hands that day, and I told her I'd reach out when, and if, I cracked the code.

A month later, while wandering down Broadway, a Nikki idea finally jelled in my head: What if she were matched with some of the most historically significant pop songwriters in history? The authors of America's songbook. What if I sent her off on the wildest writing road trip ever? Could she sit alongside those heavies and create future classics? This could be some grown folks brilliance! It was the best idea I'd ever had. Zero question. This was my *Crime and Punishment*. I hyped Nikki on it and she absolutely adored the concept. Bret walked her into Jody Gerson's office at Sony Publishing a week later, and Jody literally scooped her up on the spot. The endorsement from Gerson, the most powerful woman in the music industry, immediately kicked the project into high gear. Rob Stringer and Steve Barnett, the chairman of Sony Music and the president of Columbia Records, respectively, signed her to the company off the concept alone. As they escorted me and Bret out toward the door, Rob casually inquired about her age.

"Twenty-four," Bret replied.

In the music industry, a year or two can be easily shaved off a bio like slush off a giant cube for a Hawaiian shaved ice.

**BONUS CUT**

In hindsight, signing with Stringer and Barnett directly was probably an ill-conceived move on our part. When you start at the top of the tower, you rarely have the kids on the ground floor backing your shit. They want to make their own mark in the game. They get frustrated having these kinda acts shoved on their lap. In our case, every A&R assigned to the Nikki Jean project seemed less than enthused. They were all significantly more interested in Metro Station.

I had to make this Nikki project happen. I picked up the phone and called Carole King and Paul Williams, and they both instantly agreed to participate. Jody reached out to a slew of heavyweights. Man, she was so amazing. I couldn't believe how hard she stepped out for the project. Burt Bacharach! Lamont Dozier! Jody trotted us around at the L.A. Grammy parties that month as a precursor to that inevitable moment in the sun that was coming for us the following year.

Then the mood shifted.

The demos began to land in my email from Nikki's lengthy road trip, and the bulk of them were underwhelming at best. I'd been so consumed with the gimmick of the record when I concocted this thing, that I just assumed the tunes would arrive brilliantly constructed. Nikki certainly did her job. She brought a really unique lyrical perspective to the table. She wasn't tentative ever, which I loved, but many of these preeminents were so intent on chasing some semblance of Top 40 glory again that they suppressed the sophisticated magic that made them icons and that we desperately needed. Now, I'm not insinuating that her collaborators had lost a step creatively. I mean, these were the greatest writers of their or any generation, but they were attempting to write current rhythmic shit, without having much, if any, understanding of the Black Eyed Peas and T Pain ruling radio at the time.

Bacharach nailed it. He stayed on his brand of complex, sweeping, '60s-era chords with Nikki, and it resulted in a pretty amazing tune. Soul boss Thom Bell did his old-school thing brilliantly as well. There were others that I really dug. The rest were more or less a batch of interesting musical fragments, but as a whole, the songs just weren't competitive enough. Sluggo and I ended up doing a lot of doctoring to make it cohesive. Picture elementary school astronomy teachers editing Neil DeGrasse Tyson. It all just felt wrong.

When we delivered the finished record, the consensus from the higher-ups was that they "just didn't get it," as the music seemed a bit "more mature" than they'd anticipated. Though I had clearly explained from the project's inception that its success lay in finding an older fanbase (I think I clumsily whipped out a Susan Boyle reference), the Columbia gavel fell on Nikki Jean, and they dropped her. They did graciously give us back our masters, though. That was pretty darn generous, but it was also a solid indicator of how confident the label was that they wouldn't get burned down the road (remember, Columbia historically dropped Alicia Keys, 50 Cent, and Katy Perry, among others, before those artists went on to have massive success elsewhere).

I just couldn't let it die.

I ran across town to Steve Greenberg and begged him to take on the project. Steve, being both a loyalist and a devotee of all things high concept, signed on. I knew he didn't completely buy it, though. When the record finally streeted on S-Curve a few months later, it actually got some incredible press. The *Wall Street Journal*, *Entertainment Weekly*—she even performed on *The Late Show with David Letterman*, where I watched Paul Shaffer and the band gush all over her backstage. It was a slight taste of triumph, but in the end, none of it amounted to anything of significance for all involved. That is, other than in Japan, where the single "My Love," written by Nikki, Lamont Dozier, Sluggo, and myself, went Top 10.

Domo arigato!

The last time I saw Nikki, she was the first opener of four acts at a CMJ Showcase at SOB's a couple of years later. She was quietly doing her makeup in the middle of an obnoxiously lit basement area. While the other eager acts on the bill were buzzing with kid excitement and boisterous squads, she sat

In the studio with Metro Station, Jason Aron, Sluggo, and Sean Gould.

stoic, focused on the mask. No handlers. No posse. As we struggled through some very uncomfortable chitchat, it was a bittersweet scene for both of us. In my mind, I'd totally failed Nikki. She'd come to me so wide-eyed and excited, and I had led her down a road that, though life altering in theory, put so much undue pressure on her to deliver the next to impossible. I'd under-thought the greatest idea ever and hung her out to dry in the process. She deserved better. This was easily the biggest miss of my career, and man, it stung.

While I tried to lick my Nikki wounds, Metro Station seemed to be spiraling in the same dreary direction. Their first two singles didn't gain much traction, but then the label released "Shake It," and, amazingly enough, it blew up massively overnight. It sold over three million singles! Most excitingly (some might even say undeservedly), though, the song's success led to me and Sluggo being named *Rolling Stone* magazine's "Hot List Producers of the Year." Scooping up extra copies of that issue at the St. Mark's newsstand and racing them up to my folks' house was one of the most magical moments of my adult life.

In the end, the explosion of Metro Station and the implosion of Nikki Jean's debut made for an incredible life lesson. As Kelly Johnson, the lead aircraft engineer at the Lockheed Skunk Works, declared in a 1960 design principle, "KISS"—"Keep it simple, stupid."

We all have a Dostoyevsky inside of us, but that doesn't mean anyone wants to read it.

## BONUS CUT

By the time this book sees the light of day, I wouldn't be shocked if Nikki has already become a household name. Beyond her incredible talent, she had that rare, undefinable thing that true stars have. She lit up a room like few that I've met. For that matter, I also wouldn't be surprised to hear the news that Metro Station reunited for a much-awaited comeback, as they completely imploded after the one record! I'm serious; they never even finished a proper follow-up. I guess it wasn't totally unexpected, as they were four kids who went from creating really charming bedroom pop to being suddenly thrust into a high-stakes world of industry shit. At eighteen, I wouldn't have been able to handle it either, but as "Shake It" faded, the phone blissfully continued to ring for me and Sluggo like never before. This is one of the great reveals about life behind the musical curtain. In the end, a hit is all that matters. The acts, to some respect, are transient in our journeys. Some will have iconic careers and transcend the landscape. Others are just a tune in time. But for us songwriters and producers, every success means that we get to run *The Amazing Race* a little longer.

## CHAPTER 25

# The Footnote

The other night I finally rewatched *Searching for Sugarman*, the brilliant Oscar-winning documentary about a South African pair's attempt to discover the whereabouts of their long-forgotten musical hero. When I nodded off later, I had the craziest of dreams: I was the Australian Rodriguez, but this sad fantasy had me arriving at the Sydney airport to the emptiest of receptions. No followers. No greeters. No groupies. Nothing. As I stood on empty stages, people ignored my every move. My nocturnal confidence continued to erode throughout the night. It was gruesome. The truth is, though my songs have resonated in the Land Down Under, I'm well aware of the fact that I mean next to nothing to those lovely people on any mass level. That goes for anywhere on this damn globe. In the end, my collaborators are bestsellers. I'm basically a glorified footnote, but, honestly, I wouldn't trade it for the world.

Now, you might ask yourself, "So what, in fact, does a day in the life of this footnote look like?" That's a totally fair request, as I've danced around the intricacies of my routine so far. Though it shifts often, here's a solid Polaroid snapshot of my actual work process as we speak.

I wake up at 5:59 AM. It's some *Groundhog Day* shit. Except, in the role of Sonny and Cher, it's usually a duo of yapping dogs that stirs me. I walk downstairs and prepare coffee for me and my wife. Because I'm on an endless intermittent fast, I watch masochistically as my kid joyously devours a blueberry muffin. Then once she's hopped aboard the school bus, I collapse onto the couch and attempt to spitball five or six song titles, which I deftly type into my phone. Then it's on to a hike or something of the (low-impact) cardio variety. After I return, I swiftly shower and sail off into my lyrical abyss. This tends to kick in with an hour-long deep dive into whomever it is that I'll be collaborating with later that day. Once I've studied their work, I try to absorb their voice, tendencies, inclinations, and the like. I watch YouTube interviews. I read any press I can find. Then, when I'm finally feeling a vibe, there are two possible scenarios.

One: I begin writing over a preexisting track idea that another writer sent over.

Two: I pull out my guitar and try to find a melody or, simply, a meter and cadence that I like.

Creativity can be a mindfuck. An internal bar set so high, it's like trying to pole-vault to the clouds. By alternating between these techniques, though, hopefully I can stimulate the word flow. I guess my primary goal is a pair of song starts: just a scratch verse and a chorus on each. I usually attempt two different stabs at one title and then try a third take with a different header altogether. A little inspiration. A little desperation. This way, I'm hedging my creative bets. On a solid day, this all happens fairly quickly. I can usually actualize what I'm hearing within two or three hours. If I'm running cold creatively, I do some deep breathing and scour Pinterest, scrolling for visuals that might stimulate some different kind of vibe. Once I actually stumble upon something inspiring, it instantly unlocks the gates, and my babbling flows smoothly.

Next, it's lunch. A half sandwich of the egg salad or turkey variety usually suffices.

Then I might just google myself.

This usually has the same dicey outcome of searching your symptoms on WebMD, but I'm obviously needy and desperate for some random mention in the *Romanian Times*. On a good press day I'm greeted with a tremendous descriptive adjective inserted before my name. That brings joy. On a bleak one, I get stabbed with a prison-made shank to the throat. As I'm typing this, in fact, I've just learned that *Billboard* named Karmin's "Acapella," a song that I wrote, one of the Top 10 Worst Songs of the Decade. Hooray! It's actually a victory of sorts. I mean, it's better to be loved or loathed than ignored.

I hate being alone. Loneliness tends to engulf me fairly quickly. I'm one of those folks who thrives on nonstop social interaction. The solitary moments of the day that most cherish completely demoralize me. That's why I'm usually pretty pumped when an artist finally arrives, as well as the occasional third collaborator—usually around 1 PM. It's like a playdate for my stunted self. Now, as I'm sure you've read in books and blogs, songwriting used to be an infinitely more intimate experience. But today, with the streaming competition so cluttered, there's an all-hands-on-deck/factory vibe on most pop tunes. The bulk of the old-school writers hate it. If I'm creating with a singer-songwriter or something more esoteric, I do prefer to keep it a one-on-one experience, so the sincerity within the tune isn't lost, but for broader shit I'm completely cool with the assembly line. In the end, it's like attempting to scribe a blockbuster film. Those scripts inevitably need a pool of polishers to get 'em to that mass-appeal level.

We usually kick the writing session off with a bit of small talk. Thirty to forty-five minutes of bullshitting that serves as that much-needed icebreaker before diving into a tune. This is akin to the first ardent spirit at a mixer. Social lubrication always raises the musical comfort level. During that "feeling each other out" time, however, I've already subtly shifted to a new mode: the therapist. This is one of the hardest parts of the art. It requires listening first. The artist hints at a bunch of Easter eggs about where they're at in their personal life and creative process. You have to hit your own private "mute" button to hear the clues. Sometimes it's agony taping my caffeine-powered mouth shut, but when I do, it inevitably leads to a more productive day from the jump.

A couple of tips:

1. If a completely contrived act says to you, "I already have a stack of soon-to-be radio hits about to drop. Today, I just

wanna create something avant-garde," then, my friend, you must kick them the fuck out of the lab right then and there. If you don't, I promise you this: It will be the single most brutal day of your year. Think about it. You could be at the beach or skiing or jerking off or whatever your thing is. It would most certainly be a more pleasurable afternoon than playing second fiddle to some poseur's artier inclinations that will never see the light of day.

2. If an introspective artist tells you that she was "up all night breaking up with my asshole of a boyfriend. He's shattered my existence. I have nothing," then, whatever you do, be sympathetic to her plight, and don't try to force a "hit." On this day, if she wants to write at all, she probably just wants to write as a form of catharsis. If you happen to nail it, it'll be that big blockbuster of an emotional tune that will ruin every day of her asshole of an ex's godforsaken life when he hears it day and night on the radio. If you miss, you did a good thing karmically either way. Just follow her lead.

There are tons of musical social cues to follow, though, so that's why I spend that first half-hour focused on listening. Then it's finally time to dive in. Even though we're essentially creating something from nothing, a co-write usually takes a mere four to six hours. (In Nashville, I'd say three to four hours, as they have both craft and time-management skills completely dialed in. They don't fuck around.)

## BONUS CUT

Yes, you should always come with a hip-pocketed agenda, but wait patiently for any opening to reveal it. Don't just jam that shit in. Finesse it. Some days the window doesn't present itself. That's okay too. Just remember to ignore all of your usual inner songwriting idiosyncrasies and focus on making an actual connection with the collaborator. If the song that results is dripping in authenticity, it might just resonate on a much deeper level.

As we approach hour two, hopefully my idea or a better one is in play. If we're making any semblance of headway, then the mood gets lighter across the board. Some days, I'm paired with topline warriors who've come prepped with supercool visuals and content. On those days, my primary role in the room might be melodies or editing. On other afternoons, I've written with victims of a curious laryngitis that disables them from issuing any content whatsoever. Then it's time for heavy lifting. Either way, I still have to bring it. It all comes down to a combination of an original perspective, solid preparation, and luck.

When it's time to cut the demo vocal, I, as the spawn of MTV, sit back on the couch, close my eyes, and try to create a mental music video to the tune we're laying down. If the visuals swirl swiftly, I know we have something. Ultimately, my goal is pretty simple—a tune that's faithful to the artist's song journey to date, but has a few unique moments interspersed to help separate it from the pile.

As we say our farewells, we casually exchange social media information. That's always an awkward dance. Then we mutually follow each other on said platforms. About 50 percent of the time, we take a commemorative photo with slightly forced smiles and we share it on our respective feeds. There is indeed a certain protocol to this nonsense. That's why it truly fucks with your head when you get immediately unfollowed a day or so after a session. That's happened to me on a few occasions. The Australian singer-songwriter Dean Lewis comes to mind. Joe Jonas as well! Both unfollowed me a week or so after our co-write. Maybe I posted too many lame photos of sunsets? The fact that I even noticed these cuts says infinitely worse things about my fragile ego. As the sun slides to twilight, I usually embrace a glass of wine as my head stirs up tons of musical overthinking and a boxed set of regrets. During those final few hours before sleep takes hold, I'll rehash the day's song a hundred times in an attempt to fix whatever's broken, knowing full well that the artist

The footnote.

will be writing with another (younger and better-looking) collaborator in just twelve hours or so.

While brushing my teeth, I'll question why I'm still doing this with my life.

By the time I hit the pillow, this footnote can't wait to do it all again.

## CHAPTER 26

# The Monsters of Soft Rock

As I came of age musically, I became obsessed with the genre swivel from punk to a polished jazz/soul that Paul Weller, Elvis Costello, Joe Jackson, and even Sting had accomplished. Honestly, that 180 was fuckin' rad to me. To risk abandoning millions of angsty fans at the height of their fame was really as bold a pivot as it got, and it brilliantly paid off for them all. Well, in the late aughts, my Spidey sense started telling me that it was time to make a swift pivot as well. Every day I could sense the imminent demise of pop-punk, as the decline began to resemble the death of '80s hair bands, to use JD's original blueprint. Things were so bloated with uniformity at that point that if Sluggo and I didn't switch it up ASAP, I was sure we'd be pigeonholed when the scene inevitably imploded. If you had told me that disco-hating Chicago DJ Steve Dahl had thrown an "EMO SUCKS" night in Comiskey Park and exploded a pile of our CDs sky-high, I wouldn't have been the least bit surprised.

We initially attempted to shift genre gears with a supercool downtown NYC band called The Virgins. The record was well received (I guess "Rich Girls" is still somewhat of an East Village classic), but I just didn't get the sense that Sluggo and I would ever be accepted into the indie rock fraternity as writers/producers. I mean, we definitely had no Yeah Yeah Yeahs or TV on the Radio on our résumé.

R&B? Our tracks didn't have that Timbaland or Neptunes knock, so that wasn't gonna happen either. And we weren't Nashville cats. Props due to Kinky Friedman for paving the way, but we feared we were a bit too unfiltered New York tribe to permeate the Buckle of the Bible Belt.

**BONUS CUT**

Sluggo's first and only Music Row session ended the moment his co-writer fervently announced, "Today, we need to write a song about the scream of an unborn child being aborted!"
OK then.

There was however, one potential rebirth for us . . .
Hot AC.
I began listening to all of the pillars of Hot AC (Hot Adult Contemporary—possibly the least sexy format name in the history of radio) after numerous stays at the lower-cost, slightly run-down Le Parc Suite Hotel in West Hollywood. I probably crashed there thirty times over two years. The hotel had a fun, grimy rooftop pool scene that was just a circus of fascinating on the daily. There was Depeche Mode Dave swimming with his kid. A just-discovered Kings of Leon in the elevator down. An uncomfortable Martin Landau sighting. The paparazzi chasing the *American Idol* Top 10 who were holed up in the hotel during tour rehearsals. Every up-and-coming MC with entourage in tow. It was a bastion of trippy.

**BONUS CUT**

One early morning on that very same Le Parc roof, I was attempting to write a little something. As I furiously bashed out a lyric with my headphones on blast, my eyes couldn't help but stare at two drunken girls in bikinis sloppily making out with each other in the pool. I was probably sitting forty feet away from the action, but man, it was some gripping shit. As they continued at it, I struggled to get a better glimpse, just as the rising West Hollywood sun started exploding in my eyes. The glare completely blinded me. I closed my eyes to let them cool down. When I opened them, I saw these two silhouettes hovering over my head.

"Hi. Whatcha doin'?" one asked as I struggled to connect my corneas.

"Oh, wow. Hi. Nuthin' much. Just doing a little writing. What's up with you guys?" I awkwardly inquired.

The girls continued groping each other in front of me as they remained in this massive solar blur. Then, just as the sun fell behind the one random cloud in the sky, the drunker of the two detonated the bomb.

"We met last week on the TV show *Extreme Makeover*. We both just had $20,000 of cosmetic surgery!" she happily exclaimed.

The other interjected, "My nose used to be huge! Now it's gonna be a sweet little button!"

At that exact moment, my eyes finally regained their focus. I was staring at a sea of waterlogged bandages, bruises, and swellings. The first continued, "ABC put us up here at Le Parc until we're fully recovered for the reveal episode. We're so bored. And the Vicodin didn't kick in yet, so we decided to wake up, get fucked up, and have some fun." The other jumped in. "I love her. Isn't she fuckin' hawt?!"

It was all impeccably Hollyweird and par for the Le Parc course.

Though Le Parc was definitely the strangest train wreck of scenes, the more time I spent hanging around that roof, the more I focused on the soundtrack that blared by the pool. It was always the same loop of fifteen tunes that I referred to as "the Monsters of Soft Rock"— Train, Uncle Kracker, Sugar Ray, The Fray, Rob Thomas, et cetera. I hadn't previously gone particularly deep on any of these cats, but as they ran laps in my ears, I began to study the crafting on their hits and fell in love with the vibe. These bands had concocted timeless, multigenerational tunes. Their writing was broader than mine. A hit with one could be career altering for me. I had to get in those rooms.

And that's when I connected with Train.

Sluggo and I had cut a record with a Jersey-based singer-songwriter named Charlotte Sometimes in '08 that had received a crumb of VH1 love. Pat Monahan, Train's front man, had caught wind of it, dug it, and invited Charlotte out to open on his solo run. When the tour ended, Pat solicited the help of our mutual buddy, songwriter/producer Greg Wattenberg, in finding potential collaborators. Like the mensch he is, Greg recommended Sluggo and myself.

I met Pat at a Starbucks on Twenty-Sixth Street, and on first impression found him to be one of the more engaging yet challenging personalities I'd ever met. He had this dark, über-sardonic streak that kept you off balance (I was obviously very pro-snark and up for the challenge). Pat, Sluggo, and I began collaborating later that week. We wrote two or three things. I've gotta say, he was real good. Having spent the bulk of the previous four years throwing down with kids just north of age twenty-one, Pat's chops were on a whole other level. He basically wrote circles around me that first session. The following afternoon, I returned much sharper. We wrote a song called "Stay on Me." I fought for the "Stay on Me" lyric in the chorus. I got the sense Pat wasn't sold on it, though. As it came together, it was probably a bit too earnest for my taste, but it packed enough clever Pat-isms that it seemed like something good could come of it. We made plans to have dinner later that evening. As I set off to John's on Twelfth Street, my favorite neighborhood haunt, I texted JD. "Having dinner with Pat Monahan. Come through." JD's response was pretty muted on the scale of enthusiasm, but he decided to rally over.

And what a dinner it was!

As we dove into the avocado bruschetta, JD and I rapidly realized Pat was like a one-man eclipse. He told us he had written eighty songs over half a year or so and was now creatively confused. On top of that, he was frustrated at his label's questionable support of both Train's previous full-length and his own solo debut—both of which had kinda died on the vine. He was well aware that they had begun to abandon him for younger, flavor-of-the-month models. He even referenced our own Boys Like Girls, with a little dash of disdain. Then, about halfway through the baked ziti, Pat casually mentioned that he had already emailed "Stay on Me" over to his A&R guy, who'd immediately flung it in the junkyard. The A&R was a guy named Pete Ganbarg. Though not employed by Columbia at the time, Pete was now the go-to freelance A&R for hire, occupying the forefront of that space. It was a pretty nifty pivot. Labels would bring him in to oversee records that were slipping through the cracks internally, and he was able to work from his couch without much interference.

The following morning, JD and I went for a lengthy power walk along the Hudson. These walks were a paramount part of our dynamic. So many of our respective moves and creations were born out of our sad excuse for low-impact cardio. That AM, I told JD that I firmly believed Train could have a huge comeback. Pat's tunes were so unique in their DNA that they spoke to everyone. He was freakishly gifted both as a writer and vocalist. I concluded my passionate diatribe by stating that if we didn't start dabbling in broader genres, the Mighty Seventh Floor would ultimately collapse.

He pondered my hot take for a bit and then the conversation shifted back to a debate over the best MTV VJs of the network's first decade.

The next day, I hopped off the elevator, and who was sitting up front with JD?

Pat Monahan.

You see, that's how we all built together in those years. We trusted each other's instincts. Crush picked up Train, and JD spent days combing through the eighty or so songs that Pat had written over the previous year. Then JD noticed one title that leaped out at him from the entire batch cluttering up his stick drive. The tune was called "Hey, Soul Sister." He decided to give it a spin, and he absolutely flipped. I guess he tried to get Pete on board, but I'm not sure Pete got the song. You know what, in Pete's defense, I didn't really hear it either! I think the combination of Train and a peppy ukulele was just too farfetched for my basic ears. Still, JD was fuckin' relentless about it. He pounded on Columbia's doors until he could muster up any morsel of Soul Sister interest. In the music industry, success has many fathers and creepy uncles, but as I know firsthand, there were very few believers in that building at the time. After much hammering, the label half-heartedly agreed to release it as the first single. At the same time, Bob, a ridiculously sharp and savvy guy himself, began shaping some brilliant branding ideas with Pat for the group. He was certain that Train needed to build a culture around themselves for this comeback. He found inspiration in the Jimmy Buffett Margaritaville empire. He actually kept a large parrothead hat behind his desk to fuel the muse. Since Train had broken out of San Francisco, and had deep radio roots in the community, Bob suggested that we go back in and write a Northern California anthem. The resulting tune was "Save Me, San Francisco." One of my favorite sessions to date. It was so loose and fun. Pat and I spitballed punch line after punch line over Sluggo's fierce Stones-y guitar riff. The whole song was absolutely effortless. The Crush crew flipped. It became the album's title track.

> **BONUS CUT**
>
> Bob's inner parrothead was spot on. "Save Me, San Francisco" eventually became both an anthem for the city and the band. It was the rallying cry for the 2010 world champion San Francisco Giants, and Train played it live on the field as the team strode by to get their World Series rings.

Then, right before the album wrapped, JD played "Marry Me." It was our "Stay on Me" song, completely reworked by Pat. He did the most incredible job saving this little nugget from the scrap heap and turning it into a matrimonial classic. People thank me for it all the time, but I have to credit where it's rightfully due. By trashing my "Stay On Me" lyric, Pat elevated it tenfold.

In time, "Marry Me" went double platinum. "Save Me, San Francisco" went gold, but most importantly, "Hey, Soul Sister," the song that nobody saw coming, became the biggest-selling single in the 120-year history of Columbia Records. The rebirth of Train was just a massive game changer for all involved.

My friendship with Pat Monahan has had many perks to date (how about a 3 AM hallucinatory hotel room jam session with a revved-up Dennis Quaid, where we screamed along to Quaid's acoustic guitar covers, including his inspired take on Snoop Dogg's "Gin and Juice"?), but the crown jewel had to be the day we spent sailing with the entire Kennedy family at the Hyannis compound. As we rode those choppy waters, on a boat jam-packed with fifty or so folks, the Camelot clan prodded Pat to sing "Hey, Soul Sister" a capella. At that moment, it was the biggest song in the universe. We all cheerily sang along, and it was a beautiful, Ralph Lauren–ad worthy moment. When Pat was done, he turned toward me and deadpanned, "Hey, Sam—bet they won't ask you to sing 'Shake It.'" It was impeccably executed Monahan snark. There was only one tiny problem: He didn't factor in the junior high constituency of Kennedy spawn sitting a few feet away. One kid heard the remark, and immediately interjected, "Wait! You did 'Shake It'?" A few others started buzzing with excitement. Then another inquired, "What other songs have you done?" Now our entire end of the boat was staring at me like an old-school EF Hutton commercial. I explained that I was merely a songwriter, but I offered up the likes of Boys Like Girls's "The Great Escape" and "Love Drunk" and We the Kings's "Check Yes, Juliet." The Kennedy youth started freaking the fuck out. It was perfect. I gave Pat the slyest of winks. He started laughing profusely. This would be the one moment I ever trumped my significantly more relevant friend.

Continuing down mellower path, next I aggressively chased after Uncle Kracker. Kracker was coming off two or three singles that I absolutely flipped over. I had multiple people reach out to Kracker on my behalf, but it was actually Pete Ganbarg, who had left his consultancy at the end of Train and was now running A&R at Atlantic, who blessedly made it happen. I was pretty geeked for the session, but when Kracker arrived at the studio that day, I had to push pause.

1. He didn't really want to be there. He just seemed out of sorts in New York.
2. He looked like he had imbibed the entire Lynchburg, Tennessee, Jack Daniel's factory the previous evening.
3. He brought a "handler" with him.

Now, the word *handler* is a tricky one. I mean a "plus one" with no context added other than procuring food, beverages, or marijuana. In all honesty, I was somewhat new to the handler thing. Beyoncé (lovely, BTW) had dropped by the studio once when I was working with Kelly Rowland, and she had a few minions along those lines. Still, it felt a bit out of context for an artist of Kracker's stature. Don't get me wrong, he was coming off a bunch of hits, but it rang peculiar. In my experiences up to that point, pop-rock guys tended to run solo and kept the writing process very grounded.

The handler in question's name was JT, and within minutes Kracker sent him out to the store to grab some soda and candy. When he returned, JT and I began to kick it while Kracker fired off a flurry of texts to his management, in what I would guess were desperate pleas to shorten our session at hand. JT told me that he'd previously been signed as an artist to EMI. When that dream died, he took a gig at Tower Records on Sunset. Eventually he met Marilyn Manson, who he ran around with for a few years as an assistant, before linking up with Kracker.

Meanwhile, Kracker was straight puffed out. We were only about thirty minutes into writing, when he began to nod the fuck off. As Sluggo strummed away, Kracker's eyelids crumbled into nothingness. He actually muttered the words, "The acoustic guitar makes me sleepy" before crashing. The day was devolving at a rapid pace, but I did realize something in those moments of snore. JT was kinda awesome. He was my age and had identical influences. He was wacky, whip smart, and quite talented. We began messing around with some ideas and he chimed in with some real zingers. Why was the handler throwing out lyrics? That's a stellar question, and in any other situation, I would've booted him the hell out—but honestly, at least it was something. Eventually the caffeine kicked in. Kracker got a second wind and began to really bring it. Once he was totally coherent, he turned out to be a super fun and talented hombre as well. It was a blast hanging with those guys. By day's end, we got two songs out of the session.

A few months later, JD strutted back to the studio with an advance copy of the Uncle Kracker record in his hand. I guess one of our tunes had made the cut. Then JD said, "Look at the credits closely."

As I surveyed the sleeve, it seemed a "JT Harding" had written five songs on the record.

I was quite confused.

The handler?!

He continued, "I don't think this kid has a publishing deal. Maybe we should sign him?"

Within days, we partnered with our pals Matt Pincus, Carianne Marshall (from my DreamWorks days), and Ron Perry at Songs Music Publishing and created the joint venture Mighty Seven Songs. JT Harding was our first signing, and he went on to scribe several chart toppers, including the three-million-selling "Smile" with Uncle Kracker, "Somewhere in My Car" with Keith Urban, "Somewhere with You" and "Bar at the End of the World" for Kenny Chesney, and Blake Shelton's number one smash, "Sangria." He was the spark that launched a ten-year run for our ragtag little outfit that grew to include fifteen awesome writers. We still owe the bulk of the company's success to the handler, so lesson learned. Never underestimate the guy in the room procuring the Milky Ways and Mountain Dews. He might just two-step his way into the Country Music Hall of Fame someday.

As both Train and Uncle Kracker singles continued to dominate radio, a bunch of record labels went out and signed similar artists with whom they hoped they could follow the same roadmap of reinvention. I got a call from a guy named Stu Fine, who was running a small indie, 429 Records, and had noticed my name tied to both releases.

BONUS CUT

Back in the day, Stu helmed the influential hip-hop label Wild Pitch and had actually flirted with signing me in my early years, so I always kept a special place for him in my heart. Anyone who didn't laugh me out of the building always gets extra credit.

As Stu began his sales pitch, I learned that he had just inked Blues Traveler and wondered if I might be interested in making a "comeback" record with them. He worked me over real good. He didn't need to. I probably would've done it for free. This was life coming full circle back to those early Nightingale Bar days when Jaik Miller and I were young, wide-eyed East Village rats watching those guys jam to a packed house for hours on end. It just felt kinda destined, so we got cracking on the BT record a couple of weeks later.

Now, it was fairly obvious from the jump that these guys had zero interest in chasing Train or following any of Stu's radio playbook whatsoever. They were open to any idea as long as it was true to their musical code. In his hilarious memoir, *Suck and Blow: And Other Stories I'm Not Supposed to Tell*, front man John Popper likened our record to a Quentin Tarantino film, meaning it had that same unfiltered, experimental excitement. I had no fear of trial and error with those dudes. My only request was that all solos stay under thirty-two bars. I think it was the editing down of those ten-minute improvisations in my days of ringtone making that had exhausted my patience. To a jam band, that was a massive slap in the face, but, surprisingly, they acquiesced.

Honestly, every day was a joy with the Traveler guys. First and foremost, Popper was the definitive rock-harmonica slayer of his generation. No one could touch him. Watching him lay down his rapid-fire solos was quite moving, but that was only half the fun. John was one of the wittiest, craziest stream-of-consciousness spouters. He made the sound bite of life a little more bearable. He was one of my favorites.

We were sailing into our last week of vocals when, one morning, I was awakened with the worst news ever from New York.

My old pal Jaik Miller had died.

It was both devastating and bizarre. I mean, can you imagine how surreal it was to be working that day with Blues Traveler, the very band that lit the match for Jaik in NYC? Their scene was responsible for Jaik's (and then subsequently my) introduction to the city. I teary-eyed my way to the studio and sat the band down.

The late, great Jaik Milller.

"Guys, I've got terrible news. Jaik died last night."

The room fell silent.

A sad Brendan, the drummer, replied, "Oh, that's awful."

A shocked Chan on guitar chimed in, "Oh no."

A misty-eyed Johnny burst out, "Shit! Jaik was such an awesome guy!"

Then he paused for about ten seconds and continued.

"Hey, how many vocal takes are we going for today? I've gotta deal with some personal stuff later this afternoon."

Within seconds, they all continued conversing as if the previous exchange had never occurred. Now don't get me wrong, this was by no means a show of disrespect to Jaik's memory. It's just that this band in particular had lived through such a lengthy laundry list of tragedies by this point that they seemed 100 percent numb to this kind of news. In time, you do learn to live on without the people you've lost, but I really did feel awful for all they had endured. In some ways, I could relate, though. As I had a mom and dad who were both dancing with cancer during that time, I was beginning to get pretty emotionally calloused myself.

After the Blues Traveler record wrapped, our fam headed back east to spend Christmas with my ailing folks. We tried to spark the joy, but it was the glummest of holiday hangs. Then on December 27, as I was packing to return west, I got a crazy call from JD. NBC had just asked Train to perform the (now traditional) New Year's Eve cover of John Lennon's "Imagine" live at the top of Times Square at the stroke of midnight. He asked me if I might be interested in producing it, as the background tracks on these things are always prerecorded. I didn't even give him a breath to second-guess. I knew I needed this for my soul. Within minutes I rolled the Saw Mill straight to Broadway.

**BONUS CUT**

I was obsessed with the *Dick Clark New Year's Eve* spectaculars of the early '80s. Those year-ends were the rare occasions that my mom let me stay up late as a kid. I'd post up on the couch and soak in all the coked-up sitcom actors fumbling through abominable cue card introductions of Rick James, Rick Springfield, and such. I should've been exhausted, but all that chemical energy and the epic Times Square performances seeped through the screen right into my tiny self.

I spent the next couple of days in a furious mad dash around various downtown studios tracking Train with the help of my pal Josh Edmondson. We had simultaneous sessions in Nashville with our homie, string arranger Mark Evitts. We even threw a choir on it. From my end, I just wanted this cover to be an absolute event.

When New Year's Eve arrived, our crew and respective families were blessed to experience the ball drop from high up in the sky on Forty-Fourth Street, standing right beside the band as they performed. With the whole world watching, and the crowds of tiny, ant-like people below, we soaked in every mind-blowing second. As the confetti rained down, I couldn't help but do a ton of melancholic reflecting up there. I thought about how f'n lucky I was to experience this moment. I thought about all the years of grinding. I thought of my folks and the oncological hell they were living in. I thought about Jaik Miller. It was a pretty heavy night of auld lang synes.

## CHAPTER 27

# Burn, Hollywood, Burn

Greenwich Village was my perfect playground for twenty years or so, but as I kissed forty, the apple began to sour. I'd spent the last two years exhaustedly shuttling back and forth to Hollywood, where the industry had shifted overnight. The transient nature of it all left me feeling incredibly out of sorts. Also, as a labor of love, Jen had been writing spec film scripts for a decade—and then, out of nowhere, she sold one to Imagine Entertainment. Ron Howard! Brian Grazer! It was a huge deal. It was also another indicator to head west, so on short notice, we packed up our stuff and rented a house in the Los Feliz Hills section of Los Angeles sight unseen.

We had very little downtime to acclimate.

Within days, we toured Joey's new school, and it was indeed some surreal shit. A swimming pool. Outdoor cafeteria. This definitely wasn't NYC. Toward the end of the jaw-dropping visit, the admissions director told us that another family had just enrolled in the school from Stockholm and that they were waiting in the front office for their tour.

"He's in music, too!"

What's his name?' I anxiously inquired.

"Martin Sandberg, but I think he's known as . . ."

My heart sank.

"Max Martin."

About forty-five seconds later, we were standing awkwardly in front of the King of Pop Songwriting, exchanging pleasantries. He asked me if he knew any of my songs. I slunk my head and said, "Doubtful."

We bid adieu, and as I slowly slumped outside with my wife and kid, I provided a little context.

"Do you know those songs you really like? You know, the ones you always want me to turn up in the car as opposed to mine, which you feign interest in? Well, that's the guy who wrote them."

Needless to say, the move was initially pretty traumatic for me. I was completely discombobulated for months. Then, just when I started to settle into a routine, I got the most unexpected job offer: on the TV series *SMASH*, which was filming . . . in New York. From the moment the music supervisor, Jen Ross, now one of my closest pals, reached out to sell me on the show, I knew I was probably in for a world of hurt.

"NBC wants an edgy music producer for the season. They don't want to go safe. Can you send us a reel of anything you've done that's more cutting edge?"

Against my better judgment, I threw together a sampler of my "edgier" stuff. The Virgins. Neon Trees. Coheed and Cambria. I knew I'd get laughed out of the building, but it was all I had. The phone went silent. Then Jen Ross reached out again a week later.

"So the consensus at NBC is that your stuff is way too edgy. Do you have anything softer?"

Softer?

Oh, I could definitely squeeze the Charmin. On a lark, I shot over a revised reel with David Archuleta, Kelly Rowland, Nikki Jean, and Andy Grammer.

Guess who got hired on the spot?

Now *SMASH* was NBC's attempt at a *Glee*-like phenomenon. It was a soapy take on the inner workings of Broadway. I'm certainly no expert on these matters, but to me, at least, it felt like a network TV reach. I had a hunch that Middle America would have little interest in insider Sondheim jokes, but the executive producer was Steven Spielberg (!), and the gig would pay for me to commute back and forth to NYC, where I could see my folks—who I missed dearly. That sealed the deal.

The showrunner was Josh Safran, a veteran of *Gossip Girl* and a sweet and funny character. He explained that the *SMASH* gig would involve producing thirty-plus songs for the newly introduced rival East Village-y/Off Broadway musical *Hit List*. That meant collaborating with everyone from *American Idol*'s own Kat McPhee and the underutilized (pre-*Hamilton*) Leslie Odom Jr. to the illustrious Academy Award winners Anjelica Huston and Jennifer Hudson. When I signed on, I was under the illusion that I'd be writing tunes for the series, given that was ultimately my expertise. But from the moment my contract locked, that notion went out the window. Safran was deeply entrenched in the off-Broadway scene, so he bet all of his money on up-and-comers (future legends) like Benj Pasek and Justin Paul—who we will meet up with again shortly—and Joe Iconis (*Be More Chill*). I'd never heard of any of these folks, but they were an incredibly tight-knit bunch.

Once I touched back down in the Apple with my team in tow, Megan Hilty, the show's colead and a Broadway vet, was the first actress to track on the docket. I believe this was her first network lead in a series as well. Megan showed up to that initial vocal session with a tray of cookies for my squad. What's not to love? I'm a hooker with a heart of gold. I can be bought pretty easily.

We began tracking, and Megan was so kind and complimentary. She had the sweetest smile. This felt like the beginning of a most enjoyable spin. Then after a few vocal run-throughs, she had an issue with the song's key and asked me to lower it a full step. Megan was a terrific warbler, but the tune was sitting in a less-than-perfect place in her voice. This happens in most sessions. As a producer, you've gotta ensure that the song lands in the singer's sweet spot. As I began to transpose the key, *SMASH*'s music coordinator, sitting in the back of the control room, told Megan to wait one minute as she phoned the production office, just to make sure that the key change was acceptable to all of the higher-ups. These words were not well received, as Megan gave a slightly testy response. I didn't know how to proceed. After about four minutes of dead air, we got the go-ahead to transpose the song. And within a couple of takes, Megan killed it. When she left, I escorted her to the elevator, where she gave me a hug and suggested we grab a celebratory meal soon. *SMASH* was off to an amazing start!

Ten minutes later, my phone rang with a panicked Jen Ross on the other end.

"Okay, I know this sounds insane, but Megan already called the producers of the show. She doesn't want to work with you anymore. The fact that you didn't immediately transpose the song for her and made her wait in the booth for a response from production flipped her out. I explained to them that this wasn't your doing, but just be prepared, it's now an issue."

What the actual fuck?!

I reiterated to Jen that it was the show's own coordinator who made the phone call. I had zero to do with that individual or chain of command. The more I thought about it, the angrier I got. Then, after a little more back and forth, I bitchily replied, "Jen, they can fire my ass. This is obviously the wrong fit." Honestly, I meant it. Though the money was great, from that moment alone I could already tell this gig resembled little of what I was initially pitched. I was midway through packing my bags, when as legend (probably tall tales) would have it, Steven Spielberg and Bob Greenblatt spoke up in my defense and placated Megan, so I was asked to stay on.

I was more jazzed about working with Jennifer Hudson, anyway.

I was such a fan of J.Hud's vocals, from her first *American Idol* cover on. I knew it would be a religious-like experience working with her. Then, like clockwork, I got another frustrated text from an exasperated Jen Ross.

"I'm so sorry. I know this sounds awful, but Jennifer will only cut vocals with her personal vocal producer from L.A. NBC's flying him in."

It was mortifying. I had produced the song she was about to sing, yet I was told that I couldn't attend the session? That's not really how this shit is supposed to work. And to add insult to injury, this session was going down on my turf! Unacceptable. I decided to casually drop by anyway and feel out the vibe. I walked into my empty control room and within minutes, Jennifer's entire entourage, plus a gaggle of network execs, strutted into the room and immediately took over the place. I awkwardly attempted some casual conversation. Nothing landed. They were all pleasant, J.Hud easily the friendliest, but I got the sense that the rest couldn't give a flying fuck who I was. Finally, I asked her crew leader if there was anything else I could help with.

"Yeah, man. Is there any good food in this hood?"

"Absolutely," I replied. "There's an Italian spot on Twenty-Seventh Street that is real solid."

"Great. Hey, why don't you run over there and get us some food?"

This command was barked directly in front of the NBC bosses!

I blurted a terse response of "Hey, I think you might've gotten it wrong, but I AM NOT THAT GUY."

The room fell silent.

Translation: Nobody puts Baby in the corner.

In hindsight, I don't blame that hungry fella, nor Megan Hilty or any of these other folks, for my disappointing experience on the show. Everyone involved in the production seemed to be on edge and out of sorts. Truth be told, the behind-the-scenes show on *SMASH* was significantly more interesting than what you saw on-screen. The drama. The hookups. It was like a real-life *The Bold and the Beautiful*. I desperately fought to make it through the season, but each week my creative muscles atrophied further. When the show finally wrapped and was subsequently canceled, it was pretty ironic that a tune I produced, "Voice in a Dream," got nominated for an Emmy. It felt like a nice slice of retribution for months of misery.

Post-*SMASH*, I'd finally begun to settle back into L.A. for a few months when I got a somewhat random call asking if I'd be interested in writing a demo for a movie musical that Fox was developing. It was a reworking of the life story of P. T. Barnum. Hugh Jackman was attached, but the studio hadn't greenlit anything. They agreed to pay me a nice little demo fee, so I figured it was probably worth the moon shot. I sat down with a couple of writer pals, Boots and Shebby, and we laid down our idea of an epic opening number for this thing. It was called "Welcome to the Big Top," and it was dope. Real dope! We submitted it, and within days received a call from the film's director, Michael Gracey. He wanted to make a deal for the song! All the *SMASH* disappointment instantly dissipated. This was some big-time shit. A week later, I was flown first class to NYC to cut Hugh Jackman on the tune.

Hugh Jackman and the not-so-greatest showman.

Hugh showed up promptly to cut the vocal, and man, he was a total charmer. Kind and gracious. We spent a couple of hours shedding it together as Michael Gracey and a few of the project's producers watched with bated breath. It was a seamless experience. Tons of positivity. We wrapped, and I cheerily hopped the elevator four floors down to my pal Adam Schlesinger's spot in the same building to celebrate. The next day I rushed back to L.A. with my team to mix the demo.

Now, this Barnum project was Michael Gracey's first film. He'd been a hugely successful commercial director in Australia, but this was his entry into Hollywood. He was a brilliant guy, but communicating with him wasn't the easiest. After many revisions, he finally approved our song and decided to use it as the main theme for the sizzle reel he delivered to Fox. I must say, he did an amazing job. They *had* to greenlight this thing! Over the next few months, I resumed writing on various records and began to put the Barnum thing out of mind. But then the Barnum calls seemed to slow. Eventually, I sent a friendly check-in note to Michael Gracey, but in his reply I noticed a slight change in his tone. He kept it real brief.

Ruh-roh!

Finally, half a year later, a friend emailed me that day's headline story:

"Fox Eyes Summer Start for *The Greatest Showman on Earth* Starring Hugh Jackman; Will be the first original live-action movie musical in 22 Years. All songs will be written by Benj Pasek & Justin Paul."

As I read the piece, I literally got nauseated. I'd been *SMASH*-ed again! I immediately hit Michael, but he told me not to worry.

"Your song is still in the studio draft. I will be sure to let you know what happens as we get into rehearsal."

Famous last words.

Then Michael Gracey flew the communication coop.

The movie premiered in December 2017, and though it initially underperformed at the box office, a few weeks into its theatrical run, it found its audience and exploded. Man, it stung. Pasek and Paul are lovely guys, and their *Showman* stuff was incredible, but for me, it was completely demoralizing.

A few months later, I randomly ran into Michael on Hollywood Boulevard. He was pleasant enough, but he avoided eye contact and certainly didn't address the song. I just wish he had been direct with me earlier. I mean, look at me. Obviously, I can handle rejection. This book is like three-hundred-something pages of rebuff. I'm not sure what I was searching for on the sidewalk that day, but I went home irked and promptly unfriended him on Facebook. Yes, I am still a petulant kid.

The truth is, in most circumstances, I'm a pretty positive human. I don't want to dwell on this firing squad, but this was just a tiny sampling of my small- and silver-screen flameouts to date. There have obviously been a few scattered wins interspersed, but many more bombs than trophies. After each and every implosion, I wake up and acknowledge that I'm too old for this kind of bullshit. But then somehow, in some dark way, my inner wick gets heated up, and sud-

LA '93. Me and Don Lunetta.

denly I'm back up under the blowtorch. I guess I really do love the scald. Burn, Hollywood, burn.

**BONUS CUT**

As I type this, I've been writing and producing the songs for NBC's top priority drama *Ordinary Joe*. I think this one's got Emmy written all over it.

Editor's note: Sadly, *Ordinary Joe* was cancelled right before we went to print.

## CHAPTER 28

# Golden Ticket

Congratulations! You've just unearthed the elusive Wonka Bar Golden Ticket that you've wished for your entire creative life. Tomorrow, an honest-to-goodness famous artist will arrive at your very own factory to write a tune with you. I'm talking about a bona fide bigwig! This is huge for you, but please be careful what you wish for. **I mean, there are little surprises around every corner, but nothing too dangerous.** Thankfully, you have a pal like me who can kick these ten priceless tips in your direction. I mean, that's what friends are for, right?

1. Before the famous artist arrives, make sure your studio is clean, but not pristine. Make a little effort, but nothing that says, "You deserve the **Everlasting Gobstopper** of cleaning products." I'm a slob myself, so given that my studio is a fuckin' dump, I've often taken a casual approach instead of a spotless one. Truthfully, though, I'm not so sure my layers of dust have ever been a good first impression for me in any way whatsoever.

2. When the famous artist waltzes through the door, look enthused, but not creepily overeager. **Don't just stand there; do something.** Remember, starstruck = death. The music illuminati have been blessed with guard dog–like nostrils that can sniff out thirst a mile away! If you lock eyes and

slobber in a creepy manner one too many times, you're done before the first chord is played.

3. That being said, when you and the famous artist start to converse, do not take the sly approach of "I have no fuckin' clue who you are" or "I didn't take a minute to listen to your stuff." That's a novice trick, and it'll completely backfire. It creates a massive chasm from minute one. Notable folks crave some semblance of attention. They've earned it. Respect their catalog. **If you don't, you lose. Good day, sir.**

4. If and when you decide to openly profess your love for the famous artist's body of work, always shout out a B-side or a slept-on track as your personal favorite. NEVER harp on their hit! Don't let the outcome of my Clive Davis meeting fool you. Only a rookie spotlights the smash. **Shall we press on?**

5. When you commence the writing process, in hour one it's imperative to reassure the famous artist that their creative input is "really great," even when it's wack as fuck. **So shines a good deed in a weary world.** Honesty is a wonderful virtue and all, but you haven't arrived there yet in your bond. Do not crush the most fragile of egos until you've built up a layer of trust.

6. You? You have nothing to fear, though. You've totally earned this moment, so don't take a passive approach with the famous artist. Let the others wilt in the star's intimidating presence. When I started out, the great Nile Rodgers taught me to attack every celebrity session with the furious pen of a screenwriter crafting the artist's sequel. Quite possibly the best advice I ever received. Immediately start guiding the famous artist's next musical transition with your very own script! The more you provide this cat with an original path, the more respect and admiration you'll earn. **It's the only way if you want it just right.**

7. Like a storyteller stepping to the mic at The Moth for the very first time, you must bring your absolute "A" game. **Time is a precious thing. Never waste it.** Tons of preparation is a must. There's little wiggle room for

If the famous artist is a lead singer of a band, that means that, ninety-nine times out of one hundred, they are the ruling czar in the group's creative palace. Since the singer has most likely been the group's primary writer to date, they will fight to the death to keep the dynamic as is. He or she will never risk throwing the balance off axis. That's why you should always pass when you get a call from a label offering you the opportunity to work with the singer's bandmates sans the singer. The front person will always reject all songs written by the rest of the members without their involvement. **It happens every time; they all become blueberries!** Honestly, a complete outsider, a significant other, or a groupie has a better shot at landing a song on the record than the group's very own rhythm section!

complacency in songwriting as it is, but on this day more than any other, you better come correct. It's tough to construct your ark when the flood has already begun!

8. Many famous artists are professional charmers, but **there's no earthly way of knowing which direction they are going.** They're masters at the art of fabricating camaraderie, so there's a high probability that they will never become your real homie. On a good day, you just might have to face the fact that you only made a "glorified acquaintance," but think about it: that's not a complete whiff! As long as you receive a phone number or a social media follow at the end of the session, you did good! You'll still be able to pull a dinner-party flex on your non-industry friends by sending a friendly text to the famous artist—and who knows, you might even get a response!

9. Okay, truth is, a few of these famous artists are just dicks. Plain and simple. If you happen to get one, send 'em **where all the other bad eggs go: down the garbage chute.** Don't waste your time trying to game the outcome. Give it a solid

hour or so, and then fake a pulled hamstring or some shit and send them on their not-so-merry way. Personally, I've found famous-artist dicks to be more of an exception than rule, but if you happen to land that occasional asshole, don't let it smother your confidence. It's not you; it's them.

10. And in turn, some famous artists are absolutely wonderful. Kind, decent, selfless, first class. They'll exceed your each and every expectation. When you deal with a real one, trust me, **it's a musical lock!** Throughout this book, I've highlighted many of my favorites, but here's a few more lovely folks that miraculously landed in my own factory:

## Donna Summer

Toward the end of our run together, Duke Mushroom and I got to write a couple of songs with the Queen of Disco and our pal Mike Mangini. Those Donna sessions were hilarious. We laughed our collective faces off for three days straight. Sadly, neither of the resulting tunes were particularly special, and the label rightfully left them out with the cake in MacArthur Park. A couple of years later, though, I got a 9 PM, completely out-of-the-blue call from Donna asking me if I'd be down to roll by the Hit Factory studios on Fifty-Fourth Street so she could play me some new ideas she'd been shedding. Me? Really? In all sincerity, I didn't even think she had my phone number. But ten minutes later, Donna sent a town car to my spot that shuttled me uptown to the room where she was camped out. When I walked through the door, she greeted me with the biggest hug ever. I asked why she'd reached out to me of all people, as opposed to someone she'd actually had a biscuit of success with. She replied, "Because I loved your vibe and I thought you were real cool." How insane is that? Making a real impression on

The Queen's Court: Duke Mushroom, Donna Summer, me, and Mike Mangini.

an artist is so crucial. Even if your song doesn't see the light of day, you've left the gate open to connect again.

That night, Donna and I proceeded to bug out for hours. She was so generous and funny, and her new tunes were fabulous too. And then, when the clock struck midnight, I gave her a farewell hug and cabbed my ass back home. Sadly, that was our Last Dance. She passed a few years later, but I'm forever grateful for those few hours I spent loitering in the Queen's court. She was the shit.

## Billy Idol and Steve Stevens

Billy rolled up to the session on a Harley-Davidson Wide Glide. It made for the fiercest of introductions. His voice was still incredible. His ear as well. We knew we had something when he exclaimed that our tune-in-progress, "Rita Hayworth," had a nice bit of "Fuck You" while holding up his middle fingers with the slyest smile ever. Steve's guitar chops were obviously ridiculous. He shredded the solo in two takes. He even blasted his signature "Rebel Yell" Ray Gun effect. I kept my cool throughout the afternoon, but it was a total pinch-me session. By day's end, it would be hard to name a sweeter pair of gents than those two '80s giants whose poster once adorned my wall.

## Def Leppard

Phil Collen was one of the kindest guys I can recall. Gracious, with a great energy in the room. I had the pleasure of writing Def Leppard's "Fire It Up" with him. Phil arrived with his very own signature Jackson guitar. It sounded unbelievable. He kicked off the writing process by letting his riffs provide the initial musical bed. On some sessions, that's a topliner's worst nightmare, but Phil's choices were so tasty and spacious that it gave me tons of room to carve out a melody. Bonus points for his awe-inspiring workout regimen. I think this sexy hombre could easily bench-press my ass at will.

## Jewel

Jewel was an absolute sweetheart and complete beast in the studio. Mega talented. She had an unrivaled work ethic with zero fear of a fourteen-hour session. Obviously, she was totally self-contained as a writer, but wide open to collaboration as well. She usually started songs over sparse changes; then, once lyric phrases began to develop, she'd develop them chordally from there. She meticulously freestyled melodies until the

Deep in it with Jewel.

right lyric grabbed her. That's when the structure took place, and the resulting song flowed ridiculously easily. In sum, we probably logged a couple of weeks writing together. Couldn't have dug her more.

## Cyndi Lauper

Cyndi was a real trip. Duke Mushroom and I had a brief co-write with her back in the day, but what a kooky first impression. She sauntered through the door, looked me square in the eye, and said, "So you're the new hotshot? Well, trust me, it won't last, honey." Then she immediately dispatched me to Starbucks to fetch her a coffee. I happily obliged. I was and am a big fan. When we finally dove in, I loved her intensity and hyper-focus on our slightly world-beat-leaning tune. She layered walls of hand percussion on it. She was the most passionate of pros. Zero bullshit.

## Weezer

Crush made a career dream come true and paired me with Rivers Cuomo. We wrote a Weezer tune called "I Love the USA" that made a little noise. That might seem like small potatoes, but for me, as a Weezer fan, it was just the coolest shit ever. Rivers and I have subsequently written a few tunes since. My favorite is a jam called "Records," and hopefully it'll see the light of day before this book hits the streets. Rivers was both insanely melodic and lyrical, but open to chase any idea. He was obsessed with studying the evolution of pop songwriting. He was like a mad scientist dissecting the radio. I found that intellectual curiosity of song incredibly inspiring. He's a one-of-a-kind awesome fella.

## Goo Goo Dolls

As a writer, the Goo's Johnny Rzeznik was full analog. He was all about his pencil and notepad. That was a refreshing throwback! He was also a wonderful, talented guy. When we started creating the band's single "Miracle Pill," Johnny spit some of most intimate, honest lyrics and incredible guitar parts. The sheer volume of tunings that he used in the room was just bonkers. He even summoned his guitar tech to the session, packing endless racks of toys to record all his different parts. Since Grant Michaels was also a Buffalo kid, I brought him in to join in the fun with his hometown heroes.

## Tom Morello

The master of shred! Like his guitar work in Rage Against The Machine and Audioslave, his ridiculous riffs were all Deep Purple/ Sabbath/Zeppelin–worthy masterpieces. Tom offered up endless improvisational options to swap in and out until the puzzle pieces of our songs came together. He used this tiny Electro-Harmonix pedal to create the most massive sonic effects. His tones and feel were one of a kind, but he was also an impressive, mystical poetic lyricist, which was really interesting. Tom was completely open to all ideas with zero skepticism. Bonus points for his heavy metal trivia skills.

## Barenaked Ladies

Singer Ed Robertson was both hilarious and ultra witty. He was a pinball obsessive who, when we wrapped for the day, raced out of the session in search of some off-the-grid downtown arcade. In our session, he woodshed with his signature bright-open acoustic vibe, but he also had zero fear of modern elements. When he took the "Lookin' Up" files home with him, he added a full mariachi band, synth pop leads, hard drums, and an acoustic upright bass. I think he blew through every genre boundary in one song!

## The Violent Femmes

Folk-punk king Gordon Gano was a sweet and fascinating fella. I
ended up co-writing three Femmes songs with him (one in tandem
with Kevin Griffin, the other two with Sluggo). Lyrically, Gordon
had such a specific, incredibly visual thing that I didn't want to
overstep. His words all seemed to dance around the notion of
emptiness, which I loved. Although he was a really insular fella, he
was open to all titles, concepts, and melodic and chordal ideas. I
enjoyed our week together big time.

## Q-Tip

One evening, I actually got to throw down
with Q-Tip, courtesy of my pal Ron Perry
(now Columbia Records chairman and
CEO). We wrote a Chiddy Bang tune and
discussed obscure jazz and rock samples
and all sorts of record nerd shit. That
night was so amazing, in fact, that as
we wrapped, he invited me to catch his
impromptu DJ set at some Flatiron hipster
spot later that same evening. When I
landed in front of the guest-list clipboard
toter, I learned Tip had generously reserved

Me, Q-Tip, Sluggo.
Still reeling.

me a VIP booth. A few minutes later, he entered the room with a
tray of celebratory shots. Collaborating with one of my biggest
peer musical inspirations was pretty surreal. Drinking Flaming Dr
Peppers with him was even weirder. Feeling that I actually belonged
in that room? That was priceless.

## Liam Gallagher

I spent an afternoon writing a couple of tunes with Liam and my
pal David Bassett. Liam was genuinely sweet and amazing on the
mic. The second he sang, the room was electric. We blew through
two pretty sick tunes in record time. Unfortunately, Liam's focus
wasn't 100 percent with us. He spent every spare second between
vocal takes in a furious attempt to switch his hotel to a spot in

closer proximity to his favorite British pub. When it appeared that he was getting stonewalled, he decided to wrap the session early and head over to his desired hotel to plead his case in person. I found it all very moving.

## Neil Finn, Jared Leto, Donnie Wahlberg

These three musically disjointed gentlemen rolled over to the studio on different occasions to size me up before committing to an actual co-write. On each meeting, we ended up chatting for a few hours. I found the three incredibly engaging. Ultimately, they all decided to pass on collaborating with me, but I did enjoy the hangs immensely. I should mention Donnie broke the all-time record on my Asteroids machine. He played for ninety minutes straight while effortlessly maintaining a conversation. That was quite impressive.

## Jennifer Love Hewitt

Jennifer Love Hewitt, you wonder? Where are you going with this one? When we met Rich Cronin, he was dating the red-hot actress Jennifer Love Hewitt, who'd just spun off *Party of Five*. Love, as she was known, was also a singer at the time, and she was working on an album of her own. She asked me and Duke to collaborate on a tune, and then in the most half-baked of ideas, I got Carole King to rush down to the studio to throw down with the three of us. Immediately after, I also begged Carole to write a Trace tune with myself, Kate Mara, and Duke, which she rallied for on short notice as well. These were both massive rookie mistakes that I'd committed. Neither song was ever cut and the time wasted probably made her a bit wary of my artist curation going forward. Wisely, I never drafted her for one of these long-shot flights of fancy ever again, and thus today she still replies to my emails. Folks, if you're ever blessed with a contact list full of sexy names, it's so crucial to choose your favors wisely.

## Nile Rodgers

Crazily enough, life went full circle when I began a friendship with Chic's Nile Rodgers, the man who ultimately inspired my entire trek. We even threw down a couple of tunes together. In the studio, he played all these insane harmonic feels, and then in a flash, he'd dig hard into his signature plucking attack, the "chuck." Nile was seriously like a one-man rhythm section on his Stratocaster. He was also a wonderful guest. When we wrapped our first tune, I was literally glowing. I felt like I was finally a pro. **Round the world and home again, that's the sailor's way!**

---

I'm sure I've unwittingly bypassed a few other notables, and I could certainly expound upon the aforementioned crew of greats, but I'll save it for the sequel. Trust me, though: my fourteen-year-old, little Charlie Bucket self, miserably apprenticing that jackass at Audio Concepts, would be completely losing his shit if he knew his own Golden Ticket was coming. **Don't forget what happened to the man who suddenly got everything he always wanted . . . He lived happily ever after.**

## CHAPTER 29

# One (Brief) Direction

One afternoon, during a rare, unforecasted rain soaker, I ducked into Urth Café on Melrose for a quick bite. I'd been in Hollywood less than a year, but this felt like the first real downpour I'd encountered. I sat down at a table, and the space was so crammed that I began unintentionally eavesdropping on two folks sitting behind me. I recognized one of the voices. It was Beka Tischker, an old friend from New York, who was now a power publisher in L.A. Beka was discussing potential collaborations with a Swedish writer. The Swede mentioned his old band, and I whipped my chair around in the most obnoxious intrusion ever.

"Jesus Christ, man, you're in the Cardigans!"

The Swede looked puzzled. "Yes. You remember us?"

Then the consummate record geek kicked in. "Remember you? I saw you guys three times on the 'Life' tour. I was the fella in the front row at Tramps, who sang along to every word and probably made you a bit uncomfortable in the process. Actually, I apologize for that."

I really should have apologized. I was like Patton Oswalt in *The Fan*. If someone had suggested I face-paint the Nordic goddess Nina Persson's smile on my cheeks, I probably would've done it.

The Swede, a.k.a. Peter Svensson, and I exchanged numbers and made plans to collaborate, but Beka suggested we consider throwing a track guy into the mix. She recommended her writer, Kool

Kojak, who I knew socially but had never worked with. Kojak, a graffiti-painting free spirit, was already one of my favorite personalities in town, so I was really looking forward to it. But I was also a bit mystified. Who was the artist? The Cardigans hadn't made a record in a decade. When Beka told me it would be a pitch-song thing, the thrill swiftly dissipated. Historically, my few shots in the song-placement game had been mostly laughable. For some reason, all of the creativity and quirk in my collaborations with artists never translated to that approach. They were either too generic or too out there for the masses. I could never find my sweet spot in that formula-driven game, so I avoided it altogether. That's why this session began to feel all wrong.

The three of us linked a week later at Kojak's, and we just dove right in. After a solid minute of debate, we decided to take a stab at an idea for One Direction. Every pesky pop songwriter on earth was chasing 1D after "What Makes You Beautiful" exploded, so this seemed somewhat of a pipe dream of an exercise to me, but I guess I was down. I came with a title and concept that I thought would be in the zone for them. The guys seemed to dig it: "Rock Me." I was shooting for a sexier take on the boy band's freshly scrubbed brand of fun. It was pretty basic, nostalgic stuff. I think I wrote the bulk of the lyrics in fifteen minutes or so. Peter dug into his own brand of Swedish melodic math. As a Max Martin protégée, he was already like a Stockholm University professor at that shit. Kojak threw down a fun track, and we wrapped up the song demo in a matter of hours. It was like a revved-up Nashville write, except I could see the bluish Pacific Ocean from Kojak's deck. Later that evening, we had Thai food. Fun fellas. A day well spent.

Then something peculiar happened.

Simon Cowell heard it and loved it. Dr. Luke and Max Martin as well. Luke hopped on board to produce. The song got fast-tracked. In an instant, it permeated the track listing for 2013's hardest record to access. It was kinda like waking up to find a brand new pair of limited edition Nike MAG *Back to the Future* sneakers gifted under the bed. That One Direction album went on to sell six million copies. "Rock Me" went gold in a bunch of countries.

At that point, I began to rethink my career process altogether. Why was I only collaborating with these soul-sucking artists? It seemed like such a waste of emotional—and fiscal— time. Maybe this pitch-writing approach was truly the ticket for me as well? So I decided to throw out everything I knew and began writing blanket songs for

Pat Monahan, Harry Styles, myself, Joey Hollander, and Martin Johnson.

placement with Peter and Kojak every day from scratch. We had very few targets. Just a ton of broad strokes. "Hey, maybe this would work for Selena Gomez?"–type stuff. I think we crafted about twenty tunes.

Guess what?

They were all wack as fuck. Well, more specifically, my contributions were. My lyric ideas were all soulless and contrived—totally based on chasing whatever was happening at Top 40 at that exact instant. I couldn't connect to any of it. I'd never trailed like this before, and the results were disgraceful. The final straw was this hooky melody that Peter sent me to take on a plane trip back east. Peter wanted the chorus to start with the repeated phrase "I gotta gotta goooo. I gotta gotta goo." He demanded it, actually. There was no negotiation. This was some Iran hostage shit. I made a hundred attempts at this chorus as JetBlue crossed the states, and nothing worked. "I gotta gotta goooooo." It didn't sound like a hit. It sounded like yodeling. At the end of the day, I just couldn't connect to it, so I trashed it on the spot.

**BONUS CUT**

A few years later, Peter successfully flipped "I gotta gotta go" into "You gotta gotta gotta love me harder" for Ariana Grande, and he had a worldwide number one hit. Whenever I hear it today, my self-loathing spikes up a notch. Who's the lovefool now, bitch?

As I started losing faith in our short-lived power trio, I got the sense that both Peter and Kojak were beginning to move on from our unit as well. We really had so much fun together, but when none of the slew of tunes we collaborated on over those couple of months ever got a positive response, we all parted creative ways with an unspoken farewell. That was the end of my brief foray into the pitch-song chase.

**CHAPTER 30**

# The Tao of Steve Nash

S leepwriting.

Yes, in the days that proceeded Kojak and Peter, I started sleepwriting.

Lyrically, melodically—shit, even conversationally—I was bouncing around L.A. songwriting sessions mimicking what I thought would "work," because I was hiding the fact that I had little to offer in terms of insight. As *Succession*'s Kendall Roy put it, words were just "complicated airflow" and I was devolving into a constricted hack.

By that point, most pop songwriters had mastered both the aforementioned Swedish playbook and the agnostic singsong rap and R&B fusion of Drake. Every L.A. writer was working from that same slick grab bag of tricks. As those chart-chasing apprentices began to get all the A-level co-writes with artists across every genre, my phone went silent. I had become the dinosaur rock guy, and my lane was getting blocked like a city full of traffic cops. The rejections stockpiled and I totally understood it. I truly felt zero connection to anything coming out of my mouth.

I was sleepwriting.

Since the pop songwriting world is based on jacking whatever's currently moving the needle, sleepwriting is always gonna be an inevitable result of that desperate pursuit, but I began to see it everywhere. It was like a city of designer imposters. Sure, I'd been guilty of a phoned-in tune like everyone else, but since my lyrical quirks had been my ticket from the get-go, I had usually been able to summon up some less-generic shit even during the most nothing of sessions. Now everywhere I turned I was stumbling into studios with writers who had zero interest in high concept stuff, so I began to settle on any garden variety idea just to fit in. Hack shit. I was so scared that my style had suddenly stale milk expired. I got caught on a circuit of half-hearteds and musical bean counters. And sadly, I began to follow suit. A year or two earlier, I would've seen some of these less than inspiring sessions pop up on my calendar and promptly run for the hills. Now I was following their lead. My self-loathing had reached an apex. I know I sound like a total douchebag, but I hated that I was becoming a forgettable.

## BONUS CUT

Imagine you're an eyewitness to a musical crime. You're Plexiglas separated from a hundred songwriters that you've previously collaborated with. Take a second to affix one clever descriptor for each writer standing on this police lineup in front of you. "He's a great lyricist with incredible concepts," "She comes with really clever chords and beats," "They've got an amazing aura that lights up the room," and so on. If you're unable to summon up anything distinctive about a writer, that means they're guilty of bringing the marginal shit, and I'd highly recommend you avoid throwing down with them again. It's just too competitive out there for unmemorable. The real magic comes from the captivators. Up until that point in my career, I'd always believed that I could be one of 'em. Now I wasn't so sure.

I knew my game was off, but I didn't really understand the magnitude of nothingness my work had become. I mean, I'd also pretty much fallen out of the rotation at Crush Management. Sure, JD and Bob kindly tossed me a few co-writes that resulted in some decent tunes (my pal Matt Nathanson's "Earthquake Weather,"

Andrew McMahon's "Canyon Moon," a couple New Politics joints), but I was no longer on the Train registry. Forget Weezer. Even worse, each of these somewhat token sessions included another melodic writer as well as myself in the room with the artist. It was too many cooks in the kitchen, so I psyched out and voluntarily demoted myself to sous chef. It was quite obvious that I'd shit my own bed.

I spent a few months collaborating with Boys Like Girls's Martin Johnson, who'd grown into a first-rate writer/producer himself, but our dynamic had flipped and he was now the main alpha in every session. I love Martin like a lil' brother, but playing Ed McMahon to his Johnny Carson every late night kinda shook me. In those co-writes, I was largely relegated to the role of "lyric guy," which back in the day was a necessity, but now it seemed many of the artists we collaborated with approached lyrics as an afterthought at best. Track and melody reigned supreme. So as the words became less of a priority in sessions, I got way too comfortable taking a back seat role in all of these co-writes, as I scrambled to maintain my identity.

Now in all fairness, this wasn't an overnight descent. When I look back on it, this was probably the result of a lengthier drift. Though I tried to deny it, when I moved out of NYC, deep down inside I knew that I was beginning to tread creative water. I had begun to take my eyes off the proverbial prize. Sure, I really summoned up some solid crafting with priority acts, but on the gigs I deemed less pressing, I'd occasionally half-ass the process. That kind of thing is prone to happen when you're down to work on anything with a checkbook. How can you remain super inspired every day when you're wasting time on tunes that mean next to nothing to you and your wallet on any emotional level?

I also began to question my instincts.

My publisher pal Jake Ottmann passionately pitched me on his newest signing. I totally dug this unknown's demos. Her musical references were super cool, but I couldn't envision her haunted smoky thing working in the rhythm-heavy pop landscape of the time, so I passed. Her name was Lizzy Grant, but she'd just rechristened herself "Lana Del Rey." What the fuck was I thinking? Even worse, what was I becoming?! Sluggo and I wrote with an up-and-coming Kesha. She was kinda dope, but our song got scrapped and I didn't even flinch. We'd already spent a bunch of time working unsuccessfully with a polarizing trio called the Millionaires, who had a similar raunchy schtick. Why the fuck would Kesha connect while the Millionaires disappeared? I was obviously way the hell off target. I was beginning to miss things.

Then the move to and initial thrill of L.A. was swallowed by the insecurity of watching all the freakishly young writer kids out there nail singles and hits, while I struggled to get traction in a game and city that had completely tweaked. The circus was different in California. "Topliners." "Track guys." Assembly-line approaches. After the brief thrill of One Direction, I began to feel an ominous sense of becoming obsolete. Factor in monthly flights back to Manhattan (I believe I logged fifty-two flights back east to look after sick folks over that first four-year period in L.A.), a lost year on *SMASH*, even the harsh reality that my hits with Daughtry and Karmin had done nothing to keep my standing on any A&R call sheet, and it was all a combustible combination of creative bludgeoning. In the Pacific Ocean, I felt like an irrelevant Nemo.

Thankfully, I've blocked the bulk of the details of that early June day that I finally bottomed out, but I was collaborating with a well-known writer out in Calabasas for the first time. We'd crossed a few times on records, but never thrown down together in a room. From what I'd heard from others, he was pretty hands-on back in the day, but he was now less focused on craft, more about modeling his game after the camp mentality of Dr. Luke and Max Martin, with a bunch of underlings doing the bulk of his work while he maintained a "curator" role.

When I arrived, he seemed pleasant enough, until he instantly launched into the old songwriting dick-sword move of "I had a session with so-and-so yesterday, and we wrote an absolute smash! He wants to work with me alone for the next month! How sick is that?!"

Calabasas was apparently getting the A-list shit, and I wasn't.

In a game of alphas, this was such a subtle war tactic, but it obviously worked. My insecurities about my songwriter standing were already gnawing at me every waking minute, but this guy had managed to pry them open within a mere matter of seconds.

Soon we began the session, and it was painfully clear that Calabasas had zero interest in throwing down with me. I'm sure he took the session as a sub for another cancellation or out of some mild curiosity about my abilities. His head and heart certainly weren't in it. He must've walked out of the room at least twenty times to check on his hidden cubicle-dwelling Keebler elves who were doing the nuts and bolts work on his other demos down the hall. Was I that wack?

I tried to keep the train on track, so I swiftly spit out a rapid, generic lyric. I think it was called "Bravehearts," or "Young Hearts," or some other terrible heart. I can't recall. Then Calabasas began scatting a melody that felt equally pedestrian to me. It was just regurgitated hack. I didn't push back, though. I let myself get steamrolled by my own typicality. Calabasas feigned enthusiasm in the tune, so we sped through it. Well, honestly, he was speeding through it. At a breakneck speed. I tried to slow shit down and rework, but he was definitely racing me out of there. As I casually eavesdropped on him loudly yapping in the hall on the phone, I got the sneaky sense that he had actually triple-booked sessions for that afternoon, and I was just the first of his trifecta bets. That was the ultimate indignity.

We finished the demo in an hour and a half, and I actually thanked him profusely for taking the time. Why was I sucking up to this uninspiring individual? He had totally half-assed this session. And yet, I felt pathetically grateful. It was some Stockholm syndrome shit. I slumped into the car and sat in rush hour traffic in the deep Valley. Suddenly, and inexplicably, in that endless, smoggy traffic hell, I began uncontrollably sobbing. And I started yelling at myself, punching the steering wheel. It was so out of character; historically I'd been a pretty bottled-up cat. This time, I couldn't contain it. I'd finally hit the proverbial wall, so as soon as I got home, I grabbed a Delta ticket and flew to New York to decompress.

I still remember that trek back east and all the insecurities racing simultaneously through my brain. Was there actually a shelf life for this job? Had my moment expired? If sleepwriting was all I had left, what would be the result of me just biding my time? I didn't have a plan B.

A couple of days after I arrived in the Village, I got a call from my old friend Jeremy Piven, who asked me if I wanted to join him for dinner at the Minetta Tavern. Though I was still knee-deep in a stupor, I'd had some of the most inspiring nights of my adult life with Jeremy, so it was somewhat of a no-brainer. When I arrived, though, it seemed another fella was joining us.

Steve Nash.

That would be NBA Hall of Famer, and current head coach of my beloved Brooklyn Nets, Steve Nash.

From the moment we sat down, Steve was a lovely hang. Couldn't have dug him more. At one point midway through the meal, Jeremy asked Steve how, at the tender age of thirty-nine, he could still dominate infinitely more athletic kids—some young enough to be his own spawn. His response fascinated me. He said that back in the early days of his career, his game began to plummet, so he went to see a sports psychologist. That doctor broke it down in very basic terms. He explained to Steve that after a few years in the league, he'd probably traveled to the same cities on loop at least six times. The novelty and luster had most likely worn off. How can one stay mentally focused when every day is a shade of the same? He immediately prescribed Nash an exercise routine that included yoga, Pilates, swimming, tai chi, stretching and core, running, balance training, et cetera. The key would be no more days off during the regular season. When everyone else was partying or just sleeping it off, he would always train. From the moment he began this new regimen, his game returned to elite level, and it stayed there for two decades.

I left that dinner and walked back through Washington Square Park, letting it all soak in.

Then it hit me like a monument brick.

Why couldn't I apply this same technique to my writing?

My main writing stretch had always been Labor Day to Thanksgiving, then late January to Memorial Day. Traditionally, the summers and holidays had yielded nothing particularly fruitful because my collaborators were usually on tour or vacationing. I decided to recommit to my craft by never taking a day off during those lengthy "in-season" periods, so from September 1 to the first day back on the beach, I began putting something on paper every single day. As soon as the coffee kicked in, I'd open my dusty computer and dive into stream-of-consciousness typing. Interesting phrases and couplets suddenly flowed out of me. Lyric sheets full of more intricate wordplay. I started to sound like a creative version of myself that I hadn't met yet—lyrically sharper and melodically tighter.

In previous years, I'd start the bulk of my tunes with a title and then carve out an idea sans melody, just focusing on the narratives and the rhythms of the words. Because I'd been taking this approach my entire adult life, it was pretty easy for me to craft a lyric sheet that was so connect-the-dots friendly that any collaborator could take it and start scatting whatever of these words inspired their inner muse. I learned this trick courtesy of the great Billy Steinberg (co-writer, "Like a Virgin" and "True Colors"). It had always been a gift, and I didn't take it lightly, but the more I relied on that one skill, the more I began forfeiting my ability to throw more creative darts at the board.

On that new batch, I began messing with the guitar a bit more. I'd always had a solid six chords or so of shitty strumming at my disposal, but the melodies and, more importantly, the rhythms of the words began to take new forms as I dug in harder. I also started poring over the solos on old jazz records. I learned *this* trick courtesy of the somewhat forgotten L.A. hip-hop mic beasts Freestyle Fellowship. As I studied their intricate phrasings, my own melodic pocket started to take a freer shape.

I'd begun to turn a massive corner. I furiously stockpiled voice note after voice note. On good days, I truly felt like I was levitating. On the days I felt uninspired or just blah in general, I still forced myself to lay something down. On those (now rarer) occasions of writer's block, I'd pen a short story.

I even crafted a volume of narrative poems—seriously!

There would be no more laying back and tucking away in sessions—interjecting but not leading. That was all fear. That dinner with Steve Nash completely salvaged my career. Sleepwriting was officially deceased.

If you have a true artist's spirit, you must dare to suck. It's the only way you'll ever feel fulfilled at the end of the writing process. When creatively interfacing with others, don't hold back on pitching whatever crazy you're hearing in your head. Words. Melodies. All of it. If everyone passes on your idea, so be it. At least you stepped up to bat. I mean, James Dyson had 5,126 failed prototypes before creating his eponymous bagless vacuum cleaner. Everyone loves a Dyson. He's currently worth $4.5 billion.

## CHAPTER 31

# Dead Man Writing[1]

**W**hen *American Idol* premiered in the summer of '02, I was one of the 9.5 million folks who immediately got hooked. Kelly vs. Justin; Ruben vs. Clay; Carrie vs. Bo; Fantasia vs. Gershwin's "Summertime." For the first five seasons, I watched it with the same mystified enthusiasm as I did the first seasons of *Project Runway*. *Idol*'s musical pageantry seemed light-years away from my day job writing and producing slightly left-field-leaning pop-punk songs with kooky band kids. I was just a fanboy spectating from 2,797 miles away in New York.

One day, during the finale week of Season 6, two of my songs snuck their way into the pop radio consciousness, and my personal *Idol* odyssey took shape. In a surreal twenty-four hours, I received requests from the show's production company, 19 Entertainment, to head west to discuss collaborating with the show winners. I and my color commentary had spent the first five seasons watching the show from the cheap seats. Now, with next to no knowledge of the world of televised singing competitions, I was actively courted for fun. I was all in.

---

1 This chapter was published previously. Sam Hollander, "'Dead Man Writing': The Real Story Behind the 'American Idol' Hit Factory (Guest Column)," *Billboard*, April 6, 2016, https://www.billboard.com/music/music-news/american-idol-sam-hollander-guest -column-7325306/.

I quickly learned that the *American Idol* record-making process was madness—a panicked time crunch that kicked in the second the confetti was swept up and the cameras went black. The victor and runner-up were immediately shuttled around L.A. to collaborate with hitmakers from that specific chart year in a three-week speed-dating round of musical mayhem. The immediate goal was a handful of songs that would set the template for the musical direction of the finalist's forthcoming debut record. Then the singers would begin intensive tour rehearsals, followed by a fifty-date, summer-long, cross-country jaunt. At that point, with the artist's exhaustion level nearing hospital status, immediately after the tour wrapped they were jettisoned back west and obligated to track the rest of their entire album within a solid six-week window. The records in question usually dropped around Black Friday while the public appetite for the cast was still fresh. In the early years, the albums usually shipped gold. For the hungry writer, that meant some swimming-pool-foundation dollars. It also meant utter chaos. Every writer in the mix was whipped into a state of paranoid frenzy as we battled each other and the gruesome clock. What a competitive mindfuck.

I was first thrown into this raging fire with Season 6's quirky runner-up, Blake Lewis. Blake was so great. Totally my kind of eccentric. He wanted to make a UK drum 'n' bass record. The label wanted him to make a Justin Timberlake record. You know how that movie ends. We wrote three songs together, and to my surprise, two of them actually made the CD. I couldn't believe my luck. Even more exciting news followed. One was slated to be the second single! Damn, this dash seemed so easy.

Nope.

Sadly, I tore a hamstring before my victory lap. Blake's first single didn't make it to the podium. I learned that if the first single didn't explode on *Idol*, there would be no follow-up. But I wasn't deterred—I was excited to toss more proverbial needles into these haystacks in hopes of being found. At least I walked away with a freshly gifted Sanjaya Malakar T-shirt.

As Season 7 wrapped, my songs remained on the radio, so I received the same frantic calls again. This time, Sluggo and I were paired with the funny and earnest David Cook. The label thought he was the next Daughtry. He wanted to be the next Our Lady Peace. Uh-oh. We spent six impassioned hours together. Wrote a pretty solid up-tempo! The powers that be told us that we had an "absolute smash" on our hands. Way to jinx it, assholes. You NEVER put the "S word" out there prematurely. It guarantees a gruesome ending. When I checked my in-box a few days later, one of my peers had forwarded me an email that some clueless label fuck sent songwriter-wide to the rest of the prospective *Idol* writers with my track attached as a "template." That was the moment I learned another valuable *Idol* lesson: never deliver a song prematurely. Timing was everything. Within days, many similar, stronger numbers were written by my competitors. My and Sluggo's "hit" ended up buried at the bottom of Cook's debut as the Target hidden track.

But I wasn't done.

For Season 8 I spent a brief afternoon with the sweet and slightly disinterested Kris Allen. The label directive was to drum up something in the vein of the band The Script. As these things happen, his single ended up being an unreleased Script track. Our song was closer to "The Suck," anyway. Needless to say, it also died on the vine. Speaking of sucking, the *Idol* bosses soon set me up on a twenty-minute introductory telephone meeting with a fiery but kind Kelly Clarkson, who told me in the most specific of terms that she "did *not* want another 'Since U Been Gone.'" Three months later, her next single "My Life Would Suck Without You" was released, co-written by Max Martin and Dr. Luke of "Since U Been Gone" fame, and obviously featuring quite a few similarities to that hit. I was beginning to feel like I was stuck in a fish-out-of-water comedy.

Next, Adam Lambert recorded one of me and Sluggo's leftover tunes that was fermenting on our hard drive pile. There we go! Unfortunately, upon listening to the final mix, everyone on Team Adam agreed that his vocal performance was the wrong fit for the song, and that dream died as well.

Looking back, this was that broken moment when I was ostensibly deep-sixed from all things *Idol*. I received zero winner calls for Seasons 9, 10, or 11. Why didn't I mean anything to these damn people?! Sure, I shared three hours with the talented-yet-weary third-placer Haley Reinhart, which resulted in yet another scrap heap tune, but that was just a token. I can't forget to mention Season 9's Crystal Bowersox, who sang a duet on the Blues Traveler record I produced.

By Season 12 I had moved to L.A., so I was residing in the show's backyard, but still the crickets continued. There would be no Lee DeWyze. No Scotty McCreery. No Candice Glover. No Phillip Phillips. As far as the *Idol* powers were concerned, I was Dead Man Writing.

But wait!

Shouldn't I have received a stay of execution in the Kingdom of Cowell? I mean, I did write the first single on the Season 7 boy wonder David Archuleta's long-awaited follow-up! Sadly, it was only a hit in the Philippines. Oh, and lest we forget, I produced Season 3's own Jennifer Hudson and Season 5's Katharine McPhee, who both crooned covers for NBC's *SMASH*, but we all know how that ended as well.

Then it happened. The cadaver awakened! I wrote a Daughtry smash called "Waiting for Superman." Officially freeing me from pariah status, this tune's success resulted in a hectic eleventh-hour plea for me to write with Season 13 winner Caleb Johnson. I hopped in the car and raced over to the Venice Beach studio. I liked Caleb. He was a wide-eyed, enthusiastic kid. I dug his soulful rock thing, but I was even more thrilled to have another shot at reversing my disappointing *Idol* legacy. But something inexplicable happened between the patter that preceded the session and the song itself. I had nothing *Idol*-ish left. I got hit with another bout of sleepwriting and spit some of my blandest lyrics to date. We parted ways with a tune that was, of all things, depressingly soulless. I beat myself up the entire weekend that followed, as I wondered if all these *Idol* exercises in futility had finally taken their creative toll on me. A month later, the Batphone rang: the song had been chosen to be Caleb Johnson's first single. This would be my only *Idol* champion first single. I couldn't believe my shitty luck, or Caleb's, for that matter. He deserved better. I knew nothing good would follow. I was correct. Sadly, if you look it up, you'll probably learn that it was the fastest-disappearing single in that *Idol* era. In the early years, a song like this wouldn't cut the mustard as a Taylor Hicks Japanese B-side. By Season 13, it was the throwaway long shot. Why, you ask? Because for all intents and purposes, version 1.0 of the show was over. *The Voice* had stolen its proverbial thunder, and the industry had moved on.

And so had I.

BONUS CUT

Well, not entirely. I did in fact write an independently released single for Season 4's rock god, Constantine Maroulis, but he's a homie, so that was on the friends and family tip.

No sour grapes, though. As I bid farewell to the most bizarre roller coaster, where even the humbling lows were transcendent, everything felt weirdly perfect. For a brief, shining moment in time, this American footnote was an outsider crashing Fox's Camelot, and trust me: it was pretty f'n glorious.

## CHAPTER 32

# Posthumous Pin

I t was a sun-drenched early April morning when I got the call that my mom's health had taken one final, terrible turn. I was at LAX within an hour. It was the worst fuckin' flight of my life—a big mass of turbulent mayhem as we bounced around the Middle Atlantic. As the bumpy 747 brought on bouts of mild nausea, I wondered if this was actually my mom's spirit making a final loud statement before exiting this beautifully weird world. It sure felt like it.

To pass this miserable time in the not-so-friendly skies, I shifted my panicked focus to an old songwriting exercise that I'd usually default to in similar moments of anxiety. I attempted to write a lyric devoid of any internal or end line rhymes at all. Just an imagery-heavy, rhyme-less narrative. Suzanne Vega's classic "Tom's Diner" is a great example of this kind of thing. Simon and Garfunkel's "America." Even Kelly Clarkson's "Because of You" and my pal Lisa Loeb's "Stay" are both pretty rhyme-light overall. What do all of these songs have in common? Incredible mental imagery. Since the writers weren't boxed in by the rhyme chase, they were able to scribe powerful scene changes that resulted in timeless shit. As I dove deep into the assignment, I began to chill the fuck out. Even in the most gruesome of circumstances, music can most certainly mollify like Prozac.

When I finally touched down at JFK, I ran through the airport like pre-prison O. J. on a desperate Hertz search. I hopped into whatever sketchy rental car they had available that night and set off on the

Van Wyck Expressway. Man, I couldn't believe it. The Van Wyck was actually moving! That horrible stretch of asphalt had been stopped up every previous waking moment of my flight life. Whatever the time of day, I always factored in the inevitable twenty-five minutes I'd spend lost in this awful abyss in Queens. Oddly, this time I was sailing. Bodegas and fast-food joints blew by in the distance. I just wanted to see my mom one last time.

But then I jinxed it. I always jinx these things. I'm hyper-superstitious, so when traffic-beating thoughts like these cross my brain, I always knock on the steering wheel three times.

I forgot to knock.

Where the fuck was my head?

All of a sudden, I saw a small gridlock of brake lights stacking in front of me. It was an accident. It wasn't a crash; it was the remains of a rogue highway crosser who decided to tempt the Van Wyck fates and was now bleeding his guts out in the cold. He was killed on impact. He wasn't even covered with a blanket as I rubbernecked by.

God really does have a sick sense of humor.

I finally arrived at the hospital at midnight. My mom had just been administered morphine and was sliding away into forever. I walked through the door, locked eyes with my brother and weary old man, and completely lost my shit. I couldn't stop crying. I hugged Mom and whispered all of my love in her ear. I knew this day was coming, but it still demolished me. I had a surge of intense flashbacks to fourteen years earlier when Gramma Hilda had died in my arms.

In a matter of minutes, she was gone.

When we split the hospital and crept back to the house, my mother's long-term nurse was there to greet us, her eyes also bleary and bloodshot from hours of tears. My dad went upstairs to collapse. I sat alone with the nurse and awkwardly attempted to fill some of the emptiness for both of us. Before I could get a word out, she blurted something I'll never forget.

"Sam, your mother loved you."

Then she took a dramatic pause and leaked out the following.

"Sam, I don't know how to say this . . . Um . . . Your mother adored you, but she really didn't like your music at all. She used to tell me that all the time. But she knew you worked your butt off, and she was so proud of you for that."

Then she casually turned away and made herself a cup of tea.

It hit me like a shovel to the side of the skull. Up to that instant, my career had been a million little failings until I somehow clawed my way through. Now I was finally helium ballooning up to the sky like a Macy's Thanksgiving Day Parade float, and here was my own mother popping it with a posthumous pin, sending me right back down to earth. I began giggling uncontrollably. I mean, it really was kinda perfect. I instantly knew I had to capture that sequence on paper. No rhymes allowed.

CHAPTER 33

# Mad Owls and Englishmen

Vocally, I've always been somewhat of an Anglophile. I love a British gravelly tone. From Chris Rea to Rod Stewart to Bonnie Tyler, I'm constantly blasting a sandpaper rasp. My favorite UK singer of all was the husky-piped Joe Cocker. From the first time I heard "Delta Lady," I was hooked. Joe's raw power and soul-baring emotion was peerless. Honestly, I think he might've been the greatest rock singer of his era, so imagine my glee in 2014 when my then publisher booked me to write with a trio of collaborators for a new Cocker record.

The morning of that session, I hopped in the whip and headed straight to the Calabasas studio of Matt Serletic, Cocker's producer. I was about halfway to said destination when I got a text from a then up-and-coming, now kinda-large writer, Brian Lee, asking me if I wanted to collaborate with himself, Owl City, and Relient K's Matt Thiessen that very same afternoon. Owl City was kinda large at this point, so it was definitely an enticing offer. Because I'd been sharing a studio with Brian's publisher, they'd be writing in my place of comfort, which was a bonus. I've always tended to do my best work on my home turf. I was also in the midst of a cold streak, and I had a very strong hunch that this crew of writers might be a ticket back to the radio.

I pulled off the 101 and wrestled with it.

I played out both scenarios in my head, but in the end, since I still believed in practicing some semblance of protocol in these matters, and as I'd already committed to the Valley crew, I painfully passed.

> **BONUS CUT**
>
> All you writers out there who cancel sessions on next-to-no notice with zero remorse, you've gotta understand, it's a terrible look. Everybody compares notes in this business. Maintain your rep at all costs.

Fortunately, I ended up having a pretty bang-up session that afternoon with the Cocker bunch—Sluggo, Serletic, and my homie, the amazing Aimée Proal. We wrote a tender, melancholic mid-tempo called "The Last Road," and Joe immediately cut it. I was pretty pumped.

The next day, as the fates would have it, I strutted back into my studio, and my engineer unhesitatingly played me the tune that Owl City, Adam, and Brian had written in the room the day before. He avoided my eyes. I knew I was in for a world of hurt. The song was called "Good Time." I'm sure you know where this one's headed. In a few months, Carly Rae Jepsen jumped on it, and it became a worldwide hit.

My Joe Cocker song, you might ask?

It was only released in Germany. As a damn bonus track. Danke schön! A few years later, Cowboy Joe died. When I learned of his passing, I strapped on my crusty Bose headphones and replayed our old B-side again for the first time in ages. It was some bone-chilling shit. All of Joe's nasty, guttural vocal, fire-blazing each syllable. Such a beautiful, cryptic send-off. Sure, from that day forward, whenever I heard "Good Time," I'd drift into a momentary Monty Hall–induced tailspin, wondering what might've been if I had just chosen the *Let's Make A Deal* door #2, but I truly wouldn't trade "The Last Road" for anything. It's a pretty magnificent souvenir. My accountant might beg to differ but, for me at least, songwriting is still primarily driven by my fandom.

CHAPTER 34

# The All-New Mickey Mouse Club

**H**igh School Musical blew up in 2006, the same year my kid was born. Man, I would have loved to have written a tune on it, but Robbie Nevil, of the lost '80s classic "C'est la Vie," and pop writer Matthew Gerrard had the gig on lockdown. I didn't get a call for the Jonas Brothers' star-making vehicle *Camp Rock* either. Since I'd rolled with the JoBros years before they became a group, when young Kevin and Joe would hang out and watch TV with Jen up front at my spot while I wrote fruitless JFK List songs with thirteen-year-old Nick (then a solo artist signed to a development deal at Sony), naturally, I was kinda bummed that I missed the cut. To be awfully honest, I just really wanted to nail one of these Disney gigs as a flex for my kid. I know that sounds gross, but I had created a sweet little mental snapshot of us gleefully bopping around the living room together while the Disney Channel played one of my tunes on loop. Don't judge me. Around that time, Bret was asked to manage Nickelodeon's *Big Time Rush* in their musical endeavors. The show was a big hit for the network. I wrote and produced a couple of tunes on their debut. It went gold and was a relatively big record, but at the time, Nickelodeon wasn't Disney. It was kinda Carvel to Ben & Jerry's or some shit. I needed to experience that magic of the mouse.

BONUS CUT

1. Disney songs meant potential free passes to the park. Obviously huge in my swag-lovin' household.
2. Disney songs were a great opportunity to help up-and-coming writers find their footing in the business.

Throughout the years, I mentored, or at least attempted to mentor, a bunch of promising newbie writers. On average, those apprentices tended to come and go like network TV show pilots. When their song-writing careers didn't explode overnight, they inevitably bounced. If you ask David Frank or Mic Murphy, they'd probably tell you I was once that same restless kid. That's also probably the singular reason why it took me a lot longer to achieve success than my peers. I was too impatient. I was a musical anarchist who always thought he knew more than the next clown. That punk rock ethos is admirable and all, but if you're looking to master a craft, it helps to absorb everything you can from a mentor who's already dialed in the skills. Even if the wait is gnarly. As I shuffled through those protégés, I finally struck gold with my buddy Josh Edmondson, his girlfriend/now-wife Charity Daw, Steve Shebby, and my intern-turned-collaborator Grant Michaels, three incredibly lovely, driven, and super talented souls. Since they'd relocated out west to take shots with me on various (mostly uncertain) gigs, I had tremendous guilt when I initially failed to deliver opportunities for them. To avoid them getting engulfed by shitty day jobs, I knew I was on the clock to figure out a means for them to survive financially while they honed their chops.

Enter Disney Channel Music honcho Steve Vincent.

Steve, who I'd known loosely for years but became pals with in California, began sending me song briefs for every Disney Channel show at the time. I think he was somewhat surprised that I was open to taking on these slightly less sexy, work-for-hire gigs, but I knew those tunes would make for a great opportunity to work my squad into the rotation.

During that stretch, we collectively joined forces on songs for *Shake It Up*, *A.N.T Farm*, *Austin & Ally*, and my pal Betsy's show,

BONUS CUT

The pay for each Disney Channel tune was usually an all-in $15K buyout per track. I know that sounds bargain basement as fuck, but for anyone on the come-up, those dollars can really help lessen the Lyft shifts. Factor in the guaranteed writer's-share royalties, and it's not a terrible take-home. For whatever it's worth, it's also pretty joyous work.

*Liv and Maddie*, among others. Some stretches were bleak, but they never once complained. Most importantly, as they trudged up the ladder, all three of them went from beginner to killer at their craft (I have zero doubt they'll also pay it forward and mentor a future crew of showbiz kids the correct way).

After a few years of collectively paying our Disney dues, we got asked to write a song for the *Descendants*, the next big musical movie on the network's docket. In a sweet bit of happenstance, my friend Adam Schlesinger got the call to write a tune for the movie as well. With daughters around the same age, Adam and I were both equally stoked for a chance to win those aforementioned props from our spawn. For his tune, Adam demanded an advance fee for the demo. When I told him that I and my squad were writing ours on spec, he fervently schooled me.

"Look, you're a huge writer. Never EVER do work on spec. Always demand the money up front!"

On a business level, he was probably correct, but in this specific case, I played the game and delivered our gratis tune, "Set It Off." Thankfully, the network loved it. They only smacked us with a couple of minor revisions, and we got the gig. Adam, however, with all that freshly advanced Disney cash burrowing into his pocket, was tortured into about sixteen completely reworked versions of his tune, "Did I Mention?"

"Maybe approach it with a little more rock?"

"Can you flip it into a soul thing?"

"How about speeding it up thirty beats per minute?"

He was so f'n miserable about it.

Did I mention that I never let his ass live it down?

The *Descendants* album debuted at #1 on the *Billboard* charts, and we were brought back to collaborate on the sequel, where we wrote the hit "Ways to Be Wicked." My favorite memory of this run was being able to take my daughter to the premiere. She got to meet the entire cast (including the late, delightful Cameron Boyce),

Disney *Descendants* premiere with Steve Gold, Adam Schlesinger, Josh Edmondson, Shelly Peiken, Layla Peiken, Charity Daw, and Grant Michaels.

and we all had a great time hanging with Kenny Ortega, who directed the film (no, we did not discuss his infamous Billy Squier video from decades previous. Yes, I did celebrate him for *Xanadu*). Of course, this moment of glory coincided with Disney corporate tightening the purse strings and canceling all free Disneyland passes for songwriters. Greedy-ass mice. It was all good, though. With my own newfound Disney pocket change in my wallet, I decided to splurge on annual park passes, and me and the fam were all up in that piece on the regular. It really was the happiest place on earth.

**BONUS CUT**

God, my mom would've been horrified. She was the opposite of fun. Don't get me wrong, she was f'n incredible and I miss her every single day, but when I was a kid, she played the contrarian to most of the merrier aspects of childhood. The worst of this being a refusal to take my brother and me to any theme park. No Playland. No Action Park. And, most painfully, no Disney World. When all those other blissed-out kids returned from magical family vacations swagged out in Goofy sweatshirts, I was always left spinning in a jealous spiral courtesy of the fun crusher. But that was then. Thanks to music, I was able to jack my childhood back!

## CHAPTER 35

# Finding Someone

H oly cow, we've hit chapter 35?! How is that even possible? Before we push any further, it's time for a very brief chronological rewind. Bear with me here.

In the late aughts, after a whirlwind courtship, I signed a brand-spankin'-new worldwide publishing deal with EMI. I was quite excited to join their esteemed roster, but as these things go, the songs I delivered that first term underperformed compared to their expectations, so the head honchos (wisely) decided to decline picking up my pricier second option.

Translation: I got kicked to the curb.

Now for most songwriters, publishing deals come and go like acid-wash jeans. In my estimation, working writers sign, and subsequently part ways, with at least two or three publishing companies in their careers, unless, of course, they end up stuck in publishing purgatory. And trust me, publishing purgatory is the fuckin' worst. If you haven't fulfilled all of your contractual release obligations, you can find yourself buried in a dead-end deal for years on end. I've seen writers locked down for an entire decade. I'm serious. Songwriter friends, always make sure your lawyer carves some sort of escape route into any publishing contract before signing.

If I were to pinpoint the reason I floundered during that year at EMI, it was probably my singular, bugged-out focus on the much-hyped, Island Records–signed Black Cards, a side project of my buddy, the brilliant Pete Wentz from Fall Out Boy on which I coconspired. Originally conceived at the height of Pete's celebrity as an electronic duo, the struggle to cast his female counterpart was a fascinating case study in too many cooks in the kitchen with no applicable menu in hand.

At first, our only requirement was that she come from Europe. Pete thought it would add an interesting global vibe that would complement our tracks. It felt like a solid concept at the time, but it meant that we really needed to thread the needle in our selection.

Singer #1 arrived from London and had all the right intangibles. Great tone and energy. Spectacular style. Well, except for the fact that everyone was convinced that she was a full-on tweaker. This was never verified, but man, she was mad erratic. She blew off a bunch of sessions with the most puzzling excuses I can recall. Every other day was a flaky reveal. We couldn't risk the drama. Next.

Singer #2 was a British Beyoncé lookalike who hung in for three solid weeks. She seemed pretty even-keeled until that dreaded afternoon when the label was en route to the studio to greenlight the vocals she'd laid down on our tracks. About thirty minutes before the suits arrived, she had a full-on nervous breakdown. I'm serious. I'd never experienced anything like it. As I sat alone with her, desperately trying to console, she spun like a washing machine. She was walking in a manic circle, hallucinating. It was heartbreaking. She fled back to the UK the next day, never to be heard from again.

Singer #3 was an unknown Baruch College student writing for the first time with our (then) intern, Grant Michaels, in the B room. As I walked by, her tone stopped me dead in my tracks. She seemed very musically intriguing—kind of a stormy, kooky cocktail. JD, Bob, and Pete all agreed. Though she hailed from Staten Island, about 3,470 miles away from the UK, we decided she was worth fighting for.

Who was Girl #3?

Bebe Rexha.

Yup.

From the get-go, though, it was woefully apparent that the label higher-ups didn't share our same Bebe enthusiasm, so after a year and a half of useless, half-hearted noodling, Island buried the Black

Cards project in a scrap heap. In the end, though, I guess everything worked out fine. A reinvigorated Pete went back in with Fall Out Boy, altered their musical DNA, and had another string of hits. Bebe had a pretty tremendous run herself.

Me? Well, EMI's cutting bait ended up being the gift that kept on giving. I immediately received pretty sweet offers from the bulk of the major publishers, certainly beyond either Bret's or my own predictions. Then out of nowhere, Universal Music Publishing's East Coast head of A&R, Jennifer Blakeman, came with an eleventh-hour proposal that blew everyone else the hell out of the way. I had first crossed paths with Jennifer a few years prior when I was elected to a governor position on the NY Grammy chapter, which she headed at the time. Though the governor role was definitely the wrong fit for me (too many subcommittees of committees; once my term ran its course, I pulled an Al Gore, grew an unruly beard, and retreated from the stump for good), I've gotta say, Jennifer was pretty cool. We definitely shared a solid bond from the jump. I think she respected my snide leanings. I admired the fact that she had toured with Billy Idol on keys before she went inside the machine. Either way, our publishing deal was consummated quickly. I signed the execution copies, and Bret sprinted it over to FedEx. I grabbed Crush's Bob McLynn, and we grabbed celebratory cocktails, but as we sat there, basking in my glory and soon-to-be thickening wallet, my iPhone received an email from Jennifer Blakeman on which I was blind-copied.

The header read, "To my friends and colleagues."

My heart raced. I couldn't believe she was emailing her entire contact list the news that she'd just closed my deal! I continued soaking in the rest of her words.

"To my friends and colleagues,

"As of this afternoon, I am moving on from my job at Universal Music Publishing after 8 years . . ."

My face went whiter than the kid in *Powder*.

My A&R had been fired within two hours of my signing!

Over the next three years, I cycled through four different A&R people at Universal, before David Gray, who I'd known for years and really dug, blessedly took over the helm of my ship. David immediately landed me an Olly Murs cut, which made some real noise in the UK, and a few other album tracks on records that I dug. Nothing life altering, but certainly some solid experiences. This was still smack dab in my aforementioned frigid stretch, and he really tried to muster up some heat for me against diminishing odds.

## BONUS CUT

When you sign a publishing deal, you've gotta manage your expectations. If you're in the midst of a chart-topping run, then your ecstatic new publisher will field endless incoming calls on your behalf and plug your stuff with ease. That doesn't necessarily make them a brilliant navigator, as it's somewhat effortless work at that point, but hey, at least it's something. If your new publisher turns out to be nothing more than a professional paper pusher, they might float you emails that read, "Hey, do you want to write with Bruno Mars?" When you eagerly respond, "Obviously!" the line always goes dead. That's the lazy-ass, amateur approach. Don't fall for it. Now, if you have a loyal, hardworking publisher, and your career is cold as fuck, they will most likely get stonewalled at every possible turn they take on your behalf. That's when they prove their mettle. If you're an iceberg and they muster up a big opportunity for you, do not forget it. Send them a nice case of wine (no Trader Joe's Two Buck Chuck, you cheap ass). When all is said is done, use your gumption, as you yourself will always be your best representative. Stay relentless. Chase collaborations down. Howl as loud as you need to so you're heard over the rest of the wolf pack.

As my Universal deal wound down, I began to explore new publishing options. Max Martin and Josh Abraham, a great friend and owner of Pulse Music Group, tried to combine forces to buy out the last of my deal from Universal and set me up in a joint venture with the both of them, but Universal ultimately declined. That was obviously disappointing. Undeterred, I committed to finishing my Universal term strong, and then I planned to tempt the fates by signing with a Swedish company called Kobalt for zero advance.

**BONUS CUT**

Kobalt was primarily an administrative publishing company, so they wouldn't own any of my copyrights. That was mad enticing. Their collection fees were relatively minimal. They also developed the first online portal that allowed artists to manage their rights and royalties directly. I would say it was kinda fun watching the dollars accumulate in realtime via a phone app. It was like Robinhood or some shit. If you're signed to Kobalt, or any comparable admin company for that matter, and you have a real hit, you're making significantly more money than with a traditional publisher. It's a big gamble, though—because publishers offer sexy-ass advances that are quite enticing. By going on some Vegas shit and signing with Kobalt, you're 100 percent betting on yourself.

So I was down to my final Universal session before I inked with Kobalt. David set me up on a co-write with Nolan Sipe, a lovely and ultra-talented fella who'd just scribed Andy Grammer's brilliant "Honey, I'm Good," and an unknown seventeen-year-old British artist named James TW. Truthfully, I wasn't that thrilled about it, but since I was exiting Universal for good and, most importantly, I trusted David's instincts, I thought I might as well have one final go of it for old times' sake. Once we began that session, James pitched a really unique song concept. A year or so earlier, he'd become friends with a local family and begun to give drum lessons to their eleven-year-old boy to earn a few pocket dollars while he was in school. A few weeks in, the kid's parents told James they were planning to divorce before they had broken the news to their child. James wondered how they'd go about relaying this painful reveal to the boy, so for this song, his goal was to spin that sadness into some message of positivity for a child who was too young to understand the fragile nature and complexity of relationships. If we nailed it, James hoped the kid might listen to it cathartically to help ease his situation. Nolan and I were floored. This complex idea was birthed by a freakishly intuitive seventeen-year-old mind. We all hopped aboard this concept and began riding it.

In songwriting, the mantra is, more often than not, "Write about what you know." The things that resonate with you on an intimate level. And obviously, we do try to adhere to those guidelines, but in this specific case, I hadn't personally dealt with divorce, so I only knew marital breakups and estrangements secondhand. That meant, to really hitch on to James's vision, I needed to dive into a different emotional space inside myself, just as a screenwriter or a novelist scripting a fictional, gut-wrenching emotive tale might use any tool possible.

Well, that afternoon, the emotions came pretty quickly.

Twenty minutes into the session, Mount Sinai hospital hit my cell, alerting me to the fact that, after a good decade, my dad had finally exhausted all of his medical treatment options for his multiple myeloma, so we'd immediately have to set up a hospice situation.

Hospice.

How's that for bleak imagery?

I took a fifteen-minute breather and sat in the Universal courtyard battling hyperventilation. I knew I'd be red-eyeing back east from Burbank later that evening, but out of respect to David Gray and those two sweet gents, though, I needed to finish the session strong. I went back into the room, and we continued chasing the tale. My eyes were a shade of moist throughout the entire afternoon. As the bulk of my better songs have gone, it really flowed effortlessly. When we landed the chorus, I knew we had something stellar. After we breezed through the second verse, someone kicked around the notion of writing a bridge with a bit of optimism interspersed. I'm always down for a biscuit of positivity in a tune, but on that specific day, I saw zero sunshine. My world felt dismal. In that dark headspace, I just wanted this song to stay on the same melancholic gear for three minutes. When we parted that day, I had no idea if the three of us would ever cross paths again. I ran back to my house, packed a bag, and hightailed it back east. I'm sure you can understand how the song faded from my mind pretty quickly. I was dealing with much heavier shit. Thankfully, from his initial listen, David Gray was floored by it. Island Records UK, James's label, also seemed jazzed about its prospects. The label decided to release it as a single. I truly felt it had a zero percent chance of permeating. It's not that I didn't believe in the tune. When I finally gave it another spin, I wondered if it was one of the strongest songs I'd ever written, but to be fair, James was an unknown commodity. Also, and more importantly, this tune had a pretty sleepy mood to it. The tempo was 126 bpm, but it didn't feel up-tempo at all. I think my track record with that kind of emotional cut at that point was like one for thirty—the one being Train's "Marry Me," and, as I said, that was really Pat pulling the hitch. The bulk of my hits tended to be louder, with more joy and bombast. That wasn't just my forte, but my passion. I had very little belief that I could actually create a song that resonated with people if the vibe was slower and sadder than dial-up internet. I often wonder how the song would've been altered if Mount Sinai hadn't called that day. Would I have fought more aggressively for a more chipper reveal in the bridge to lighten the vibe? Shit, would I have campaigned for Imagine Dragons–like stomps and claps to bump up the groove? A year later, the tune finally dropped as is and immediately caught fire worldwide on Spotify. As I'm typing this, the song has been streamed over 500 million times. Pretty nutty. Even trippier, I received a bunch of really sweet emails and messages from fans of the song who thanked me for my role in its creation. The fact that it affected folks to this extent was quite moving. Up to that point, I couldn't recall birthing a song that held such a deep emotional vibrancy for people.

On the day the song really hit its zenith, James debuted it on *The Ellen Show*. Watching that taping, I listened to it from a different perspective. I just wanted to hear it as a fan. As James passionately sang the hook, I began to focus on the tag, specifically the word "someone." The way it hung over the last bar of the payoff sounded so beautiful in James's tone. There was just something about the phonetics of that word that soothed like perfection in that butter British accent. Adele's "Someone Like You." Hozier's "Someone New." Lewis Capaldi's "Someone You Loved." All of those cuts packed a similar punch.

BONUS CUT

Sluggo and I were such shameless fucks. For a moment in time, we always attempted to jam the word "tonight" at the end of our choruses. The word was just so easy and warm. The more we threw "tonight" into the hopper, the quicker the song raised its hand. In the '80s, the word "rain" did a similar thing—"Purple Rain," "Can You Stand The Rain," "Blame It on the Rain," "It's Raining Men"—even Toto blessed the rains down in Africa! There were no two ways about it—"rain" definitely made shit rain!

Taking that into consideration, I decided to part the clouds to see if I could cook up another "someone" smash. I just needed another perfect British muse. Enter again Steve Yegelwel, who was now managing A&R duties at Island. One of his newer signings was an up-and-coming Liverpudlian named Michael Nelson, who performed under the moniker Banners. Michael had a pretty kooky backstory himself. His father, Ken Nelson, produced the three seminal Coldplay albums, as well as classics by Badly Drawn Boy and Snow Patrol. I guess Michael wanted to pave his own path, so he fled to Toronto of all places, and that's where the Banners project was born.

When I met Michael, he was beginning to build a decent streaming base, but he hadn't really broken through in any significant way. His voice was stellar, though. It had a yearning quality that totally slayed me. He'd just spent an entire month writing in L.A.—twenty-five different speed-dating rounds of writing sessions back to back with a new collaborator every day. Nothing had come of it. At that point, he was both frustrated and lonely. I was his last write before his flight home. He called Steve to bail on our session. Steve talked him out of it. When he arrived at my studio, Michael's excitement level was somewhat below muted. As we began to talk, he was quite open and honest about it all. He led with, "Man, I'm sorry, but I feel burned out. I'm definitely struggling a bit." My response was pretty blunt.

"Ignore all that shit. Erase the last month. Today, we're going to write a hit."

The craziest part of this (in hindsight, cheesy-as-fuck) statement was that I was 100 percent convinced that we would. As a writer, there are just those rare days when you know you have it. I can't recall what fueled my tank that day, but whatever it was, I felt freakishly energized and supremely confident. Grant Michaels, my wonderful ex-intern turned engineer and occasional collaborator, started a track the night before that had a really wonderful foot-stomping groove. Michael and I decided to mess with it. We began trading verse lyrics and melody. We played with words of vulnerability—the innate need to love and be loved that burns within all of us. Then it was time to land the chorus. This was my chance to inject the magic word. I began waltzing around the room singing the phrase, "I wanna be somebody to someone oh," and thankfully, Michael didn't flinch a bit. He just wailed it right back, and we continued building. Man, it was so on. The rest of the day was magic. We cut ELO-inspired backgrounds all over the demo. When we wrapped the resulting song, "Someone to You," I called Steve, bursting at the seams. I knew it was special. He instantly agreed. For the tune's production, Steve decided to give a very hip British producer the first crack at it. The guy was given the following simple directive from Steve:

"The demo is exactly the vibe. Just re-create it with a little more polish."

The production came back as . . . a ballad!

A ballad?!

Yes, for some inexplicable reason, this uncoachable bloke went rogue and slowed it down 80 bpm to a passionless pit. It was unlistenable. Thankfully, Steve trashed it on the spot and Banners finished the production in Toronto with his boys, and they completely crushed it. The only problem was that the bulk of the label, beyond Steve, had next to no interest in this developing act (déjà Bebe). They were top heavy with the likes of Shawn Mendes, Demi Lovato, and Nick Jonas. An unknown, poppy alternative kid who would struggle to pack a small club was doomed to languish on the lowest rung of their roster. So as you'd expect, "Someone To You" didn't get a radio shot. Instead, it was uploaded to Spotify with zero fanfare. Surprisingly, to me at least, it got next to no playlisting. That meant death on arrival. Truthfully, I was a bit bummed about it, but I had little recourse. As the industry had finally shifted into a streaming-based game, you had a very brief window to make a dent, or it was on to the next. The song quickly disappeared, and we all resumed life. Then something funny happened. An *American Idol* executive heard it and pushed it through as the theme for the 2018 season. Soon the tune began to sell like crazy on iTunes. It also started to stream. *Idol* even brought Banners to L.A. to perform it live. Island still refused to work it. Jerks. Even worse, Steve Yegelwel's contract wasn't renewed. Yet despite the act having few champions in the building, the song just refused to die. It got a film trailer for some Netflix teen thing, and the streams began to raise their hand again. Ten million became 40 million! Island stayed silent.

Finally, in 2020, a full three years after its initial release, "Someone to You" exploded thanks to TikTok. Kids started making videos to the tune, and, within a year, 40 million streams grew to 500 million. The song finally became a worldwide hit. It was also the slowest climb of its sort I'd ever experienced in my life. Four years. So many false starts. I can't express how proud I am of this little tune and, for that matter, the James TW song as well. Having success with established artists is a really powerful feeling, but being a part of *someone's* rise into relevance is the most thrilling shit of all.

### BONUS CUT

Trust me, folks: the fun never stops. Two years ago, I signed my current admin deal with Sony Publishing. An old friend, senior VP Rich Christina, brought my deal in. A couple of days after closing, I rolled by Rich's office for the signing photo. Big smiles all around. It ran in the trades a few days later. One week after it hit the newsstand, however, on the Jen Blakeman tip, Rich was fired! Undiscouraged, the next day I loaded the signing photo into some shitty iPhone app and (sadly) proceeded to completely photoshop Rich out of the shot. Then I replaced his head and torso with that of my freshly assigned publisher, Jennifer Knoepfle (another old pal) that I found on Google Images. I went to a copy shop, printed it out, framed it, and gave it to Jennifer as a gift for posterity. It still hangs in her office. At the end of the day, we all just orbit each other endlessly on a loop in this business. Folks will come, go, and return again to your career.

## CHAPTER 36

# The Band that Almost Saved Christmas

J ews rule Christmas music. We're seriously like Baryshnikov in this dance. Look at our track record: "White Christmas," "Rudolph the Red-Nosed Reindeer," "Silver Bells," "Let It Snow," and "The Christmas Song (Chestnuts Roasting on an Open Fire)." Even "Santa Baby" was birthed in the tribe. I learned all of this as a kid via proud family musings. These reveals were repeated every year around the holidays, which of course was immediately followed by a very brief game of Great Jews in Sports (Sandy Koufax, Rod Carew, Hammerin' Hank Greenberg! Umm . . . ?).

From the jump, I always loved Christmas music. Coming from a tiny fam with very few traditions and celebrations, I viewed the indomitable Yuletide sing-along spirit as a thirsty spectator, secretly wishing that I had a membership card to the exclusive North Pole club. What about Hanukkah jams, you might inquire? I wrote a Festival of Lights anthem with the Orthodox Jewish reggae boss Matisyahu (and "Rock Me"'s Kool Kojak) called, appropriately enough, "Happy Hanukkah." The tune caught a bit of holiday shine on release. Matis performed it on *The Late Show with Jay Leno*, where Kojak and I snuck around the set snapping Instagram gold. Though "Happy Hanukkah" did earn me some solid top-tier points from the descendants of Abraham, that pie-in-the-sky

Mariah-Carey-Christmas-enormity was still looming in my dream sightline.

Now, it was a brutally hot late-winter Los Angeles AM, when Kevin Griffin, he of the '90s rockers Better Than Ezra, rolled by my crib. Kevin was not only a fantastic talent but also one of my closest pals. He'd begun segueing into a successful career of co-writing, so we were on the same grizzled circuit—the 150-plus-songs-a-year Ferris wheel of endless co-writes—hoping that something worthy materialized (and paid the mortgage to boot). Kevin was thinking we should write a pitch song. At that point, I'd mostly stopped doing anything of that sort, so when we dove in, it's fair to say I wasn't really dripping with inspiration. We kicked around a few bland ideas for a bit, but then we both lost interest, and for some inexplicable reason we randomly segued into thrashing out the merits of Band Aid's "Do They Know It's Christmas" versus USA for Africa's "We Are The World," and the current nostalgic worth of these two charitable, holiday-ish classics.

**BONUS CUT**

Writing with folks who share your perspective of music history is a godsend. If a similar frame of reference isn't there, it's tough to break down those first walls of collaboration. "Hey, Sam! What's your favorite Aztec Camera single?" When someone can actually engage in that debate ("Oblivious," duh), I know we're gonna be fast friends.

As our holiday convo continued, on an '80s, Very Special Christmas–inspired whim, we decided to write our own Christmas number. Shit, what better place to channel Santa's sleigh than in the middle of the sweaty sauna that is Hollywood? Pulling from a sack of yuletide tools, the resulting tune, "Must Be Christmas," was effortlessly written in under an hour. Then we began cooking up ideas on how to birth it into the world. Our initial thought was to pitch it to Kelly Clarkson, because any time either of our publishers sent us a "Who's

Looking" list, Kelly Clarkson was one of the names that was ALWAYS on there. The chance of Kelly cutting your song? Infinitesimal.

**BONUS CUT**

"Who's Looking" lists are industry-insider tip sheets full of major label artists who are "looking" for new material. Music publishers spit them out to writers as a form of carrot dangling. If you scour these things closely, however, you'll typically find singers who've completed their projects months earlier and aren't looking, bands that have long since been dropped from their labels, as well as the occasional deceased artist. It's all a big jerkoff to me, but others might disagree.

So with the pitch prospects looking their usual bleak, we began to kick around the notion of recording the song ourselves as our very own philanthropic posse cut. We figured we both had healthy Rolodexes of friends and collaborators who might sign up to guest on the song. Kevin was deeply involved in the charity MusiCares, so we thought we could put out the single and kick some cash to them in the process. Who knew; maybe it could grow into something fun! I phoned the brilliant Tyler Glenn from Neon Trees. Kevin hit Charles Kelley from Lady A. They were both down to jump on it. Then Kevin locked in Michael Fitzpatrick, a.k.a. Fitz from Fitz and the Tantrums (that call would, in time, significantly alter my song-life). One by one, shit continued to align—311's Nick Hexum, Owl City, the Mowglis, 3OH!3, and a host of other friends agreed to guest on the tune. By the time we tracked and mixed it, we had a pretty swell little holiday jam! We just needed a home base for it. Thankfully, Kevin had a tight relationship with The End, an indie label in Brooklyn, who backed it and agreed to put it out. Joyeux Noel!

"Must Be Christmas," by the Band of Merrymakers (as we christened ourselves) dropped right before the 2014 holiday season commenced. And it actually got a smattering of press—solid reviews in *USA Today* and *People* magazine. It also made its way onto something called the Spotify Christmas Pop playlist. That was the long and short of it. Then it melted into the sand.

As January rolled in, we both settled back into our respective writing rodeos. One February morning, though, my phone rang from a 212 number. I instinctively answered, and it was a real blast from the past: Winston Simone. I hadn't spoken to Winston since an impromptu lunch a decade previous. He managed the Hall of Fame songwriter Desmond Child, and together they formed the publishing company Deston Songs (Desmond/Winston) and built it into an absolute powerhouse. They were both bosses and, from what I could recall, really sweet guys. That being said, I had zero notion why he was reaching out.

"Hey, Sam, I was walking through Central Park a few weeks ago, and I heard this wonderful song on the Spotify Christmas Pop playlist. Can you tell me more about this Merrymakers thing?"

Wait, was the Spotify Christmas Pop playlist really a thing? Remember, this was back when Spotify was still more of a young gun than the semiautomatic it is now. I proceeded to spew the passionate pitch on the Merrymakers concept that Kevin and I had thrown together to induce our pals. We were "a rotating-cast holiday supergroup" (I know, that's a VERYYY bold term to be loosely tossing around, but fuck it, days were desperate . . . ). There were obviously bigger problems with this toss than my descriptive liberties. There was no group! We had no artists locked into promoting this group beyond the generous vocals they had cut on the one song. This did not deter! After a lengthy chat, full of exaggerated promises from my end, Winston concluded the call with the following statement: "I'm doing some A&R for Sony Masterworks. I'd love to sign the Band of Merrymakers, if you're interested?"

Holy mistletoe!

The Band of Merrymakers were in the major-label business of Christmas!!!

Then we nabbed the game-changing Merrymaker . . .

Sugar Ray's own Mark McGrath.

Since the "Fly" days of the band, I'd always been a big McGrath fanatic from afar. Back in 2008, I'd collaborated with Sugar Ray on a song called "Girls Were Meant to Love." We never hung hard, though—only casually crossed paths a few times in L.A.— but he always seemed so genuinely warm and humble. Also, a little self-doubting. That perplexed me. It was almost like he was viewing his career through a foggier lens than the rest of us. Mark came over to my house to hang, and then, on a whim, the three of us spontaneously wrote "Holiday in L.A." It was a blast. We spit-take-laughed the entire afternoon. As we wrapped, Kevin boldly asked Mark if he wanted to partner with us on this band, fully expecting him to pass. Remarkably, he was down.

The forty-something holiday *Three Amigos* was born.

From the moment the Masterworks deal was signed, it was a psychotic sprint to finish our full-length debut. We were now in mid-April. Christmas albums were usually wrapped by late summer at the latest. That gave us an adequate three months or so to set up press and TV appearances before the eventual release (usually in October!). The timeline was further complicated by the fact that we chose to write a bunch of original songs for the record. We were chasing The Waitresses instead of phoning in karaoke Nat King Cole. It was a lofty goal; still, we began attacking this mistletoe beast with reckless abandon.

We effortlessly wrote seven originals—at a song-a-day pace—and brought in radio staples like Christina Perri and Bebe Rexha to join in the joy. We were also the beneficiaries of some incredible heavy lifting from Josh & Charity. They gave their everything to this project. Josh coproduced it, and Charity sang many of the backgrounds. It was a total labor of love. We delivered our full-length debut to Sony Masterworks in mid-July, and the label seemed genuinely pumped. As the project continued to take shape, Winston told us that we should start configuring the live show. The live show? Honestly, we'd never even factored performance into the equation. Suddenly we were formulating this thing on a whole other level. We decided to model our visual after old UK *Top of the Pops* clips of Slade and Wizzard performing during the early '70s. We loved the visual of those glam bands dressed in goofy-ass plaid costumes while lip-syncing over TV tracks. That was our spirit in a nutshell. We ordered a bunch of goofy

Christmas suits from an upstart Dutch company called Opposuits. We mixed and matched their tacky plaid garb until we began to look like a colorblind, crackhead Christmas. For our live appearances, we miraculously locked in a lineup of Mark, Kevin, Fitz, Tyler Glenn, and Natasha Bedingfield. Charity sang occasional leads and backgrounds, and Josh and Blair Scinta, of Alanis Morrisette's band, held down the rhythm section. Me? I was the Happy Mondays-like dancing mascot in the background, holding it down with a keytar. A Christmas-light-adorned keytar.

I know that optic should've been the deal breaker, but a week or so later, ICM signed us, and we were booked to perform at *The Today Show*, the Hollywood Christmas Parade, *Jimmy Kimmel Live!*, and, most incredibly, the NBC primetime *Rockefeller Christmas Tree Lighting Special*! We couldn't be stopped! ICM mapped out a thirty-date run of performing arts centers along the East Coast. We were even floated a Vegas residency. Insanity!

As the holidays whipped into a frenzy, we began workshopping our live show at a soundstage in Atwater Village, but we hit our first hiccup almost immediately. The main problem we faced was that our guaranteed money on these dates was low. Ridiculously low. I didn't want or deserve any cash, but my cohorts all stood to make substantially more dollars doing solo gigs than singing their fa-la-las with our ragtag ensemble. How could we ask McGrath to pass on an opportunity to judge Miss Hawaiian Tropic or some shit for $10K on the very same night he'd only be making back his basic expenses with our holiday troupe? Anyone else would've dipped at that point, but Mark was beyond a trouper. He believed in the end game and took one (in his wallet) for the team.

Our first performance was at the Glendale Americana Mall in front of ten thousand festive shoppers. It was so bizarre. I hadn't set foot on a stage since my youthful rapping disasters. Now here I was decked out like a holiday acid trip, and the crowd seemed to love it. I guess everything was forgivable during the holiday season. Mark and Kevin grabbed my ass and pushed me to the front row for comedy. I merrily bounced around as we triumphantly blew through the set and sprinted to the backstage area. We all hugged and celebrated, while receiving tons of love from the grinning mall bigwigs and car-dealership-owning sponsors.

Next we performed at the Hollywood Christmas Parade. So campy! So strange! So Hollyweird! Our dressing room was located smack-dab in the middle of the Church of Scientology Information Center. There were L. Ron Hubbard photos everywhere. That was something. The Hollywood Christmas Parade lineup was indeed some *Battle of the Network Stars*–worthy gold. TV's Erik Estrada, Montel Williams, and Dean Cain hosting, gawking at the likes of Lou Ferrigno, Jerry Mathers, and Burt Ward, and hangs with Kenny G, Olivia Newton-John, and Cyndi Lauper, who I hadn't seen in fifteen years since our one brief co-write. It was like reliving my childhood in a delirium state. It was awesome. I felt like I'd hopped on the Further bus with Ken Kesey and the Merry Pranksters.

The following morning, we were off to the Big Apple.

We landed in NYC that Monday with a jam-packed itinerary. We'd booked one final rehearsal before dinner, and then our first performance was the following AM at the *Today Show*. I was a complete bundle of nerves. I only crashed for a couple of hours before the dreaded 3:30 AM lobby call. As I exhaustedly made my way down, Mark was already posted up and rehearsing banter. What a pro!

**BONUS CUT**

If you're watching your favorite artist perform on these morning talk shows and they underwhelm, keep in mind that they're probably operating on three hours of shut-eye, tops. The lack of sleep is utter brutality on the vocal cords, so please calm your bitter Twitter fingers the fuck down.

That morning we arrived at 30 Rock and changed into our festive uniforms. It was during the soundcheck (at 5 AM) when it really hit me. I was actually gonna be performing on the *Today Show*! I marveled at how tiny the actual studio actually was. It seemed like a Matchbox car version of what I'd envisioned. And the entire *Today Show* production staff were wonderful to us. The crew, the executives, even our fellow guests. The Property Brothers for one were some spirited fellas. They seemed very supportive of our ragtag holiday troop. Amanda Peet was promoting some film and she was both nice and extremely brief. She did appear a bit puzzled by our whole thing.

Then it was showtime.

We launched into the "Must Be Christmas" intro, and the multiple cameras began speeding back and forth with rapid-fire zooms on each of us. It was pretty dizzying. I pondered puking. I felt so self-conscious and exposed as I held down the end of the front of the stage with these infinitely more gifted pals of mine. Mark noticed and whispered in my ear, "It's easy. The camera that's shooting is always flashing red. Just follow the light. That's what they're seeing at home." In a flash, I actually began to get it. It was like an insane game of Pong. About halfway through the first verse, I finally loosened up and became an elastic version of myself. I'd like to believe I was channeling the fluid spirit of my old man. His movements were poetry. My movements were inarticulate, but I did do my thing that day in front of a smiling Al Roker. I even incorporated my own version of the *What's Happening!!* Rerun dance (Rerun was always my spirit animal).

After the song wrapped, we did a quick Q&A with Matt and Savannah. Then they name-dropped me on national TV! God, I wish my folks had witnessed it.

But there was no time for a victory lap.

Within an hour or so, we were filming an interview for *Extra* that was beamed across Times Square for everyone below to view. Next we taped an hour-long radio interview with Hoda Kotb. She was quite cheery and sweet. This was followed by Vevo and SiriusXM The Pulse interviews. Then we sprinted up to Montefiore Medical Center in the Bronx so we could go room to room, performing acoustically for patients, their families, and staff for Musicians On Call's Bedside Performance Program. Finally, we made it back to Times Square and ran around with a massive NBC film crew shooting our escapades. This footage was used for network promos. It was damp and raw, but just seeing huge crowds of folks' faces light up as we performed our snippets was just the coolest shit ever.

After a quick disco nap, we returned to 30 Rock later that afternoon for the *Rockefeller Center Tree Lighting* taping, and it started to sleet like crazy. As we got dressed in our costumes, we marveled at the enormous (and sopping-wet) crowds that were already forming. Suddenly, the show's line producer stepped into our greenroom and asked, "Which one of you is Sam?"

I froze.

I knew this was the moment when I was gonna be sent back down to the minors where I belonged. Honestly, I felt a sense of relief. I really didn't deserve to be on any stage with my seasoned friends. I was simply a present that looked much better unwrapped.

"Sam, follow me," he said.

My bandmates seemed equally puzzled.

I was about to get fed to the peacocks.

As we marched to my execution in silence, the producer turned to me and casually uttered, "So we're giving you your own riser. We saw the *Today Show* and liked the keytar visual. You're gonna kick the tree lighting special off on camera."

I couldn't even reply.

I was so dreadfully terrified.

Also, it was now full-blown ice conditions as they hoisted me up to this dangerously slick, five-foot-square riser that had to be toweled down every two minutes. If I gyrated in any wrong direction, it would be game over. The rest of the group were on the main stage laughing at my predicament. I'm sure there was a solid over/under bet on me falling off this damn thing and going viral forever. As I attempted to get my bearings, I teeter-tottered high in the air, anxiously waving to the crowds below, who obviously had no idea who I was. I was a fake Christmas star and I loved every second of it. The countdown began.

5-4-3-2-1!

The camera zoomed toward my face. The red light shined, and the director waved his arms frantically. All I had to do was throw a handful of snow at the camera. Guess what?

I shotputted that damn powder like an Olympic gold medalist!

This was my greatest sports achievement!

From that point on, the performance breezed by. I attempted to hop around a little, launching every step judiciously in hopes of avoiding a broken neck. The camera gave me more love than I needed. In three minutes and change, it was over.

The greatest prime-time snow toss of '16.

After the taping, we all gleefully hopped back in our sprinter van and headed to Winston's spectacular Fifth Avenue townhouse to watch the prime-time broadcast. I only wish that I could freeze that memory then and there, and end on that joyous note, but sadly, that was the end of the merry.

As we sat in Midtown traffic, one by one we began getting frantic texts from friends alerting us of a mass shooting in San Bernardino, California. It was horrific. Fourteen dead. Twenty-two seriously wounded. NBC immediately pulled the plug on our peppy performance and we were preempted everywhere in America, except the Northeast region, where we all watched our remarkable, barely seen effort in stunned silence.

The next evening, we performed a show in Times Square at B. B. King's nightclub. The following night at a performing arts center in Morristown, New Jersey. We even headlined the Troubadour in Hollywood and, in hindsight, that was all indeed pretty sweet, but there was a significantly lower level of morale in our ranks. We spent the remainder of the holiday season licking our wounds.

We did merry on, though.

We were offered a 2016 endorsement from the Opposuits CEO, who, in doing so, also berated the shit out of us for mixing and matching their outfits on camera. Then said CEO was fired, and our phone line to the Netherlands went dead. Fitz and Natasha moved on. The ultra-rad Kay Hanley and Lisa Loeb slid in. We continued to hit the Hollywood Christmas Parade, but just like the Merrymakers lineup, the event's celebrity booking began to thin out as well.

"Hey, look, it's Ruben Studdard . . . again!"

The following year, we released a cover of a holiday tune written by my late pal Jaik Miller. On a personal tip, that song choice meant the world to me. I think Jaik would've loved it as well. By 2018, though, there was little merry left. We had only one Merrymaker show on the books. It was the Thousand Oaks Christmas Tree Lighting. Mark, Kevin, and myself were all unavailable, but Josh and Charity cobbled together an amazingly talented lineup of some of their closest friends to headline this thing. Alas, this was immediately after both the tragic Woolsey fires and Borderline Bar mass shooting, so it was probably not gonna be the most festive of nights. The show opened with a local magician. It was a far cry from 30 Rock.

As the Charity-fronted, ever-evolving Band of Merrymakers strutted up the ramp to the makeshift stage to greet the few hundred or so revelers, Josh's kid brother, Blake, the newest Merrymaker drummer, took an errant step on the poorly configured setup and proceeded to fall through the ramp and break his left leg. Literally shattered. Here's the wild part, though. In true Merrymaker form, the kid hammered away and played the entire set. Sure, at times it seemed like he had morphed into the Muppets' Animal, drumming in unknown time signatures, but on heart alone, he absolutely sleighed it. That night ended with an ambulance ride and a fitting end to the Band of Merrymakers as we knew it. In the years that followed, I was convinced that my holiday road to Christmas record glory had reached its rightful dead end, but strangely, in time, as sure as Salvation Army bells ring along Fifth Avenue in December, it would snow on my ass yet again.

Band of Merrymakers in Times Square.

CHAPTER 37

# The Clapper

When I was a tyke, I first heard Shirley Ellis's classic "The Clapping Song" on an oldies station and flipped. Then, as a teen, I soaked in Kurtis Blow's "The Breaks" with his "clap your hands everybody" call to arms, as well as the still ubiquitous, "Clap on, Clap off, The Clapper" TV commercial. Clapping was the shit. Then, somewhere along the timeline, the clapping died and the world's fingers dropped. I knew somebody had to fill that void. Civilization was in desperate need of an a new clap anthem.

I was beach strolling on Cape Cod one autumn sunset when I began hearing a goofy little phrase that sat stubbornly in my head. I kept scatting "I can make your hand clap" to myself for hours on end. I didn't know what it was, but it sure sounded like something special. I'd had a similar electric reaction with the genesis of Karmin's hit "Acapella." I walked around L.A. humming the "I'm a do it acapella" thing for months before I actually got to throw down the idea with Martin Johnson and the duo.

As I flew back west, I began to ponder potential outlets for this "handclap" idea. I knew that the bulk of the artists I worked with at the time would dismiss the novelty of the concept in a millisecond. Over the next couple of months, I had a bunch of sessions with various bands and singers, but none of them felt like the correct fit for this thing, so I kept it tucked in my hip pocket.

Then one morning, I finally got the text that I had been hoping for. My new pal Fitz was wondering if I was interested in taking a stab at a Fitz and The Tantrums tune with him. Though I'd initially met Fitz at a couple of industry events during my first few years in L.A., I'd never broached the topic of collaborating with him. Even when he sang on the Merrymakers record, I didn't really go there. Since his band's *More Than Just a Dream* album featured co-writes by Sia and my friend David Bassett, who was coming off a banner year, I just assumed it was "Out of My League." I know that sounds a bit unnecessarily self-deprecating, but it was the truth.

**BONUS CUT**

Knowing where you stand in the songwriter marketplace is a very valuable skill. If you're iceberg cold, suppress your false optimism and don't expect the hot-lava sessions. If you're writing Florida Georgia Line singles, you might not get a call to throw down with Arcade Fire. Don't take offense and leave the entitlement at home. It's on you alone to alter others' perception of your work.

The morning of the Fitz session, I had Grant Michaels, who blessedly engineered for us that day, scour his sound banks for a distorted bagpipe patch. I know that sounds a bit mad and specific, but I wanted to create some sort of earworm in this track to emulate the power and immediacy of House of Pain's stadium banger, "Jump Around." A sonic blast that would create visceral chills up and down forearms when it dropped. Grant unearthed a supercool bagpipe/horn hybrid right before Fitz walked through the door.

Okay, so I don't do blow, but trust me: I do know white pony energy. I deal with it all the time in sessions. That day, my inner caffeine had me jittery like a snow fiend, so the moment Fitz sat down on my couch, I couldn't contain myself. There would be no time for chitchat. I literally blurted out, "I think I've got something, man!" I sensed Fitz was appreciative of the fact that I'd actually made the effort to pregame an idea. I could tell he was burned out from the usual treadmill of co-writes.

I began scatting the first verse. He stared at me wide-eyed. I was convinced he was eyeing my nostrils for the residue of rails. The last words off my lips were, "I can make your hand clap."

Then he did the strangest, most spontaneous thing.

He replied, "You don't even know," and clapped five times.

1, 2, 3, 4, 5.

Not a Patrice Rushen "Forget Me Nots" disco clap-clap.

This was like some extra clapping shit.

Every time I sang "I can make your hand clap," Fitz's hands went "clap clap clap clap clap!"

Then he sat down at the keyboard and began manipulating Grant's horn/pipe instrument into a melody. Fitz has always had such a sophisticated ear for musical hooks. That iconic whistle on "The Walker." The chopped-up vocal on "Out of My League." As someone who had bounced around the industry for as long as I had, he'd also logged long years creating music for commercials and other synchs, and in the process, he'd mastered the art of catchy.

**BONUS CUT**

Randy Newman. Paul Williams. Barry Manilow. A. R. Rahman. Sluggo! All of these legendary writers did time in the jingle game. The chops they acquired in that world were priceless. I'd also say the same thing about writers who logged long miles in cover bands. They were forced to go under the hood of hits and learn to re-create them brilliantly. I can't over-emphasize how important it is to understand how and why great songs work.

As Fitz began to play an 808 drum pattern against his horn/pipe melody, I started scribbling a verse B section. Fitz stopped me dead in my tracks.

"Nah, let's just repeat the verse A section twice."

I was a bit rattled by the idea, but Fitz referenced "Mr. Brightside" as a song where the second-verse lyric was just the first verse repeated. Two thousand listens to that jam, and I had never noticed it. And I had the nerve to call myself a lyricist.

Celebrating "HandClap" backstage in Anaheim with Fitz, Noelle Scaggs, and Grant Michaels.

We banged out the bones of "HandClap" within thirty minutes! I approached the words as a lost '80s plea of desperation. In my retro mind, I pictured Jon Cryer as the lovelorn Ducky in *Pretty in Pink* falling to the floor in front of Andie at the high school dance, screaming, "Get on my knees and say a prayer, James Brown," with the goal of cock-blocking that dull-as-a-doorknob Blane. My inner nerd always related to Ducky's thirsty plight.

**BONUS CUT**

When this song became a hit, a TV director friend of mine actually brought me to hang with Jon "Ducky" Cryer in his production company office! That was amazing. Hollywood is most definitely high school with credit cards.

Then the chess match began. I envisioned the production as a retro Motown rave-up number. Quarter-note snares. Think "Stop! In the Name of Love" by The Supremes. Fitz heard it exactly like the demo. Minimal electro-pop. Though we had a shared love of new wave's Martin Fry and obscure mid-'80s electro records, it still reeked of musical suicide to me. It was such a radical departure from the band's indie-soul catalog of hits. I was petrified. Though I'd always pushed the pop envelope with most groups, and it had certainly worked many times before, occasionally I'd feel the wrath of superfans who were all up in arms about their favorite band's directional shift.

A few years ago, me and one my closest pals, Tim Pagnotta, wrote a blink-182 single, "Blame It on My Youth," with Travis Barker and Mark Hoppus that was crucified by a portion of their fanbase. I've gotta give props to Travis and Mark, who stood by the tune. They wanted to try something new artistically and were willing to take the hate for it.

At their core, I think authentic artists like blink, or Fitz for that matter, are always willing to alienate fans to push the creative envelope. They have the same spirit as Ricky Nelson did at his infamous 1971 Madison Square Garden gig. For those who are too young for that ancient reference, ex–child star Ricky Nelson played one of the first "oldies" shows ever at MSG. He began his set hitting his '50s classics, but then he ripped into a Rolling Stones cover and the boos rained down. Completely pissed, he sang one final tune, then broke the fuck out and refused to appear onstage for the show's big finale. Shortly thereafter, the frustration of that gig prompted him to write the classic "Garden Party," which became his first US Top 10 hit in almost a decade. The song expressed the importance of trusting your gut no matter the circumstance. It was just the best clapback ever. I love the tune so much that I actually interpolated it on the Tarsha Vega single!

Happy days with Mark Hoppus, Travis Barker, and Tim Pagnotta.

As "HandClap" began to roll down the assembly line, Fitz grabbed our files and brought 'em over to Ricky Reed to finish the track. I'd always been a big admirer of Ricky's aesthetic. He was blessed with ridiculous retro R&B chops. Given his pedigree, I was expecting him to add a bit more throwback soul to the production, but he didn't mess with the demo's electro DNA—and now I was truly terrified. Once the tune was mixed and mastered, most of the folks involved with Team Fitz just didn't seem to get it either. There were many whispers that if it was released as the first single, this was a potential kiss of death for the band— and I was their Jack fuckin' Ruby! Fitz refused to hear any of it. He wouldn't back down on his vision. Thankfully, Craig Kallman (my first boss!) at Atlantic Records agreed with him. He only had one note, but it was huge: We needed to make the "hand" plural. As Craig put it, "You don't make your hand clap; you make your hands clap!" God, I felt like a buffoon. He was totally right! I was so stuck on making the title "HandClap" work that I wasn't really following the laws of plurality.

Fitz re-sang it, and the song was rushed to release.

In a mere matter of months, the tune exploded. It began to synch like crazy. TV shows. Commercials. It hit #1 on *Billboard* & Clio's Top TV Commercials Chart for three months. I had never experienced anything like it. It was even the most-played song of the year on Amazon's inaugural Alexa Chart ("Alexa, play that annoying song with the five handclaps!"). It blared at the Super Bowl, the World Series, the NBA Finals, the Stanley Cup. Literally every high school sporting event in the US. I'd finally created a Jock Jam! It even exploded globally. South Korea. China. Japan. Over a billion Far East streams later, it was now part of the worldwide pop consciousness. More importantly, this weird little tune validated me in this short-term memory of a biz like nothing had before. For the first time, it felt like folks finally saw the totality of my career as a complete body of work and not just a slapdash assortment of hits. I can't even explain how incredibly fulfilling that was. I could only hope Shirley Ellis was clapping back at us from a dance floor in heaven.

CHAPTER 38

# The High Life

anic! at the Disco's *Death of a Bachelor* album was released in January 2016. It debuted at #1 in the US, selling just under 200,000 units that first week. The record got some stellar press and, in time, a Grammy nomination. I co-wrote four songs on *Death of a Bachelor*, including "Emperor's New Clothes" and "Crazy=Genius." Though both were quite successful, platinum and gold respectively, the tune I was proudest of was "Impossible Year." That lyric encapsulated all of the frustrations of watching my dad's final lap around the sun. I was especially thrilled that it made the cut, even though I knew it'd never be a focus track. For me, at least, it was just some mega-cathartic shit.

So as Panic!'s Brendon Urie started gearing up for the *Death of a Bachelor* follow-up, he also took over the lead in *Kinky Boots* on Broadway. Man, he was spectacular in the role. The morning after his fantastic performance, I began to wonder how surreal a journey it must've been for that dude to date. Chart-topping at eighteen. Rebounding at twenty-two. A rabid, slightly divided fan base who hung on his every word. Now here he was, on the edge of thirty with five albums under his belt and bigger than ever. Plus, throw "Broadway star" into the résumé. What a loopy roller coaster! I spent the next six weeks freestyling a pile of ideas inspired by Brendon's voyage to date. I really had no idea if I'd get another Panic! call, but I was motivated, and it seemed like a worthwhile time suck. I sent the heap to Crush, but all I heard was crickets. Then Evan Taubenfeld, one of my closest amigos now running A&R for the company, broke the news to me that Brendon had decided to kick off the record's co-writes with many of the usual suspects of *Death of a Bachelor* (Jake, Lolo, Ilsey Juber, Morgan Kibby, etc.), but alas, I didn't make the initial list. Though I had zero sense of entitlement with the project, it was still a bit of a downer. Since this wasn't the first time I'd been back-burnered, though, I tried not to take it as a slight. I just continued to lay down ideas, and as the voice notes built, the more I believed that I had a super-solid vibe on where this record could go.

Finally, after a few of months of silence, there seemed to be an opening, as JD sent me a killer track that had everything Panic!-worthy except that the chorus was unfinished. The payoff of the hook was a big chant of, "Oh . . . it's Saturday night." That part was sick, but there was nothing framing it conceptually in the two lines that preceded it. If this was stand-up comedy, it was like the perfect punch line that was completely missing the setup to the joke. I sat down and started typing all sorts of nonsense. Almost immediately, I spit out the words, "I pray for the wicked on the weekend. Mama can I get an amen." Everyone involved seemed to love it, and shortly after, I was told they were gonna roll out the record with this track. I liked it fine enough, but I wasn't particularly sold on the tune's long-term prospects. I certainly had no idea that the phrase "pray for the wicked" would land as the title of the record. That was pretty neat. Then I got the Batphone call I'd been waiting a solid decade for.

"Brendon wants you to come over and write in person."

I was over the fuckin' moon.

You see, on *Death of a Bachelor*, I'd sent Brendon and producer Jake Sinclair my lyric sheets, but I never got invited to collaborate in person. Though I definitely dug Brendon's melodic choices that he matched with the words, like any other control freak of a writer, I just wished I could've been there to pitch a suggestion here or there. Now I'd finally be able to construct a tune with this legend from the ground to the sky.

I rolled up to Brendon's crib with Roman candles shooting through my veins. I pelted into his garage studio, where he was holding court with Jake and Suzy Shinn, a wonderful engineer/producer. The day before, Brendon, Jake, and Morgan Kibby had pulled one of my lyric sheets, and flipped it over this incredible Dillon Francis track. Brendon played the resulting chorus, "Hey Look Ma, I Made It," for me, and it sounded disgustingly big—but they hadn't messed with the verses yet, so he cracked open that session, and I began scatting verse lyric vibes with him. The words came from a somewhat perverse perspective. Since the track had more of an uplifting dance floor thing, I thought it would be fun to balance it with some acerbic, less obvious shit. For better or worse, I always aim for that kind of sweet/sour juxtaposition. Brendon ran with it, and we paper airplaned it back and forth melodically for an hour. Finally witnessing his skills in the room, I learned quickly that he was as freakishly gifted in the lab as onstage. Both melodically and instrumentally, he was a fuckin' monster, but his production chops were no joke either. His beats were pretty sick.

Over the next few weeks, me, Brendon and Jake banged out eight songs. I can't recall ever being so creatively dialed in. I just had a hunch that we were on some next level shit. When the tunes made their way to label and management, everyone seemed pretty joyous across the board. I could sense a real buzz on the record, but there was still one massive puzzle piece missing. JD and Evan were holding on to an incredible hook and track that had been written in a hot tub—yes, a hot tub—at a "writing camp" in Colorado a couple of years previous by the über-talented Ilsey Juber, Jonas Jeberg, Cook Classics, and Tayla Parx. I can't overstate how epic this chorus was. The first time I heard it, I was covered in goose bumps. I believe all involved originally envisioned it as the perfect hip-hop feature, which it easily could've been, but every single rap A&R had passed on it.

It was called "High Hopes."

**BONUS CUT**

A writing camp is a small congregation of topliners and producers who spend a week fraternizing in some semi-exotic locale while attempting to craft songs for a specific artist. Publishers and labels typically kick in for these things.

**CONT.**

Some camps consist of chart-topping heavyweights, but most are lined with up-and-comers. I've only attended one. It was for *The X Factor US* champs Alex and Sierra, and, surprisingly, I flew home with three tunes that made their debut! From what I've heard, though, that's definitely the exception to the rule. I once had an A&R guy proudly exclaim that he booked writing camps solely as a form of song bidding for records that he had zero direction or excitement for. Once he heard a solid tune at the camp, he'd send it out to the entire industry as "his" blueprint for the project. What a dick. In time, that one writing camp cut that had raised its hand would inevitably die on a dusty bunk with the rest (remember my David Cook/*Idol* dance?). That's why I still avoid these things like syndicated reruns of *How I Met Your Mother*.

So as the clock continued to tick on the record, and still feeling that it was desperately in need of a monster of a tune, the team brilliantly pulled a pre-chorus/bridge from a short-lived Brendon idea, fused it with the hot tub hook, and the foundation of "High Hopes" began to form. Nowadays, this sort of Frankenstein cut/paste thing happens on the regular, but in most cases, it rings kinda false to me. On this one, however, they completely nailed it.

It just needed verses.

There were no verse words or melody. Just a long, lengthy instrumental section. I couldn't fathom why they wouldn't let me have a whack at it. I was totally convinced I could deliver, as I'd now written eight songs in a row with these cats for the record, but it was always radio silence when I inquired, so I let it be.

It was the day before Joey's twelfth birthday, and I was lying on my back porch when I finally got the go-ahead to give the verses a shot. The album was set to master within a week! I slapped my headphones on, shut my eyes, and blasted the track on loop. I knew my job was pretty pivotal on this joint. Beyond the time sensitivity, I had to be the glue to bring this thing home. There was zero room for error.

I decided to frame it in a narrative. This meant threading the most delicate of needles—to keep it aspirational, but not preachy or contrived. The words came flooding from head to hands instantaneously. In totality, the verses took a solid thirty minutes to write, tops. The first was a conversation with my late mother. The second was a dialogue with my soon-to-be twelve-year-old. I guess in my head, the sum of the parts was the passing of the generational torch. I hoped it would drip of that '70s lyrical optimism that I loved as a kid. Most importantly, I could see Brendon absolutely exploding on a whole other level, if he did his thing on the track. It felt like fire.

An hour later, I drove over to Jake's house on the Silver Lake Reservoir and sang it to those cats. Evan really responded to it, which was an awesome indicator. That night, Brendon dug further into the melody and totally elevated it. Shit was a wrap.

Two months later, "Say Amen (Saturday Night)" was released as a set-up single. Unexpectedly to me, at least, it did some damage and eventually topped the Alternative chart. The *Pray for the Wicked* album dropped later that spring and, like *Death of a Bachelor*, it also debuted in the top spot. Brendon threw a party at his house to celebrate. Honestly, I was just thrilled that I made the guest list. Brendon was/is an absolutely delightful kid, but I'd be lying if I ever claimed that I was a part of his inner circle. No matter how much time I've spent with this legend, I still feel like somewhat of a gatecrasher.

I'm not sure anyone in the room that night knew what was in store, but *Pray for the Wicked* just exploded. More importantly, though, the buzz grew for "High Hopes." People seemed to *love* this tune. TV shows, movies, commercials. The song was even the campaign anthem of 2020 Democratic Party presidential candidate Pete Buttigieg, who played it on loop at his rallies and speeches. His staff and campaign volunteers created a goofy dance to the song and it went viral (truthfully, this was not some Debbie Allen in *Fame*–style shit). It was also jacked by Democratic candidates Amy Klobuchar, Cory Booker, and Julián Castro. Even then-president Donald Trump swiped it, blasting it at a June 2020 reelection rally. Like "HandClap," it entered the zeitgeist, but on a substantially louder level.

In time, the song would reach #1 Pop, #1 Alternative, and #1 Hot AC, breaking a decade-plus record with its reign atop Billboard's Adult Pop Songs radio chart, and ruling the Hot Rock Songs Chart for an unprecedented seventy-six weeks. Now, over one billion streams later, it's hands down the biggest song of my career. It's hard to express how in debt I am to Brendon Urie and Crush. They really gifted me the greatest year of my musical life. At the height of the "High Hopes" hysteria, the aforementioned blink-182's "Blame It on My Youth"

With Brendon Urie backstage at *Kinky Boots*.

was a hit at Alternative as well. That was immediately followed by the release of "Hey Look Ma, I Made It," which caught the "High Hopes" tailwind and completely smashed across formats as well. That tune ended up being my 21st Top 40 hit. I should've been basking in that most exhilarating of moments, but deep down inside, I couldn't help but feel like this stretch of success was just another fleeting cycle. Like any other neurotic creator, I've always viewed the glass as half full and rapidly cracking. In that way, I guess I'm sort of my own self-defeating prophecy. It doesn't matter what you achieve in this business; you can never escape the dragging self-doubt.

CHAPTER 39

# Benjamin Buttons

One sticky September night, I attended an ASCAP event called Lovefest, a once-a-year gathering of L.A. songwriters. It was held poolside in the backyard of a slick Toluca Lake abode. Now, I was no regular Lovefest attendee by any means, but these annual rallies were usually pretty decent soirees. It was always kinda fun seeing the excitement of up-and-coming writers attending for their first time. That youthful, unadulterated bliss in their eyes as they swarmed the free tacos and cocktails warmed my frigid heart. I remembered feeling that same rush when I started out. Those vaunted moments of glory, bumrushing a recording studio guest list at Platinum Island or Chung King for some "industry mixer," and subsequently siphoning off the gratuitous drinks until the night got hazy.

That evening at Lovefest, as the kids proceeded to get sloppy, I hung on the other side of the pool with the older guard. After many years, I'd finally graduated into that upperclassman fraternity of writer. The veritable OGs. Picture the senior section in a high school cafeteria of music nerds. It was such a fascinating crew chock-full of glorious reveals.

"This is the man who wrote 'Wind Beneath My Wings,'" or "Do you know her? She wrote Tiffany's second single in '87!"

I say that with no shade whatsoever. I live for that kind of shit. I'd usually coerce these folks into lengthy chats about whatever it was that inspired their biggest tunes. I've always found any nugget of songwriting wisdom a blessing.

Unlike previous years, though, this particular Lovefest was becoming somewhat of a snoozefest—until I saw Loretta Muñoz, the glorious grande dame of ASCAP, waltz into the proceedings with the Beach Boys' Mike Love in tow.

**BONUS CUT**

Aspiring writers! When you're starting out in this insane game, beyond mastering craft, rubbing elbows is the most crucial shit. Go to showcases, writer rounds, industry parties—basically anywhere you might make a real contact or connection. One immediate way to get it going is to utilize your performing rights organization. There are many incredible networking events and opportunities (writing camps, scoring workshops, etc.) available through ASCAP, BMI, and SESAC. These are unsung industry heroes—the ultimate songwriter advocates who love mentoring young talent. Do not sleep on them!

As I stood by the pool chatting with old friends, Loretta escorted Mike Love my way for an introduction. We chatted briefly, and, surprisingly, I found myself really digging him. It's hard to articulate, but I could just sense from his energy that he was pretty self-effacing. We took a couple of press pictures together, and he moved on down the reception line like a British royal.

And yes, obviously I was well aware of the Beach Boys' spot in the popular imagination. In this view, Brian was the one and only supreme being. A once-in-a-generation musical demigod who plunged deep into the depths of his tortured soul and subsequently fried in the never-ending quest for musical perfection. Mike Love? He was the evil, preening hack who'd sullied the band's legacy with his refusal to let it die with any semblance of grace. It's always impossible to un-hear narratives like this, but I'd never really let that kind of rock 'n' roll mythology impact my personal takes on people. I've met too many "douchebags" who were wonderful and too many "brilliants" that were fifty shades of contrived.

At that point in their storied career, the Beach Boys were basically Mike's machine. Carl and Dennis were gone, and Brian was in his own dimension, so Mike single-handedly kept the longboard afloat. Though this Mike-driven outfit ushered in a new generation of fans with his 1988 smash "Kokomo," to which I did happily dance at my prom, many purist Beach Boys fans despised every bit of it, which led to a nonstop barrage of media criticism. In all fairness, Mike's train wreck of a Rock & Roll Hall of Fame induction speech didn't help his cause.

It was about four weeks post-Lovefest when Winston Simone reentered the picture. Coming off the Band of Merrymakers ride, my friendship with Winston had blossomed into something special. He was now one of the few industry fellas I truly trusted.

I was halfway up my tri-weekly Griffith Park hike when my annoying ringtone started chirping. You know the one with the acoustic guitar that everyone seems to use? I was stunned. My iPhone never rang on that path. I have such distinctly awful memories of weekly mid-hike calls from my ailing mom that would drop every ten feet or so. By the time I'd finally make it back to my car, there were probably fifteen failed call attempts between us. With that in mind, the fact that I was actually receiving this call from Winston, with a solid four-bar reception at that, blew my damn skull. I answered, and, after a brief catch-up, he told me he was now doing a little advising for Mike Love and the Beach Boys organization, and wondered if I'd be interested in writing a Christmas song with Mike the following week.

Obviously, this was a no-brainer.

From Carole King on, my experiences working with music legends had mostly been monumental for me, both as a fan and a creative. The wisdom that flowed from those hangs had given me endless inspiration throughout the years, as well as some stellar dinner-party tales for old friends.

About a week later, Mike Love arrived at my garage studio.

We began the afternoon with a little prerequisite small talk. Before we knew it, four hours had blown by. It was one of those spectacular hangs. Just an effortless, flowing conversation. He was such a funny character. The ego was infinitely lower than I'd anticipated. Sure, politically we seemed to dance in different arenas, but at the core, he was just really witty and a completely open book. He blessed me with some incredible Paul McCartney, Marvin Gaye, and Charles Manson tales, most of which are in his autobiography. Buy that shit. It's pretty great.

When it came time to write, Mike knew exactly what he wanted. I brought Grant in on the session, and Mike rode him pretty hard as he threw down the bass line and we dialed in the groove. As for the melody, I sang him all sorts of variants, but he chose to use only the bass line as the melodic springboard. I couldn't recall any other writer using that trick. We ended up creating a festive little holiday number called "Celestial Celebration" and made a plan to write and record some more down the road. Within a month, I was producing Mike's full-length holiday album on a budget that probably wouldn't pay my Uber bills. That's how much I enjoyed hanging with this fella. We recorded the remainder of that Mike Love holiday record in an old, dusty studio deep in the Valley. He was a consummate pro throughout. Every day he arrived promptly, excited, and draped in a different Robert Graham designer shirt. He had two hundred of them. No lie. Oddly enough, at the same time we were recording Mike's album, my pal Adam Schlesinger was tracking a Monkees Christmas album down the street. We'd meet up for meals and discuss how perfect this bit of happenstance was, and also speculate how significantly more monumental it would've been if we'd been blessed to make these dueling holiday joints during Nixon's first term. I'm joking!

Pacific Pioneer Broadcasters with *Full House* creator Jeff Franklin, "Shotgun Tom" Kelly, Mike Love, Michael Lloyd, and John Stamos (and a tardy Mark McGrath, who missed the photo by 30 seconds).

(Kinda.) Upon its release, Mike Love's *Reason for the Season* record actually hit #4 on the iTunes Holiday Charts. Alas, it landed two spots behind Adam's Monkees record! He totally rubbed it in too. Bastard! Mike's label, BMG, was pretty thrilled. Most importantly, though, Winston Simone was ecstatic too.

**BONUS CUT**

One of the other great joys of the Mike Love run was when he invited me to sit on my very first dais, alongside Mark McGrath, John Stamos, *Full House* creator Jeff Franklin, and Michael Lloyd (*Dirty Dancing*!) at the Pacific Pioneer Broadcasters' Lifetime Achievement tribute in his honor. I couldn't have been more thrilled (and slightly petrified) to spill a few words in his honor in a room full of radio legends.

Right after that holiday season dissipated, Winston was in the middle of a lunch with Ringo Starr's lawyer, Bruce Grakal, when Bruce casually mentioned that after years of writing and recording his albums with a very closed-door crew of his closest friends (his brother-in-law Joe Walsh, Steve Lukather, Men at Work's Colin Hey, etc.), Ringo was potentially open to tossing a new collaborator into that mix. Without pause or any skin in the game, Winston pitched me. How cool was that? He knew how much it meant to me—a fellow colossal Fab Four fanboy. Bruce ran the idea by Ringo, and, astonishingly enough, he was open to meeting me. When Winston relayed the news, I was literally freaking the fuck out.

A week or so later, I hopped in my car, fixed my lid in the rearview, took a deep breath, and slowly crawled my car toward Beverly Hills' foothills, trying to avoid arriving prematurely, thirsty for the hang. When I pulled up to the gate, I was immediately buzzed in, and nervously climbed the long driveway, attempting to maintain my cool. At the top of the hill, I was greeted by a handyman who escorted me to the house.

Then the door flung open.

There he was.

Sir Ringo Starr.

He took a few steps in my direction and went in for a hug. I really felt like I was tripping my face off. I enjoyed every millisecond of it. Ringo led me into the living room of his beautiful estate. Man, this spot was majestic. We sat on couches across from each other and exchanged pleasantries. Then Ringo grabbed a stack of fax machine pages with my face adorning the cover. He looked me in the eye and spoke.

"So your team has been working very aggressively to get you over here . . . Why?"

I was totally blindsided. I mean, there seemed to be a bit less peace and love in his tone than I'd anticipated. As my eyes surveyed the packet in front of him, my mumbled response was an awkward attempt at some off-the-cuff humor.

"Wow . . . Um . . . I don't recall anyone on my team actually owning a fax machine?"

Wait! I had just tried to out-funny a Beatle! What the fuck was I thinking?

Ringo continued: "Hmm. Okay. So let me ask you something. What instrument do you play?"

Uh-oh.

"I fumble with guitar," I anxiously replied, "but I'm pretty miserable."

"Well, how could we write a song together, then?" he countered. "I mean, I'm just a drummer."

I felt like I was chess-boxing the entire Wu-Tang Clan.

I took one final deep breath and lobbed the proverbial Hail Mary.

"Just give me twenty-four hours, and I'll come back and sing you an idea. If you like it, we can mess around with it, and if you don't, we can hug and part forever?!"

He remained mute for a solid five seconds.

Then he smirked and said, "Two PM tomorrow."

I pulled down the driveway and sped toward Santa Monica Boulevard. My mind was racing on some Mario Andretti shit! Does Ringo Starr hate me? Do *all* humans despise me?! Maybe I can't read a room?

Now, if I haven't made it abundantly clear by this point, I've always disliked meetings. Loathed them, actually. It's never the specific interactions per se, just the mental time suck that takes me away from creating (or hiking, or eating my favorite sandwiches, etc.). Industry hangs do drum up the occasional gig, so they are a necessary evil, but at this point, after thirty years or so of the dog-and-pony bullshit, the novelty had indeed worn off. Since I was always whining about this sort of thing, Bret would mercifully book a couple of long-ass days a year for meeting madness so I could just run through them in a string.

Unfortunately, the day I met Ringo was one of those days.

I spent the rest of that afternoon uneasily tolerating four run-of-the-mill A&R visits with folks who would most likely never hire me, and it pretty much robbed me of any time to take on this once-in-a-career assignment. By the time I'd walked the dogs and dined with the fam, it was 7 PM, and I had zero brainstorms for Ringo. I was on the clock, but I knew not to force it, so I took a long stroll and waited for inspiration to strike.

After a few minutes, I began to hear something.

I started humming a chorus that summed up my entire thirty-year journey in song. The payoff was "Thank God for Music." A pretty cheesy title, but I connected to it. It read like the cover of one of John McMahon's dusty old K-Tel records that I had traded for a lifetime ago. It was also somewhat of a personal mantra. Without these tunes, I'd certainly never have had the opportunity to hang at Sir Ringo's palace.

Once I got back home, I whipped out the acoustic and began dialing in the song. Then I hit Grant and had him meet me at the studio at 10 PM. Normally, I avoided evening sessions like the Domino's Pizza Noid, but this was definitely a worthy exception. We began laying down a demo, and Grant took my sketch and went ham. He instantly flipped my pedestrian changes into something decidedly more Randy Newman. It seemed like a real vibe.

The following afternoon, I returned to Ringo's with a very spellbound Grant in tow. Ringo gave us both warm hugs. He had the best energy. He led us on an impromptu tour of his entire property, including his art studio, where he painted Pop Art portraits using beetroot juice as a primer. Beetroot juice! Who knew?

After a couple minutes of chitchat, he halted the conversation and said, "Okay, you got a song for me?" Grant instantaneously broke out his acoustic and began strumming his face off. And I began to sing. I sang like I was auditioning for *The Voice* in front of Blake Shelton or some shit, but I can't even express to you how hard I committed to this performance. I steamrolled through a verse, pre-chorus, and chorus, and then stopped on a dime.

Ringo deadpanned me for a few seconds and responded, "That's horrible."

Oof.

Then he smiled and continued, "I'm kidding! That's a fun little tune there, Sam. I like it! But what do you want me to do . . . just sing it as it is?"

My response was simple.

"Well, in all fairness, there's no second verse. Why don't you hop on it?!"

Ringo laughed. "Well, okay then!"

Within minutes, Ringo began shouting out lyrics and we nailed verse two. Then, with a little prodding, I convinced him to lay down the drums and percussion and sing the vocals to boot. I really can't express to you how surreal that was. When he pounded on the kit, it was absolute Ringo magic. The snare/tom/floor-tom double-stops. The peerless groove and epic fills that held down the melody. His pocket was nasty, and he brought such ridiculous bounce. After each take, he'd rush back into his control room area and pogo jump high in the air like kids at a Flogging Molly show. His zeal, physicality, and, most importantly, positivity were bonkers. He was incredible. We finished tracking a few hours later, and, as we wrapped, Ringo and his awesome engineer, Bruce Sugar, said they'd "work on the song."

Suddenly, that awkward air breezed back into the proceedings.

Ringo didn't offer up any contact info.

Honestly, I was pretty decimated, as I had a sinking feeling that this was probably the end of my Fab Four journey. I hastily scribbled my email and number on a piece of paper and hightailed it home.

A couple of weeks went by, and there was radio silence from Team Ringo. I sent a feeler email to Ringo's lawyer, Bruce Grakal, but he didn't offer up much in return. It was irking me big time. I mean, I just wanted to have a souvenir or keepsake of the experience. It would've been the coolest possible trophy in my mental case! There was only one choice; I had to be proactive. I went on a deep dive of interviews Ringo had given over the previous decade. I grabbed any pull quote that dripped in Ringo speak. Some YouTube. Some print. There were some real gems sprinkled everywhere I scoured, but a 2015 *Rolling Stone* feature was the icing on the cake.

**BONUS CUT**

If you're prepping for a session with a particular artist and you're attempting to get a handle on his or her lyrical voice, follow this song hack and comb through their old interviews. You might just stumble upon a nugget or two of inspiration. It's that extra diligent step that most of your competitors will lazily avoid.

Then I hit Grant and gave him a simple directive: "Send me a vibe that's just straight-up riffy, bluesy fun." I wanted to write a greasy little number as a complete about-face from "Thank God for Music." Hedge the bets. A few hours later, Grant sent me a nasty-ass guitar riff. I combined Ringo's words about his journey with my own flavors and came up with the tune "Better Days" in an hour or so. I wasn't gonna take any chances. I called in my friend Garen Gueyikian to sing the demo. He crushed it. We mixed the hell out of the track. The demo sounded properly greasy. I typed a last-ditch note to Bruce Grakal.

"Hey, Bruce! Hope all is well! Started a second idea for Ringo that I thought he might want to rip into! If interested, I can send a scratch demo?"

Bruce replied within minutes, "Send it over and I'll forward."

At least it was an opening! The song exited my outbox and then that awkward waiting game resumed. Two weeks sailed by until I got a response.

"Can you run back over to Ringo's this afternoon? He wants to work."

I jumped up and down, immediately grabbed Grant, and we rolled back up to the gates of Peace & Love. When we entered the studio, Ringo exclaimed, "Guys, I love the new song! Let's work on it today, but I also want you to hear something." Bruce Sugar pushed play on Pro Tools, and there was "Thank God for Music," finished with Steve Lukather on guitar—holy Toto! I was bowled over! We finished writing and tracking the "Better Days" basics that same afternoon, and once again, Ringo was the warmest cannonball of positive energy. I wanted that session to go on forever. It was some pinch-me shit. A few months later, he phoned me on my birthday and sang a vocal rendition of the Beatles' "Birthday," and I actually teared up. The fact that I can proudly call Ringo Starr a friend—that's some serious craziness right there. Soon after, the press announced the album's upcoming release, and I learned both songs had made the cut. In a *Billboard* interview, they asked Ringo about my involvement. His response was some headstone-worthy gold.

Sir Ringo and fan.

**BILLBOARD:**
You also brought in some new collaborators, like Sam Hollander, who cowrote Panic! at the Disco's "High Hopes" and Fitz and the Tantrums' "HandClap."

RINGO STARR:
Sam Hollander is the best prize a boy could have.

"The best prize a boy could have."
I still get teary-eyed when I re-read that quote.

At the time, it seemed like the absolute peak of a thirty-year journey in song, but the high was truly elevated a month later when I got a late-night call from Bret to alert me that I was now **THE #1 ROCK SONGWRITER IN AMERICA** on the *Billboard* Songwriter Charts (I don't wanna overdo it, but that is worthy of a little capitalization and boldface, right?!). Somehow I ended up holding down that top spot for nine weeks in 2019, which was a year-end record! The climax of the insanity was the weekend when Richard Curtis's Beatles homage *Yesterday* opened at the box office, and though a pair of no-names, Lennon & McCartney, saw their catalog bounce tremendously on Spotify, and nipped at my heels from the #2 spot, they couldn't overtake my ass on the chart. Better luck next time, freshmen!

With both a Beatle and a Beach Boy in my songwriting treasure trove, I thought it was probably time to resume working with some younger, developing acts, but then things took one more legendary turn.

I was lazily watching *CBS Sunday Morning*, and the show ran a feature on the Philly soul kings the O'Jays. It was a career retrospective, and it absolutely floored me. As the segment concluded, the O'Jays announced that they were planning to call it quits at the end of that year. Could you blame them? They'd been together since 1959! Seven decades! I grabbed my phone and speed-dialed their manager, Toby Ludwig. Toby's office was only three blocks away from our studio on Eleventh Street in the Village, so we'd hang on occasion. I immediately pressed him about who was signed on to make the O'Jays farewell record.

"I guess you are," he replied.

Now, frankly speaking, the O'Jays hadn't recorded anything particularly big over the previous twenty years, so this wasn't the kind of situation where Toby, or Bret for that matter, could simply layup a new record deal. There was only one real option. I hit S-Curve's Steve Greenberg and pitched him the O'Jays farewell record. He replied, "I'm in!" before I could spit the pitch out of my mouth. Steve signed them on the spot, and we agreed to helm the record together.

BONUS CUT

If you put Steve Greenberg's career under a microscope, you'll see it sits in very rarefied air. He's like a lost child of Mo Ostin and Lenny Waronker, Chris Blackwell, or Seymour Stein. I can name very few executives in 2022 to whom I can apply the same glowing descriptive. Don't get me wrong, there are definitely some brilliant heads running labels right now, but in this era, when master recording rights revert back to the artist in an instant, most execs will hedge their bets on a kid with massive social media numbers over taking the time to break an infinitely more gifted artist with a minuscule following. Greenberg is still all about patience and gut. Though the O'Jays's Tik Tok numbers were anemic, thankfully Steve was not thrown.

Me, Steve, Mike Mangini, and the "Cleanup Woman," Betty Wright, recorded *The Last Word* in Brooklyn, Miami, L.A., and Las Vegas. The task of attempting to decipher the brilliance of Gamble and Huff was both intimidating and awfully fun. The O'Jays' Eddie Levert and Walter Williams were two of the warmest, funniest cats I've ever come across. They were absolute sweethearts. On the mic, Walter Williams crooned with a butter-smooth tenor, and Eddie Levert had the rawest baritone ever. They could both sing their faces off. And the great Miss Betty? She redefined force of nature. She waltzed into our first session and promptly handed everyone in the room, the O'Jays included, Betty Wright T-shirts! That was the most punk-rock shit I'd ever seen.

The late, great, Betty Wright, myself, and the O'Jays.

The peak of the O'Jays experience for me was attending the record release concert at the World Famous Apollo Theatre in Harlem. The concert was beyond monumental, but the cherry on top was Eddie stopping the show to shout me out a few times in front of the packed house. It was certainly another one of those what-the-fuck-is-my-life moments. After the concert, I linked up with Eddie, Walter, and their families, and we all kicked it in a midtown hotel bar until 3 AM.

These guys were seventy-eight at the time!

As I looked back on that run of Mike Love, Ringo, and the O'Jays, beyond their general awesomeness and incredible work ethic, the one thing that truly blew my mind about that crew of Rock & Roll Hall of Famers was that they were all on some Benjamin Button shit. It was probably the most life-affirming reveal of my career. As the great cigar chomper George Burns put it, "You can't help getting older, but you don't have to get old."

## CHAPTER 40

# $280 Electric Lady Satin Bomber Jacket

avid Wolter was an A&R guy who'd been in the game for as many years as myself. He was a genuinely nice fella who I'd run into at playgrounds and industry events as we continually orbited each other for decades. Now I can't really recall where David and I initially met, but I do believe we were both in our mid-twenties when he first hipped me to his own crazy music backstory: His father had previously been both chairman and CEO of Columbia House (Remember those "8 CDs for a penny" ads?). My nostalgia-loving nerd-self thought that was just the coolest shit ever. Most of you youngsters reading this won't appreciate the significance, but in the '70s and '80s, this mail-order music club had a membership of 10 million people attempting to game their system. For me, my brother, and all of our collective friends, there was a brief moment in time when Columbia House was literally the gift that kept on giving. I guess to some extent, David could probably say the same. Since he was born with the biz in his blood, David had inherited an incredible innate ability to navigate the industry, which most "outsiders" never fully master. I say this with complete and utter sincerity. Working at a record label is like surfing the pipeline in Oahu. It's a graveyard of a wave. Unless you have both the correct positioning and survival skills in your DNA, you will undoubtedly end up fucked. Though I marveled at David's lengthy ride to date, it was always from a distance, as we'd never really worked together. That's why I was kinda puzzled when he decided to offer me, of all people, what appeared to be the Holy Grail of holiday fun: the *Jimmy Fallon Christmas Mixtape* album!

Huge, right?!

The *Jimmy Fallon Christmas Mixtape* had been concocted a few months earlier, when David hired Billy Jay Stein, a Grammy-winning producer of Broadway cast recordings, to helm the talk show host's holiday CD. But after a month or so, Wolter got the sense that Jimmy also wanted a guy who'd "written hits" added into the mix. I guess I was that guy? Keep in mind, I was a big Fallon fan. He was my absolute favorite of the late night hosts! Jimmy sat with all the cool kids at the industry lunch table. I sat with the stoners in the smoking section. I wanted Taylor, Ariana, and McCartney in my clique too. More importantly, knowing that Jimmy's platform at NBC was massive, I sensed that the record could be my last shot at riding *The Polar Express* to holiday gold. Though I did ponder the gig for an hour or so, I decided it was indeed worth chasing, thus the following day I had an intro Zoom with Jimmy and pitched my unfulfilled Christmas obsessions with the maddest of passions. By the time I was done shooting my shot, Fallon applauded, laughed hysterically, and told me he was actually a huge fan of my work! I'm not sure I believed him, but man, it sure was flattering. Immediately after our convo, he fired off an email to the label that read, "Love him." On the bonus tip, Billy Stein and I had previously worked together a couple of times on *SMASH* and I knew that he was both a sweetheart and a studio beast. This record seemed like a layup. It was more of a flagrant foul.

# Night 1

I rolled down to the famed Electric Lady Studios in Greenwich Village, and Jimmy greeted me with a warm hug, some beer, and a gift: a $280 Electric Lady satin bomber jacket.

A $280 Electric Lady satin bomber jacket!

Can you believe that shit?!

Artists had rarely, if ever, lavished me with anything at all. Thankless bastards. Here was the uber-famous Jimmy Fallon delivering that first-class swag right from the jump. It was pretty monumental.

Now Fallon rolled with two collaborator homies in tow at every session. Evidently, they were both *Tonight Show* writers, one of whom might have been his college roommate as well? From the jump, they seemed like nice enough fellas, but they were masterfully poker faced. It made for a flimsy dynamic between us. They rarely spoke unless Jimmy initiated. I got the sense that they were hella wary of all musical interlopers in Fallon World. I couldn't blame them. I'd always had "interloper" tattooed on my endless forehead.

As we discussed the potential direction for this thing, Jimmy really impressed. He was quite a charmer, and his music history knowledge was ridiculously legit. He introduced a bunch of clever track references. Billy and I excitedly followed his lead. Then, about an hour or two into the festivities, when no one was noticing, I took a quick break and swiftly slipped into the studio bathroom to try on my $280 Electric Lady satin bomber jacket. Shit, it didn't fit! Jimmy had purchased me a size large, not taking into consideration the genetic failings of my freakishly elongated torso. I definitely needed an XL. As we all said our farewells that evening, I loitered around the sidewalk as the two writer guys chatted their way toward Sixth Avenue and Jimmy hopped in his chauffeured SUV limo and raced off into the night. I think I waited a full ten seconds before I ran back into the studio and sheepishly inquired about exchanging my jacket for the larger size. The studio manager kindly obliged. I nodded off that night with Jimmy texting me at 2 AM inquiring if I'd seen the Style Council *Long Hot Summers* documentary. We nerded back and forth on the band for a bit. He even wished me luck on my first colonoscopy. That was very sweet. Evidently, I'd made a new famous friend.

# Night 2

Billy and I had been grinding on Jimmy's stuff 24/7 for ten straight days. We were completely underwater. We had a stack of Fallon's chosen Christmas cover songs to track with a slew of first-call NYC session cats. Wolter had also tasked me with writing choruses for Jimmy and his boys' original holiday tunes, which, though quite funny, were all a bit dynamically linear, so I broke out the guitar and went all in. To me, Christmas music has always been about a big-ass sing-along payoff. I have cheeseball leanings; I just needed to summon that holiday fromage. As I raced toward Electric Lady, I was super thrilled with the pile of ideas that Billy and I had shed and was obviously chomping at the bit to play Jimmy everything we'd laid down thus far. I strolled through the Electric Lady studio doors with an extra pep in my step, but in a mere matter of seconds, I stopped dead in my tracks. The two writer guys were sporting their very own $280 Electric Lady satin bomber jackets. Why didn't anyone give me the heads-up that this was a mandatory uniform?! I'd left mine on a dusty-ass closet hanger. I apologized profusely, but I'm not sure it registered. I did bring Magnolia Bakery banana pudding to share. I thought that was a classy, yet slightly unoriginal, move. For whatever it's worth, Jimmy did seem to enjoy the pudding.

Then it was time for our first listening session.

The Electric Lady house engineer proceeded to blast each of our musical offerings through the speakers. After every tune, while one of the writers furiously scribbled notes on a pad of paper, Fallon exclaimed, "Yes! This is sick!" or "Wow! That's amazing!" Fist bumps all around. He seemed fuckin' thrilled. David phoned me after and said, "Jimmy absolutely LOVES you and the tracks!" He also related that Jimmy called me a "genius"! Of equal importance, Wolter whispered that the record was a lock to get us both an exclusive invite to Jimmy's famed holiday party at his swanky town house. What up, Macca!

# Night 3

It was ninety-two degrees in Manhattan. I debated wearing the $280 Electric Lady satin bomber jacket down to the studio. It was a touch-and-go decision. I decided to gamble and leave it in the closet.

Massive mistake.

I parked my car on Eighth Street and watched Jimmy slide out of his chauffeured SUV limo wearing his very own $280 Electric Lady satin bomber jacket. At that very moment, I knew I was completely fucked. Instead of acknowledging my heinous lack of protocol upon studio entry, I swiftly attempted to flip the subject to the New York Islanders' miraculous playoff run. Unbeknownst to myself, the previous evening, Jimmy, a self-proclaimed Rangers diehard, had caught Twitter wrath for attending the game in Islanders swag and boldly hopping on that fanwagon. I didn't see any problem with it, but it seemed like a touchy subject, so I wisely went mum. After regaling us with some fun *Tonight Show* taping tales from earlier in the evening, Jimmy loosened up and began cutting his lead vocals on a Christmas-friendly cover of the *National Lampoon's Vacation* theme, "Holiday Road." Fallon called out some really clever harmonies and his pitch was super tight. Like most singers, he was a bit insecure about his tone, but I reassured him that he sounded great. He really did, but I'm not sure he bought it.

But then I committed another ginormous social faux pas.

After his last vocal take, Jimmy waltzed back into the control room to join us. The writer guys had strategically plunked down in the two available Aeron chairs, leaving the couch as the only other viable seating option. Since it was Jimmy's castle, he justly held court there, but in what I sensed was a sign of humility, he burrowed his body tight on the right-hand side.

Let me state this clearly: Jimmy Fallon was no spatial monopolizer.

When I boldly sat down on that couch beside him like the overgrown man-child that I am, my leg crossed over to inhabit the 60 percent of the free space between us. As I type this, I still wonder why I went in so hot? As we all know, in a normal, human couch-sharing dynamic, it should be a 50/50 territory thing, but factoring in Jimmy Fallon's fame, I'd say he certainly deserved a solid 70 percent of the couch. I should've been satisfied with my 30 percent and kept my overstepping legs in check, but I was greedy, and both of the writers noticed it. I locked eyes with the notepad-wielding writer and he immediately jotted something down. There was zero merry in that moment. Shortly thereafter, the session wrapped, and Fallon had the engineer email him a link to all of the tracks we'd created to date. Then, as the clock struck midnight, Jimmy offered up one final, somewhat cryptic aside. He said his chauffeur, in the SUV limo, was the critic that mattered most on his material. If the driver cast a thumbs-up or -down, it was usually a deciding vote. I paid it no mind. Jimmy's chauffeur didn't scare me. I knew we were creating holiday magic, and there was no fuckin' way the man behind the wheel could Scrooge our shit.

**BONUS CUT**

For what it's worth, I'm a bit envious that I've never had a song-evaluating chauffeur at my disposal for critiques, just the occasional UberX guy who tries to pawn me vitamin supplements.

The evening concluded with me and Jimmy cheerily reciting rap bars from Nice & Smooth's lost classic "Funky for You" together on Eighth Street at 1 AM. Then he gave me a pound and hopped in said SUV limo. And to all a good night.

# Night 4

I did it.

I finally remembered to exit my crib in the $280 Electric Lady satin bomber jacket.

I was quite proud of this achievement.

I gleefully raced down to Electric Lady, but as soon as I neared the Village, I got a panicked text from David Wolter that read, "No session tonight. Jimmy's out." I had an instant bad premonition, but when I finally got him on the phone, Wolter said it was much ado about nothing.

"Sam, he really LIKES you."

(Note: no longer "loves.")

"He just has some minor contractual issues he wants to address. I promise, it has nothing to do with you, though."

Now keep in mind, this was the same week that Jimmy's ratings bottomed out, and he'd just drawn the smallest *Tonight Show* audience since 1986, so the bloodthirsty press was kinda going for the jugular. I kinda hoped those dwindling numbers were the sole reason for the work stoppage, but my paranoia built nonetheless. I waited impatiently for a reschedule, but, using his years of industry savvy, Wolter creatively began to duck all of my neurotic calls.

**BONUS CUT**

There is in fact a delicate art to the duck.

I'd always been the best (and worst) kind of optimist. A wiser soul would've phoned in this novelty of a gig and removed all emotion from the equation, but my inner Christmas lights weren't wired like that. I really cared about this record. I knew we were under the tightest of deadlines to get this thing in the can, and I wanted it to be epic, but as the days came and went, I felt like I was a kid who'd been mistakenly put on the naughty list. I was both hurt and stumped. I sat frozen in my house in the most awkward limbo ever.

One week became two.

Three became four.

I wore my $280 Electric Lady satin bomber jacket over my pajamas to breakfast every AM just to cheer myself up.

Finally, I reached a boiling point and summoned up the nerve to hit Jimmy directly to ask what the deal was.

He replied instantly. "My man! Let's goooo!!!! What song to tackle next?!"

Alas, there would be no more tackling.

That very same day, Wolter finally reached out and alerted me to the fact that only a few hours earlier, Fallon had decided to ask the significantly hotter hand, Mark Ronson, to take over the reins of the *Jimmy Fallon Christmas Mixtape* sleigh.

What a fuckin' gut punch.

I didn't even know how to reply.

As Wolter awkwardly attempted to break the tension, I stewed in silence, pondering the dead months ahead. You see, most functioning humans have jobs with salaries. They're blessed to have glimmers of stability. Songwriters and producers are forced to hustle gig to gig. We're self-employed. There are no sexy stock options, 401(k)s, or offices with panoramic views of the park. The scrounge never stops. I'd like to believe an industry lifer like David understood that I'd totally wasted the front half of my summer on this thing, and as songwriting pairings are usually booked a month or two out, I would now also be forced to sit on my couch with no compelling sessions until after Labor Day. It was a lot to unpack. After a few more minutes of forced small talk, the brutal truth finally hit me. I had no right to blame Jimmy Fallon at all. I mean, if I had the same opportunity, *I* would've bounced me for Mark Ronson in a millisecond. He was both a significantly bigger producer and blessed with incredible hair. That's just the way the game works. It is what it is. The hottest hand wins. I could sense David anxiously fidgeting to end the call, but like the dick that I am, I had to ask him if Jimmy's chauffeur had provided any useful musical feedback that I could use to rectify the situation. The line went dead.

## (There Would Be No) Night 5

I never heard from Jimmy Fallon again.

Nor the two writer guys.

Nor David Wolter, for that matter, who I assumed was probably more focused on protecting his (now tenuous) hold on a Jimmy Fallon holiday party invite like a Brink's truck guardsman watching the bank. No judgments. In the end, the *Jimmy Fallon Christmas Mixtape* was just another shiny ornament of music industry punishment that I signed up for the day I began scribing songs. We think we're immune to it, but at some point or another, we all get kicked to the South Pole. That being said, though, as I sit here cheerlessly typing this, I must make this final offering à la Columbia House:

*Dear Jimmy Kimmel,*

*My ABSOLUTE favorite late-night talk show host.*

*If you're reading this, I've got a rested and ready $280 Electric Lady satin bomber jacket and an incredible unfinished ten-song record of Christmas bliss eagerly awaiting your vocal stylings for only a penny.*

*Let me hear you say "Ho ho ho"?*

THE $280 Electric Lady satin bomber jacket.

CHAPTER 41

# Farewell, Randy Newman

I loved L.A. Both the glitzy historic spectacle and the dark comedy of it all. I spent many a morning power walk on Hollywood Boulevard trying to unearth the most random of stars on the Walk of Fame. Hoot Gibson? Johnny Hayes? I just loved the notion that somewhere alongside the Lucille Balls and Cary Grants were a bunch of folks who made incredible entertainment contributions that were completely lost to time. At the core, that felt very "professional songwriter" to me.

I guess that's why I was so incredibly moved when the wonderful writer-advocacy organization SONA (The Songwriters of North America) threw a concert at The Hotel Café in Hollywood featuring a stack of my songs performed by various vocalists. A bunch of old friends from assorted stretches of my existence rallied to celebrate my ass. It was both dreamlike and a bit humbling to get a little recognition from my peers in real time. As I stood there staring out into a crowd full of old-schoolers and up-and-comers, it was one of the most emotional scenes for me to date. For all the times I'd given up in my head, I was so grateful that I never quit.

Still riding that high a couple of months later, I sold my entire career catalog of 499 songs to Hipgnosis Music. Though I did debate the deal for a minute, it really was a no-brainer. For the first time in my entire life, I could finally stop spinning the endless song roulette wheel and simply create whatever the fuck I pleased without any semblance of thirst. It was one of the greatest days of my life. I felt like I was starring in a feel-good movie!

Then one afternoon, my new agent at WME, Amos Newman (Randy Newman's kid!), hit me in a bit of frenzy.

"Where you at?" he exclaimed.

I replied that I was driving around East L.A. with my kid. His reply was rather succinct.

"Get over to the Fox lot in Culver City at four sharp. I'll leave your name at the gate. Don't be a minute late."

I'd just begun working with Amos, who was repping me for movie tunes. Though I'd been on a pretty sweet run, relatively, it was somewhat of a dice throw on his part. Most agents like Amos repped composers, not songwriters.

After dropping Joey off at home, I rolled up to the gates at 3:57, and I was given a walk-on pass. The lot was super overwhelming for my ADHD brain, but Amos grabbed me and escorted me through doors that, as I'd soon learn, led to the studio's famed Newman Scoring Stage.

**BONUS CUT**

The Newman Scoring Stage was built in the 1920s for filming, but was later converted into a recording studio where Amos's great-uncle, the famed composer Alfred Newman, who headed Twentieth Century Fox's music department, held court. In time, every Newman-family composing giant (all of whom have their own Walk of Fame stars) did their work there, as well as legends like John Williams, who scored *Jaws* in that very same spot.

When we entered the Newman control room, the first thing that caught my eye was a line of champagne bottles, probably about thirty deep, along the back wall. There were balloons everywhere, and the space was densely packed with the cheeriest of folks. This did not resemble any session that I'd ever partaken in!

Then Amos clued me in.

Randy Newman was in the process of leading a 110-piece orchestra in the last-ever live scoring session for *Toy Story 4*, which would put a wrap on the franchise as we knew it! Seriously, the final Toy Story orchestra date! I'd had many

I Love LA with Randy Newman and Amos Newman.

near-religious experiences in music, but nothing could compare to this moment of Pixar perfection.

Amos led me into the live room, where I sat less than five feet away from one of the harpists, and I got to experience this momentous occasion in the front row! As that massive ensemble dug in, which was strangely less sonically bombastic than I'd expected given my proximity, every cue was executed with machinelike precision. Then the room would fall eerily quiet between takes. After the last cue was laid down, the entire studio began crying and cheering as Randy gave the most powerful farewell speech. It's still so hard to express how much it meant to me, getting the opportunity to crash that once-in-a-lifetime event, but it was easily among the most beautiful experiences of my life.

To infinity . . . and beyond . . .

. . . or to 2020.

That's when shit went haywire. First, my friend Allee Willis died. It was so sad. Allee was not only one of my favorite songwriters, she was also the most uniquely creative human I ever met. No one could touch her. Only a couple of months earlier, she'd been in the house at that SONA tribute. It meant so much

With the late, spectacular Allee Willis.

to me that she'd rallied on my behalf. Now she was gone. Suddenly things began to feel real ominous.

Then only a couple of months later, COVID-19's initial wave of destruction kicked in, and Adam Schlesinger was tragically among its first victims. Losing Adam was one of the saddest days of my life. He was simply the greatest. I have stacks of memories of nights running around together. Japanese wings in the East Village. Piano karaoke with a Bill Murray cameo. Drinks

Adam Schlesinger.
Man, I miss this fella.

with a somewhat indecipherable Peter Wolf of the J. Geils Band. Our discipling of both the soft-rock god Stephen Bishop and the gimlet-eyed jazz pianist Dave Frishberg, whom we celebrated equally like Deadheads dancing to Bobby Weir. Every night with Adam was full of thrilling twists and turns. Though we'd written a couple of tunes together for fun earlier on, our first real collaboration was on an ill-fated demo for the 2011 Disney film *The Muppets*. Man, we wanted in on that Henson action. That session, I noticed a dynamic in our friendship that I'd rarely experienced with a peer before. Adam was willing to tolerate my misfires, my wack ideas, without any judgments or one-upping. He was completely secure in his art. As the years went on, it seemed like Adam and I always ran on parallel musical tracks, and yet he never once flexed any sort of competitive bullshit with me. He was one of my biggest backers, and I was obviously one of his superfans.

Immediately after Adam's passing, I started to spiral in my head a bit as I began to feel disconnected from myself and my surroundings. Though my wife and kid had been pushing to move back east for a few years, I had always resisted. But in those endlessly bleak early-pandemic weeks, I started to wonder if I also needed some sort of Hollywood hiatus as well. Maybe the novelty of writing songs with less-than-inspiring (or inspired) influencers was wearing off. Maybe it was the trauma of stumbling upon a powderhead who had broken into and was subsequently squatting in our crib. Or maybe it was our fancy Beverly Hills Realtor, who blew off our first crucial open house, choosing instead to walk on fire at a Tony Robbins seminar somewhere in Florida. One of the most imperative human abilities is knowing when the fuck to say "when," so by the time July arrived, the moving trucks were packed and set course for New York. Yes, in the midst of the worst year on record, my family and I relocated back to the state that Randy Newman labeled "cold and damp" and that's where I'm frostfully typing this as we speak.

## CHAPTER 42

# Overlook Drive By

On May 27, 2022, the morning of what would've been my father's eighty-eighth birthday, I took a ceremonial ride to Overlook Drive, the same street where my pops made his book pronouncement a lifetime ago. As I parked my car on a road that I had long forgotten, the memories began to flood. I thought about my folks and lost amigos. I thought about my once spectacular Jewfro (RIP) before it went full Garfunkel. I thought about how lucky I'd been to get to watch my incredible kid come of age. I thought about how incredibly blessed I'd been to spend my life doing the one and only work I love. And though I really had zero idea where my voyage would go from there, as I silently took it all in, I knew, no matter how trivial the detail, there was only one rule: I had to keep writing it all down.

You see, while birthing these chapters, it finally dawned on me that my pop's greatest joy in life was simply the chronicling of his own journey. Though I couldn't understand this notion as a kid, for my old man, his writing was never about the finish line. He was artistically, and humanly, fulfilled simply by freeing the thoughts from his head and deploying them to his hard drive. It was the process that made him whole. Maybe that's true for most creative souls out there. I guess in the end, it doesn't really matter if you're undiscovered or an up-and-comer, a not-yet or a gonna-be; every damn day you've just gotta put pen to paper and persevere, even when

**303**

your saner side tells you to pack it in. Sure, there will be heavenly highs and soul-crushing crashes along the way, but document all of it. Who knows where it will lead? For whatever it's worth, I'm so stoked to read YOUR story!

# Acknowledgments

I just want to send a boxed set of gratitude and love to my family, friends, collaborators, and heroes; Matt Holt, Katie Dickman, Mallory Hyde, Brigid Pearson, and the entire Matt Holt/BenBella Books team for this mind-boggling opportunity; and any kind soul who ever cheered me on along the way. Thank you, Casey Kasem. Thank you, MTV. Thank you, K-Tel Records.

The author will be donating 100 percent of his proceeds from this book to the charity Musicians On Call.

Bringing a dose of joy to the hospital experience for nearly one million people since 1999, Musicians On Call (MOC) delivers live and recorded music directly to the bedsides of patients, families, and caregivers in health-care facilities nationwide. People of all ages in facilities including children's, adult, and VA hospitals, hospices, behavioral health, and memory care facilities, and others have enjoyed live music in the hospital thanks to MOC Volunteers. When pain, uncertainty, and exhaustion take center stage, MOC's goal is to bring comforting and enriching performances that transform discomfort and stimulate recovery. MOC believes that all patients, families, and caregivers should have access to and benefit from the healing power of live music. It has been demonstrated that music has a direct effect on people and can manage stress, alleviate pain, and improve pain tolerance, blood pressure, outlook, and overall mood.